THE CONCEPTUAL FOUNDATIONS
OF TRANSITIONAL JUSTICE

Many countries have attempted to transition to democracy following conflict or repression, but the basic meaning of *transitional justice* remains hotly contested. In this book, Colleen Murphy analyzes transitional justice – showing how it is distinguished from retributive, corrective, and distributive justice – and outlines the ethical standards that societies attempting to democratize should follow. She argues that transitional justice involves the just pursuit of societal transformation. Such transformation requires political reconciliation, which in turn has a complex set of institutional and interpersonal requirements, including the rule of law. She shows how societal transformation is also influenced by the moral claims of victims and the demands of perpetrators, and how justice processes can fail to be just by failing to foster this transformation or by not treating victims and perpetrators fairly. Her book will be accessible and enlightening for philosophers, political and social scientists, policy analysts, and legal and human rights scholars and activists.

COLLEEN MURPHY is Professor of Law, Philosophy, and Political Science at the University of Illinois at Urbana-Champaign. She is the author of *A Moral Theory of Political Reconciliation* (Cambridge University Press, 2010), and the coeditor of *Engineering Ethics for a Globalized World* (2015), *Risk Analysis of Natural Hazards* (2015), and *Climate Change and Its Impacts: Risks and Inequalities* (forthcoming).

THE CONCEPTUAL
FOUNDATIONS OF
TRANSITIONAL JUSTICE

COLLEEN MURPHY

University of Illinois at Urbana-Champaign

CAMBRIDGE
UNIVERSITY PRESS

CAMBRIDGE
UNIVERSITY PRESS

University Printing House, Cambridge CB2 8BS, United Kingdom

One Liberty Plaza, 20th Floor, New York, NY 10006, USA

477 Williamstown Road, Port Melbourne, VIC 3207, Australia

4843/24, 2nd Floor, Ansari Road, Daryaganj, Delhi – 110002, India

79 Anson Road, #06–04/06, Singapore 079906

Cambridge University Press is part of the University of Cambridge.

It furthers the University's mission by disseminating knowledge in the pursuit of education, learning, and research at the highest international levels of excellence.

www.cambridge.org
Information on this title: www.cambridge.org/9781107085473
DOI: 10.1017/9781316084229

First published 2017

Printed in the United States of America by Sheridan Books, Inc.

A catalogue record for this publication is available from the British Library.

Library of Congress Cataloging-in-Publication Data
NAMES: Murphy, Colleen, 1974- author.
TITLE: The conceptual foundations of transitional justice / Colleen Murphy, University of Illinois at Urbana-Champaign.
DESCRIPTION: Cambridge, United Kingdom ; New York, NY, USA : Cambridge University Press, 2017. | Includes bibliographical references and index.
IDENTIFIERS: LCCN 2016054369 | ISBN 9781107085473 (hardback : alk. paper)
SUBJECTS: LCSH: Transitional justice–Philosophy.
CLASSIFICATION: LCC K5250 .M87 2017 | DDC 340/.115–dc23 LC record available at https://lccn.loc.gov/2016054369

ISBN 978-1-107-08547-3 Hardback

Contents

Preface and Acknowledgments

Dealing with past wrongdoing is a prominent and recurring issue for many societies. The United States continues to struggle with its legacy of slavery and Jim Crow–era segregation as well as ongoing tensions between the police and blacks heightened by recent police shootings. Canada continues to deal with the legacy of its residential schools for indigenous peoples. Discussions about how, whether, and in what way Spain should face the abuses from the Franco era, and Northern Ireland should face the legacy of The Troubles are ongoing. At the time of writing, the brutal civil war in Syria continues into its fifth year, amid calls to establish processes to deal with rights abuses committed to date. The work of the Tunisian Truth and Dignity Commission to deal with gross human rights violations during the period of repression starting in July 1, 1955, and prior to the 2011 revolution is ongoing, as is Nepal's Truth and Reconciliation Commission and National Commission of Inquiry into Disappearances focusing on gross human rights violations committed during armed conflict from 1996 to 2006. The Supreme Court of El Salvador just invalidated a 1993 amnesty law covering atrocities committed by government forces and guerillas during its twelve-year civil war (1980–1992). The International Criminal Court currently has ten situations under investigation, including in Georgia, the Central African Republic, Mali, and Uganda, as well as ongoing trials in the Ongwen, Banda, Ntaganda, Bemba et al., Gbagbo and Blé Goudé, and Al Mahdi cases.

The moral questions raised in these cases are similar in some morally salient respects, but not identical. One of the primary aims of this book is to clarify these similarities and differences. While past wrongs place moral demands on particular perpetrators and generate moral claims of particular victims, the appropriate satisfaction of these claims is context dependent. What it means to properly acknowledge wrongdoing depends on who is doing the acknowledgment and the particular kind of wrong being acknowledged. Moreover, the overarching moral point and purpose of responding to past wrongs is in important respects also context dependent. In some cases, the overarching moral point is fostering societal transformation. In other contexts, societal transformation may not be necessary to pursue, and the main moral point in dealing with past wrongs may be simply to respond justly to perpetrators and victims of wrongdoing. The moral point and purpose in dealing with past wrongs in turn shapes the moral standards a response to wrongdoing must satisfy in order to qualify as just. Over the course of my book, I discuss the various moral aims that dealing with past wrongs might have and the corresponding standards of justice such aims require be satisfied.

This book has taken seven years to write, and over the course of that period of time many individuals and audiences provided invaluable feedback. I am particularly grateful to the Princeton University Center for Human Values (UCHV) for the time and support provided through my Laurance S. Rockefeller Visiting Faculty Fellowship during the 2010–2011 academic year. My project on transitional justice was in its very early stages, and conversations and presentations throughout the year were critical in shaping the direction it ultimately took. I am especially grateful to Chuck Beitz, Corey Brettschneider, Tom Christiano, Alex Guerrero, Liz Harman, Adrienne Martin, Alan Patton, Jon Quong, Kim Lane Scheppele, and Peter Singer for the feedback they provided. Chuck also deserves special mention not only for his intellectual feedback but also for the support he provided in his capacity as director of the UCHV. My first son was born in January of the year I spent at the UCHV, and I was able to remain engaged with the center because of the way in which Chuck encouraged and welcomed me to bring my son with me to my office as well as UCHV talks and events.

I also presented different parts of this book at Illinois Wesleyan University; the Midwest Political Science Association; the Department of Philosophy and the Mershon Center at The Ohio State University; Osgoode Hall Law School at York University; the Law and Philosophy Program at the University of Texas at Austin; the Comparative Politics Workshop and the College of Law at the University of Illinois at Urbana-Champaign; the S. J. Quinney College of Law and Tanner Center for Human Rights at the University of Utah; the University of Virginia's Institute for Practical Ethics and Public Life and the Program in Political Philosophy, Policy, and Law (PPL); the Robina Institute on Criminal Law and Criminal Justice at the University of Minnesota Law School; the Department of Philosophy at Illinois State University; Queen's University Belfast; the University of South Florida; and the Society for Applied Philosophy.

These audiences provided insightful and rich feedback for which I am grateful. I also thank the hosts for these events, including David Archard, Neha Jain, Hugh LaFollette, Francois Tanguay-Renaud, John Deigh, Deen Chatterjee, Alan Silverman, and Mark Criley.

Formally and informally, a wonderful group of scholars provided invaluable comments on various draft chapters. I thank in particular Lorraine Besser-Jones, John Deigh, Andy Engen, Erika George, Pat Keenan, Dan Korman, Alice MacLachlan, Simon Stacey, Susanne Sreedhar, and Daniel Weinstock. Paul Morrow, Kathleen Murphy, Linda Radzik, and John Tasioulas deserve special mention, as they each provided extensive feedback on multiple chapters, especially as I was finalizing the manuscript. Finally, I am very grateful to Dan Philpott for pressing me in his review of my first book on the question of the relationship between political reconciliation and justice. It is his questions that in many ways provided the impetus for this book.

I thank Hilary Gaskin for her superb editorial guidance throughout. Parts of different chapters have been published in other venues. The introduction was published as "Transitional Justice: A Conceptual Map," in *Theorizing Justice: Novel Insights and Future Directions*, ed. Krushil Watene and Jay Drydyk (Rowman and Littlefield, 2016). Excerpts of Chapter 2 are taken from my chapter "Transitional Justice, Retributive Justice and Accountability for Wrongdoing," in *Theorizing Transitional Justice*, ed. Claudio Corradetti, Nir Eisikovits, and Jack Rotondi (Ashgate Publishing, 2015). Parts of Chapter 3 are taken from my "Reply to Critics," in *Criminal Law and Philosophy* 10.

I dedicate this book to Paolo, Peter, and Patrick, the rocks in my life who make all else possible.

Introduction

In recent decades, dozens of countries emerging from long periods of repressive rule and civil conflict have attempted the difficult transition to democracy. South Africa after apartheid, Rwanda post-1994 genocide, and Egypt following the end of the Mubarak era are examples of such societies. Although the precise markers of a successful transition to democracy are a matter of ongoing dispute, scholars and policy experts alike agree that societies must explicitly address their legacies of violence, which typically include systematic and brutal human rights abuses.

The term *transitional justice* is generally taken to refer to formal attempts by postrepressive or postconflict societies to address past wrongdoing in their efforts to democratize.[1] Societies in transition have enacted a range of measures to confront these legacies of violence, such as amnesty, criminal trials, truth commissions, and reparations. However, there is little consensus about which responses are appropriate and morally justified.[2] Many important studies on transitional justice concentrate on specific cases and employ social science methodologies to understand the social outcomes of different legal responses to wrongdoing, such as whether the establishment

---

[1] This definition is reflected not only in academic discussions but also in international documents on the subject. See, for instance, the UN Secretary General's Report, "The Rule of Law and Transitional Justice in Conflict and Post-Conflict Societies," which defines *transitional justice* as "the full range of processes and mechanisms associated with a society's attempts to come to terms with a legacy of large-scale past abuses, in order to ensure accountability, serve justice and achieve reconciliation"; see de Greiff, Pablo, "Theorizing Transitional Justice," in *NOMOS LI: Transitional Justice*, ed. Melissa S. Williams, Rosemary Nagy, and Jon Elster (New York: New York University Press, 2012), 31. As I note later in this chapter, the necessity of including a democratic aspiration is the subject of debate; I ultimately defend the inclusion of democracy in our understanding of transitional justice in Chapter 4.

[2] See, for example, Leebaw, Bronwyn Anne, "The Irreconcilable Goals of Transitional Justice," *Human Rights Quarterly* 30, no. 1 (2008): 95–118; Fletcher, Laurel E. and Harvey M. Weinstein, "Violence and Social Repair: Rethinking the Contribution of Justice to Reconciliation," *Human Rights Quarterly* 24, no. 3 (2002): 573–639.

of a truth commission has an impact on the rule of law.[3] For example, Jack Snyder and Leslie Vinjamuri examine thirty-two postconflict countries and find that truth commissions were either irrelevant or harmful except when established in countries that had already made significant progress in democratization.[4] Such studies also consider the factors that explain the particular choices specific communities make and the constraints that influence decision making. These examinations enrich our understanding of what does or does not happen within various transitional communities and why.

My focus in this book, however, is different. My interest is in the moral evaluation of the choices transitional communities make in dealing with wrongdoing. Both members and observers of transitional communities form moral judgments about the responses to wrongdoing that communities select. These judgments are expressed in reactions such as, "It is unjust to grant amnesty to perpetrators of human rights abuses" or "A truth commission achieved justice." There is great variation, and at times incompatibility, in the judgments individuals make. Scholars, international organizations, victims, and citizens of transitional societies disagree on how we should morally judge measures adopted to deal with past wrongdoing in such contexts.

To illustrate, consider South Africa and reactions to the Truth and Reconciliation Commission (TRC) established as part of the transition from apartheid to democracy. In 1994, South Africa began to transition from a forty-year period of institutionalized racism to democracy. All South Africans were placed into one of four racial groups: white, Indian, colored, or African.[5] During the apartheid era, the African, colored, and Indian

---

[3] See, e.g., Fletcher, Laurel, Harvey Weinstein, and Jamie Rowen, "Context, Timing, and the Dynamics of Transitional Justice: A Historical Perspective," *Human Rights Quarterly* 31 (2009): 163–220; Van der Merwe, Hugo, Victoria Baxter, and Audrey Chapman, *Assessing the Impact of Transitional Justice: Challenges for Empirical Research* (Washington, DC: United States Institute of Peace Press, 2009); Olsen, Tricia D., Leigh A. Payne, and Andrew G. Reiter, *Transitional Justice in Balance: Comparing Processes, Weighing Efficacy* (Washington, DC: United States Institute of Peace, 2010); Shaw, Rosalind and Lars Waldorf, *Localizing Transitional Justice: Interventions and Priorities after Mass Violence* (Stanford, CA: Stanford University Press, 2010).

[4] Snyder, Jack and Leslie Vinjamuri, "Trials and Errors: Principle and Pragmatism in Strategies of International Justice," *International Security* 28, no. 3 (2003–2004): 5–44. For a critique of the analysis used to generate these findings, see Thoms, Oskar N. T., James Ron, and Roland Paris, "State-Level Effects of Transitional Justice: What Do We Know?" *International Journal of Transitional Justice* 4, no. 3 (2010): 344.

[5] I follow the racial categories used by the South African Truth and Reconciliation Commission in its final report. "Generally in this report, black Africans are referred to as Africans. Coloured people, people of Indian or Asian origin and white people are referred to as such." (www.justice.gov.za/trc/report/finalreport/Volume%201.pdf at paragraph 13).

South African populations were subjected to systematically unequal treatment, and racial segregation governed every aspect of daily life. The white South African minority constituted approximately 20 percent of the overall population. The government, run by the ruling National Party (NP), maintained apartheid by relying on a brutal system of repression carried out legally and extralegally by state security forces. Black South African resistance, largely led by the African National Congress (ANC), was initially nonviolent. However, after the 1960s, the ANC increasingly relied on violence as a form of resistance. After decades of protracted conflict, negotiations between the ANC and NP paved the way for the first democratic elections in 1994, when Nelson Mandela became the first black president of South Africa.

Many observers and citizens worried that civil war would follow the end of apartheid. A product of the negotiations to end apartheid, the Interim Constitution of 1993 contained a commitment to amnesty for parties responsible for offenses during the preceding conflict.[6] Recognizing the high stakes of this transition to democracy and respecting the commitment to amnesty, the South African Parliament subsequently passed the Promotion of National Unity and Reconciliation Act, No. 34 of 1995, which created the TRC.

The TRC's directive was to "investigat[e] and document gross human rights violations committed within or outside South Africa in the period 1960–1994," specifically killing, abduction, torture, and severe ill treatment. The TRC investigated instances of direct violations as well as any "attempt, conspiracy, incitement, instigation, command or procurement" to commit such violations.[7] The TRC comprised three committees: the Committee on Human Rights Violations, the Committee on Amnesty, and the Committee on Reparations and Rehabilitation.[8] More than 20,000 individuals testified as victims (or as family members of deceased victims) over the course of its proceedings. The TRC also made recommendations regarding reparations for victims. The TRC was not empowered to punish perpetrators, although the TRC was given the legal authority to grant amnesty to perpetrators – on both sides – who testified

---

[6] Dyzenhaus, David, "Survey Article: Justifying the Truth and Reconciliation Commission," *Journal of Political Philosophy* 8 (2000): 475.

[7] Ibid., 476.

[8] The TRC also held institutional hearings to determine the role of the media, law, health sector, business, and religious communities during apartheid; these were designed to understand how the system was sustained. The radio, newspapers, and television media covered the public hearings of the TRC extensively (see ibid., 479).

fully to what they had done. The amnesty provision was such that a perpetrator could apply for and be granted amnesty if he or she fully disclosed the acts for which he or she was responsible and demonstrated that the acts were committed for political reasons. By individualizing amnesty, the TRC allowed for a measure of accountability for human rights abuses; this contrasted with previous commissions preceded by a blanket amnesty that allowed general impunity for human rights abuses. Nonetheless, perpetrators granted amnesty were immune from civil or criminal liability. More than 7,000 amnesty applications were submitted, and eventually amnesty was granted to approximately 850 individuals. Like other such commissions, the TRC was charged to produce a report that summarized the findings of their investigation. Following the conclusion of its work, the TRC produced a five-volume report detailing its findings and recommendations.

In a powerful account, Antjie Krog, one of the journalists who covered the TRC, recounts a range of judgments expressed about the commission.[9] Here are a few examples:

According to a black South African journalist: For me, justice lies in the fact that everything is being laid out on the same table ... The Truth that rules our fears, our deeds, and our dreams is coming to light. From now on, you don't only see a smiling black man in front of you, but you also know what I carry inside of me. I've always known it – now you also know.[10]

According to an international observer: It will sometimes be necessary to choose between truth and justice. We should choose truth, he says.[11]

According to an applicant for amnesty: Where does culpability rest? I believe I cannot be held solely responsible for the death of Anton Fransch. And the role played by the security police must be exposed. [*cries out*] I wish! To be recognized! For who and what I am! So that the falsification of my history can be rectified.[12]

Krog recalls thinking that the imprisonment of the apartheid era prime minister, P. W. Botha, could only be an empty spectacle of justice – that his arrest could hardly compensate for the vast injustice of the regime over which he and his predecessors had presided. In her words, "A commission for truth? ... What would be the effect of a manacled P. W. Botha,

[9] Krog, Antjie, *Country of My Skull: Guilt, Sorrow and the Limits of Forgiveness in the New South Africa* (New York: Three Rivers Press, 1998).
[10] Ibid., 60.
[11] Ibid., 32. These were the words of philosopher Jose Zalaquett at a conference Krog attended in early 1994.
[12] Ibid., 73.

stripped of his little hat and forefinger, on his way to long-term imprisonment, other than astonishment that anyone could regard this as the final
proof of justice? But immediately I'm ashamed."[13]

These perspectives represent a wide range of moral viewpoints. While
for the black South African journalist exposing the truth is itself a form of
justice, the international observer claims that transitional societies must
choose between truth and justice. The amnesty applicant complains about
unjustly being held liable for crimes in which others should also be
implicated, while Krog reveals her own skepticism – which many others
shared – about what is achieved by holding anyone, even leaders, responsible for collective crimes, liable through criminal punishment. Through
these impassioned responses, we can begin to see how differently members
of societies in transition respond to the legacy of wrongdoing and attempts
to address that legacy. Confronted with decades of horrific and systematic
violations of human rights, black and white South Africans had to decide
how they would deal with the moral aftermath.

This book takes as its point of departure the range of such complex
reactions, which exemplify the moral judgments we all make about justice.
It is not obvious which – if any – of these judgments is correct. Each
expresses a different, and yet plausibly legitimate, point of view. The
justice of having the truth finally known and acknowledged seems compelling, as does the need to do more than just know what happened in
order for justice to be achieved. It does seem intuitively unfair to hold one
individual responsible for the actions of many, as well as intuitively futile
to hold anyone accountable for wrongdoing that an entire society permitted. It simply is not clear what justice means "in the wake of massive
abuses" when "'ordinary' expectations concerning what justice requires will
not be satisfied."[14] Expectations in this context refer not to predictions
about how justice will in fact be meted out in any given case; rather,
expectations are normative in character and reflect the standards of behavior to which individuals and communities should appropriately be held.
Equally unclear are the moral value and justifiability of *any* response to
wrongdoing in such circumstances.

At the heart of debates about how societies in transition should deal
with wrongdoing is the following question: *What are the appropriate
standards of justice to use when evaluating various legal responses to wrongdoing in transitional contexts?* This is a question about the general standards
or principles that any response to wrongdoing must meet to qualify as *just*.

[13] Ibid., 31–32.   [14] De Greiff, "Theorizing Transitional Justice," 58.

In order to explain why responses other than criminal punishment do or do not meet the standards of justice, we must first understand what justice requires. The overarching objective of this book is articulating what transitional justice demands. My analysis aims to provide philosophers, lawyers, and other theorists engaged in scholarly debates about transitional justice, as well as policy makers and citizens of transitional communities, with the conceptual tools to morally evaluate options for dealing with and decisions about legacies of violence and wrongdoing.

All human beings care about whether justice is achieved. Individuals and communities react to injustice and failures of justice with various reactive attitudes, such as anger, resentment, and indignation. Such attitudes are one way that human beings hold others accountable for what they have done or failed to do in meeting our moral demands and expectations. Reactive attitudes are a form of communication, and implicit in such attitudes is an invitation for individuals or communities to respond to the judgments being expressed.[15] Critically engaging the moral judgments underpinning such attitudes is a way of acknowledging the humanity and moral agency of the victims and communities expressing them.

Before developing a new positive theory of transitional justice, it is important to establish why such an account is needed. This is the primary task of this introductory chapter. In Section 1, I provide an overview of the pragmatic and moral challenges confronting transitional communities that explain why "ordinary" expectations of justice will not be satisfied. In Section 2, I explain why it is erroneous to think of justice in transitional circumstances as involving a moral compromise between truth and justice, in the way that the international observer, quoted in the preceding, suggests. In compromise views, transitional justice entails the balancing of specific (retributive/distributive/corrective) justice-based claims against competing moral and/or pragmatic considerations. Finally, I discuss limitations of equating transitional justice with restorative justice. At the core of the limitations with compromise and restorative justice views is a failure to acknowledge the context-sensitive nature of claims of justice. This failure matters, I argue, because ignoring the background context presupposed by theories of justice undermines distinctions between kinds of justice. As a result, the normative point for making such distinctions is undercut.

---

[15] On reactive attitudes, see Strawson, P. F., *Freedom and Resentment and Other Essays* (New York: Routledge, 2008); David Shoemaker, "Moral Address, Moral Responsibility, and the Boundaries of the Moral Community," *Ethics* 118 (2007): 71–75. On the second-person standpoint more generally, see Darwall, Stephen, *The Second-Person Standpoint: Morality, Respect, and Accountability* (Cambridge, MA: Harvard University Press, 2009).

After discussing limitations with conceptualizing transitional justice as a moral compromise or as restorative justice, I argue that the most promising theoretical route to explore is the idea that transitional justice is a distinctive form of justice. Yet, as I discuss in Section 3, this idea remains undertheorized and in need of greater conceptual clarification and articulation. Section 4 provides an overview of the positive account of transitional justice developed in the succeeding chapters. The problem with justice in transitional contexts, I claim, is not the same as the problem of justice with which theories of retributive justice, corrective justice, or distributive justice are fundamentally concerned, nor, consequently, are the demands of justice that must be satisfied in transitions reducible to the principles of such theories. Transitional justice is ultimately concerned with the just pursuit of societal transformation, and that objective becomes salient in a specific set of circumstances of transitional justice. The rest of the chapters in this book articulate the circumstances of justice and flesh out the moral requirements for pursuing societal transformation justly.

What Is Controversial about Transitional Justice?

Modern democracies generally hold that criminal punishment is the "first-best" moral response to wrongdoing, especially in the case of egregious wrongdoing such as rape and torture. Trials establish guilt and determine punishment, giving perpetrators "what they deserve." Justice is achieved when wrongdoers are punished.[16] Then President Barack Obama articulated the basic idea that perpetrators of wrongdoing must be punished in the aftermath of the killing of the U.S. ambassador to Libya in 2012: "Make no mistake, we will work with the Libyan government to bring to justice the killers who attacked our people."[17] More generally, the criminal justice system in the United States, as in many states around the world, is designed to mete out justice so conceived.

For the purposes of articulating why justice is controversial in transitional contexts, I assume the claim that punishment can satisfy standards of justice.[18] Criminal punishment is not entirely without its critics; some

---

[16] For the purposes of this chapter, I take *punishment* to refer specifically to "legal punishment" by the state.

[17] Kirkpatrick, David and Steven Lee Myers, "Libya Attack Brings Challenges for the U.S.," *New York Times*, September 12, 2012.

[18] I am using this example for purposes of illustration to set up why there is a question about which standards of justice are salient in transitional contexts. In doing so, I recognize that there are a range

skeptics charge that punishment simply masks the brute desire for revenge that human beings harbor when wronged. However, such skeptics are in the minority among the general population and among academics; the consensus view is that punishment can be a legitimate response to wrong-doing and can satisfy standards of justice.

For many, at least part of the moral point of punishing criminals is to give them what they deserve. Many people also believe that desert is not the only justification for punishment (deterrence counts, as well); how-ever, what is crucial for my purposes is that few are willing to say desert plays no part at all in the justification of criminal punishment. Appeals to desert are characteristically appeals to retributive justice. The core claim of retributive justice is that perpetrators deserve to suffer and it is intrinsic-ally just to inflict such suffering.[19] For retributivists the amount of suffering should be proportional to the wrong committed. Retributivists differ in the explanations offered for why suffering is what is deserved. Some take this to be a bedrock moral intuition; others offer competing accounts of why suffering is deserved. Michael Moore argues that the intrinsic goodness of punishing wrongdoers best accounts for our intuitive judgments in particular cases. Jean Hampton argues that by countering the false moral claim implicit in wrongdoing suffering restores the moral equality between perpetrator and victim that wrongdoing disrupts. By contrast, Herbert Morris argues that suffering restores the fair distribution of benefits and burdens that wrongdoing upsets, and in particular the burdens of self-restraint that abiding by rules requires. Punishment takes

---

of theories of the moral point of criminal law to which one might subscribe, not all of which link the purpose of criminal law to desert. For an overview of such approaches, see Duff, Antony, "Theories of Criminal Law," in *The Stanford Encyclopedia of Philosophy*, ed. Edward N. Zalta, http://plato .stanford.edu/archives/sum2013/entries/criminal-law/. For a sophisticated account of a pluralist theory of punishment, see John Tasioulas, "Punishment and Repentance," *Philosophy* 81, no. 2 (2006): 279–322. I use retributive theories of the criminal law because I believe they best capture a core source of the dissatisfaction with responses other than punishment in transitional societies. When objecting to the justice of alternative responses to wrongdoing, one typical core concern is that perpetrators are not getting what they deserve because they do not suffer the infliction of punishment. For many, this means that victims consequently do not receive the recognition and entitlement they are owed.

[19] All retributivists agree that it is morally wrong to inflict more suffering than is proportional to the crime or to intentionally punish the innocent. Some retributivists may view proportional suffering as setting the ceiling on the suffering that is permissible. Alternatively, retributivists may see an obligation to inflict suffering up to the point of proportionality such that it is morally wrong to inflict less than proportional suffering. Negative retributivists argue that desert is not a sufficient reason to punish; some other moral good (e.g., deterrence) must be achieved through punishment as well. Positive retributivists see desert as providing a reason or justification for punishment. See Walen, Alec, "Retributive Justice," in *The Stanford Encyclopedia of Philosophy*, ed. Edward N. Zalta, http://plato.stanford.edu/archives/sum2015/entries/justice-retributive/.

away a wrongdoer's unfair advantage.[20] The differences among these accounts do not matter for my purposes; what is important is the underlying thought that punishment is an intrinsically fitting and appropriate response to wrongdoers.

In transitional contexts both pragmatic and moral obstacles preclude the straightforward application of trial, conviction, and criminal punishment to many, indeed most, instances of wrongdoing. The sheer number of crimes can overwhelm even a mature criminal justice system created to deal with statistically infrequent wrongdoing. Numerous human rights abuses are characteristically committed during repression and conflict, and so criminal justice systems face the task of potentially prosecuting tens of thousands of cases. According to one estimate, between 170,000 and 210,000 individuals actively participated in the Rwandan genocide in 1994.[21] In the words of South African lawyer Paul van Zyl, "Criminal justice systems are designed to maintain order in societies where violation of law is the exception. These systems simply cannot cope when, either as a result of state-sanctioned human rights abuses or internal conflict or war, violations become the rule."[22] There are furthermore obstacles to the successful prosecution of even a portion of alleged perpetrators. It is not unusual for evidence to be systematically destroyed by government officials prior to a transition. Lack of trust in state agents may make the possibility of getting ordinary citizens to testify against wrongdoers practically impossible. Corruption as well as insufficiently trained and funded police and legal staff often undermine the ability of courts to effectively distinguish the guilty from the innocent.

Even when such pragmatic obstacles are not as severe in a given context, moral obstacles remain. During conflict and repression, the state is often complicit in wrongdoing, and the criminal justice system colludes in preventing agents of the state from being held accountable for wrongs

---

[20] See Hampton, Jean, "Correcting Harms versus Righting Wrongs: The Goal of Retribution," *UCLA Law Review* 39 (1992): 1659–1702; Herbert Morris, "Guilt and Suffering," *Philosophy East and West* 21, no. 4 (1971): 419–34; Moore, Michael, "Justifying Retributivism," *Israel Law Review* 24 (1993): 15–49. The views of both Hampton and Morris have been subject to extensive critique. For a critique of Morris, see Hampton, "Correcting Harms." For a critique of Hampton, see Gert, Heather J. Linda Radzik, and Michael Hand, "Hampton on the Expressive Power of Punishment," *Journal of Social Philosophy* 35, no. 1 (2004): 79–90.

[21] Straus, Scott, "How Many Perpetrators Were There in the Rwandan Genocide? An Estimate," *Journal of Genocide Research* 6, no. 1 (2004): 85–98.

[22] van Zyl, Paul, "Justice without Punishment: Guaranteeing Human Rights in Transitional Societies," in *Looking Back, Reaching Forward: Reflections on the Truth and Reconciliation Commission of South Africa*, ed. Charles Villa-Vicencio and Wilhelm Verwoerd, 46–57 (Cape Town: University of Cape Town Press, 2000).

committed. This collusion calls into question the authority of the state to prosecute such wrongs following a transition. The practical impossibility of charging all – or even most – who are guilty of wrongdoing has led to charges of arbitrariness and bias in the case of the few who are held to account. It is claimed that punishing a few while the many go free is unjust, especially when among the many going free are those responsible for issuing the orders that the punished followed. Finally, in some contexts, including South Africa, the possibility of a transition itself may have been conditioned on the granting of amnesty to those who participated in wrongdoing in the past. Amnesties preclude legal liability for a crime for either an individual or class of individuals and are granted prior to a criminal trial. Amnesty thus precludes punishment, and so pursuing punishment in a transition becomes morally controversial insofar as it violates a prior commitment.

Against this background, it is unsurprising that many communities in transition have sought out means other than criminal punishment to deal with the wrongs of the past. Amnesty was granted following the Dirty War in Argentina, apartheid in South Africa, and the civil war in Guatemala. Truth commissions have been established in dozens of countries since the 1970s, including Ghana, Fiji, Sierra Leone, and El Salvador. Truth commissions are officially established committees directed to investigate and document patterns of human rights abuses during a specified period. Commissions produce a report that summarizes the findings of their investigation but do not punish perpetrators. Reparations, offered to victims in Chile, Cambodia, and Morocco, provide some form of compensation to victims of wrongdoing, including "financial compensation to individuals or groups; guarantees of non-repetition; social services such as healthcare or education; and symbolic measures such as formal apologies or public commemorations."[23] Finally, the barring of individuals from holding certain offices via programs of lustration has been implemented in countries such as Czechoslovakia, Poland, and Bulgaria.

Legal scholars, international organizations, victims, and citizens of transitional societies disagree on whether any legal response other than criminal trial and punishment does in fact achieve justice. Such disagreements are unsurprising given that alternative responses do not hold perpetrators accountable in the same way as criminal punishment. Amnesty in exchange for peace can grant rapists immunity from criminal and civil

---

[23] See International Center for Transitional Justice, http://ictj.org/our-work/transitional-justice-issues/reparations.

liability, thus severing the link between accountability and hard treatment. Truth commissions document the actions of torturers but do not punish them. Furthermore, truth commissions do not focus primarily on individual perpetrators and victims in isolation, but rather on patterns of interaction and structures of institutions that permit, sanction, or promote such patterns. Reparations shift the emphasis away from the perpetrator to those who have suffered and been wronged, but reparations only offer material compensation for what in many cases is irreparable harm.

Transitional Justice as a Compromise

Many scholars view transitional justice as a compromise among familiar forms of justice (e.g., retributive justice) and competing moral considerations. In this section I critically evaluate different ways of conceptualizing transitional justice as compromise found in the literature. Scholars differ in how they characterize the compromise made and whether they take the compromise to be justified. Despite these differences, however, there are two general features of compromise views. First, such views implicitly or explicitly define justice as "all-things-considered justified." Scholars may analyze what particular kinds of justice (e.g., retributive justice) demand in the course of their analysis, but what makes a response to wrongdoing justified is that it strikes the appropriate balance among competing values. The claims of commonly recognized types of justice, such as retributive justice, are one of multiple moral (or in some cases pragmatic) inputs that must be taken into account to determine whether a particular response to wrongdoing is just. Second, compromise views also generally assume that moral demands are context insensitive,[24] that is, the

---

[24] The context sensitivity of demands of justice is the key issue in the extraordinary-ordinary transitional justice debate in legal scholarship. In defending the justifiability of truth commissions and/or amnesty, some legal scholars have claimed that justice in transitions is "extraordinary": transitional contexts are exceptional contexts in which distinctive standards of justice apply. On the idea that justice is different in transitions and in some respects extraordinary, see generally Teitel, Ruti, "Transitional Jurisprudence: The Role of Law in Political Transformation," *Yale Law Journal* 106 (1997): 2009–80; Teitel, Ruti, *Transitional Justice* (Oxford: Oxford University Press, 2000); Gray, David C., "Extraordinary Justice," *Alabama Law Review* 62 (2010): 55–109. However, other legal scholars claim that justice in transitions is "ordinary": although the contexts are not identical, whatever standards of justice apply when evaluating responses to wrongdoing in the ordinary context of a stable democracy also apply in the context of a transition. See, generally, Dyzenhaus, David "Judicial Independence, Transitional Justice, and the Rule of Law," *Otago Law Review* 10 (2003): 345–72; Posner, Eric and Adrian Vermeule, "Transitional Justice as Ordinary Justice," *Harvard Law Review* 117 (2004): 761–825. In what follows I use the labels "context sensitive" and "context insensitive" rather than "ordinary" and "extraordinary" to refer to the question of whether – and in what way – context influences moral demands. The "extraordinary"

same moral principles apply across all contexts. Thus, the same set of principles or standards needs to be satisfied in all contexts for a response to wrongdoing to be justified. I argue in this section that some versions of compromise views are insufficiently nuanced in their understanding of the justice component of the overall compromise, failing to recognize that justice is a scalar concept and assuming rather than demonstrating what justice, as one moral value, demands. The most nuanced compromise views avoid these limitations, but in trying to identify how justice specifically is satisfied such approaches collapse important distinctions among kinds of justice; as a consequence, the normative point for making such distinctions in the first place is undermined. A source of this latter problem is a failure to recognize the context sensitive character of justice claims.

Compromise views are most commonly found in the literature in political theory and philosophy; such discussions are dominated by one case study in particular: South Africa.[25] Some scholars focus exclusively on South Africa, while others reference additional examples. Because South Africa has been so influential in philosophical discussions of transitional justice as compromise, I use it as the case study to illustrate competing versions of compromise positions. A central moral question debated in discussions of the TRC in the literature is whether and for what reasons the granting of amnesty to perpetrators of gross human rights abuses is morally justified.

According to the *simple compromise* position, alternative responses to wrongdoing, such as the South African TRC, sacrifice justice. The realist version of the simple compromise view claims that justice is sacrificed out of expediency.[26] This position is realist in the sense of the traditional

and "ordinary" labels imply that either transitional justice is exactly like justice as we normally conceptualize it or it is exceptional and in some ways alien from justice normally understood. The completely common or wholly foreign divide is not helpful. It suggests that in order to demonstrate that there is something theoretically different about transitional justice, we must identify something about transitional contexts that is wholly "other" from ordinary democratic contexts. Unsurprisingly, the debate in legal scholarship has focused on whether there are unique dilemmas or features in transitional contexts that are not present in democratic contexts. An underlying assumption of this dialectic is that differences of degree are not morally significant: identifying the same feature as present to different degrees in each context does not explain why justice is different. I argue in Chapter 1 that this assumption is false.

[25] One prominent version of a compromise view in the legal literature is Posner and Vermeule, "Transitional Justice."

[26] Mendez, Juan E., "Accountability for Past Abuses," *Human Rights Quarterly* 19, no. 2 (1997): 255, disapproves of the sacrificing of justice on these grounds. For this characterization of political compromise, see Jonathan Allen, "Balancing Justice and Social Utility: Political Theory and the Idea of a Truth and Reconciliation Commission," *University of Toronto Law Journal* 49 (1999): 315–53.

approach in international relations that claims morality does not extend to relations between states. All is fair in war – and the aftermath of war. Justice is defined by the powerful. Choices are a function of merely political compromise. "From the realist perspective, the question of why a given state response occurred is conflated with the question of what response was possible."[27] Pressing prudential considerations, such as concern regarding the resumption of violence should alleged perpetrators be prosecuted, dictate the choices of particular communities. At first glance this characterization of the choices that transitional societies make seems apt. Indeed, transitional contexts can give rise to the same thought that realists articulate in the context of war or that underpins justifications for the suspension of ordinary rules by a government in a state of emergency. Justice is taken to be a luxury that communities cannot afford or that does not pertain to such contexts.

However, the realist version of the simple compromise position is too sweeping in the permission it grants. Although many find it intuitively plausible to claim that actions not ordinarily sanctioned may be permissible in moments of crisis, few are willing to permit any action whatsoever. Killing may be justified in war, but massacre is not. Similarly, establishing a truth commission may be justified in a transitional context, but summary executions are not. Moreover, the realist version of the simple compromise view does not capture or recognize the moral salience of the various pressing considerations that transitional societies confront. A concern for reducing or ending violence is not only of pragmatic interest for those potentially targeted but also reflects a moral concern with preventing unnecessary suffering.

The moral version of the simple compromise view acknowledges the moral weight that should be given to many of these countervailing considerations. In the moral version, when transitional societies establish a truth commission or grant amnesty they sacrifice justice for the sake of achieving competing moral values, such as peace or reconciliation.[28] This version has the virtue of acknowledging the moral salience of many of the factors influencing decisions concerning how to deal with past wrongs. However, the moral version is too simplistic in its conceptualization of the various

---

[27] Teitel, "Transitional Jurisprudence," 2011.

[28] See, e.g., Moellendorf, Darrel, "Amnesty, Truth, and Justice: AZAPO," *South African Journal on Human Rights* 13 (1997): 283–91; Wilson, Stuart, "The Myth of Restorative Justice: Truth, Reconciliation and the Ethics of Amnesty," *South African Journal of Human Rights* 17 (2001): 531–62; Lenta, Patrick, "Transitional Justice and the Truth and Reconciliation Commission," *Theoria: Journal of Political and Social Theory* 96 (2000): 52–73.

values at stake in these choices. This view implicitly assumes that values such as justice and reconciliation are completely distinct and incompatible. *Either* one promotes justice *or* one promotes reconciliation, so the thinking goes. Moreover, the moral version of the simple compromise view assumes that justice is achieved in an all-or-nothing manner. *Either* the demands of justice are satisfied and satisfied completely, *or* justice is sacrificed. The possibility that justice may be satisfied to some degree is not considered.

Nuanced compromise views complicate the moral landscape.[29] The basic strategy of such views is to demonstrate that alternative responses to wrongdoing are or can be sensitive to the moral concerns at the core of retributive justice. Similarly, the extent to which such responses respect the moral concerns at the core of other values, such as reconciliation, is considered. Nuanced compromise views demonstrate that choices to adopt responses other than punishment do not simply sacrifice justice for the sake of another value that is distinct from and unrelated to justice (e.g., something we could name reconciliation). Instead, alternative responses may serve both the values of justice and reconciliation to some degree. At the same time, nuanced compromise views recognize that alternative responses to wrongdoing entail a moral cost and sacrifice. However, the moral cost and sacrifice is principled and one that can be justified.[30] As Jonathan Allen writes about the South African TRC, "Although we may still have a sense that something has been lost in the transaction, we can resist the conclusion that a simple sacrifice or trade-off has occurred. . . . The question, rather, is whether punitive justice has simply been sacrificed to some or other conception of an overridingly important social goal or

---

[29] This way of assessing the justice of responses to wrongdoing is not utilitarian. To see why, consider explanations of the justice of punishment offered by mixed theories. For a classic example of such a mixed theory of punishment see Hart, H. L. A., *Punishment and Responsibility* (Oxford: Oxford University Press, 1968). Mixed theories justify punishment on the grounds of both desert and consequential considerations. However, unlike in discussions of transitional justice, the explanation of the justification of punishment by mixed theorists is not necessarily explained as a compromise between competing moral considerations. In mixed theories desert serves as a side constraint, restricting who is properly subject to punishment. Punishing only those who are guilty ensures that only individuals who deserve to be punished are punished, and avoids the moral problems associated with punishing the innocent that plague purely utilitarian theories of punishment. Positive social consequences such as deterrence must be achieved for punishment to be just in a given case. In this interpretation of the justice of punishment, multiple moral considerations bear on punishment's justification, only one of which is a desert-based consideration.

[30] Examples of such nuanced compromise views include Allen, "Balancing Justice and Social Utility"; Posner and Vermeule, "Transitional Justice"; May, Simon Cabulea, "Moral Compromise, Civic Friendship, and Political Reconciliation," *Critical Review of International Social and Political Philosophy* 14, no. 5 (2011): 581–602; Allais, Lucy, "Restorative Justice, Retributive Justice, and the South African Truth and Reconciliation Commission," *Philosophy & Public Affairs* 39, no. 4 (2012): 331–63.

whether some respect for justice might still be thought to be embodied in this institutionalized encounter."[31]

Nuanced compromise views take a more sophisticated view of justice than simple compromise views. They recognize that specific moral concerns underpin the basic principles of justice associated with different kinds of justice. They also draw attention to the basic rationale for specific injunctions of justice. Many such views also recognize that there are multiple kinds of justice about which we may speak and that may be fostered to varying degrees by alternative responses to wrongdoing in transitional contexts. For example, Lucy Allais discusses both restorative and retributive justice, while Jonathan Allen considers punitive justice, compensatory justice, and "justice as ethos."[32] Finally, nuanced compromise views acknowledge the complex relationship between justice and other moral concerns such as reconciliation, noting that such values are not necessarily incompatible and may in fact be promoted by the same process.

An assumption underpinning nuanced compromise views is that extant theories of justice provide the requisite conceptual resources for understanding and evaluating the moral questions that transitional societies confront. Nuanced compromise approaches generally recognize that transitional contexts are not identical to ordinary contexts; rather, transitional societies are frequently characterized as exhibiting more-pronounced or acute versions of features found in other contexts.[33] For such theorists, more-acute versions of problems or features of stable democracies may lead to a fuller appreciation of the basic moral concerns at the core of, for example, the retributive injunction to punish those who have done wrong. However, such differences do not alter the fundamental moral framework of justice that we should use to evaluate responses to wrongdoing in transitional contexts; the appropriate framework is the same one we use to evaluate responses to wrongdoing in other contexts. In this sense moral demands are context insensitive.

In the chapters that follow, I reject the assumption that we can sufficiently adapt theories of familiar kinds of justice to be applicable to all contexts. In my view, theories of justice always presuppose a set of background conditions, conditions that explain and shape the justice problem to which specific principles of justice are responsive and that

---

[31] Allen, "Balancing Justice and Social Utility," 325–26.

[32] Jonathan Allen describes justice as ethos as a disposition to protest or resist injustice. It is this disposition that is corrupted in contexts in which widespread wrongdoing occurs. See ibid., 335.

[33] See, for example, Posner and Vermeule, "Transitional Justice."

influence the plausibility of arguments for a given set of justice principles. Moral claims, and in particular justice claims, are context sensitive in the sense that they are salient only when such background conditions obtain. Here I begin to motivate my opponent's view that extant theories of particular kinds of justice can be adapted to all contexts by considering an influential attempt to adapt a theory of retributive justice so that it can be used to evaluate the justifiability of truth commissions in transitional contexts. I then argue that there is a significant cost in pursuing this strategy: the distinctions among kinds of justice collapse.

Advocates of nuanced compromise views generally recognize that the moral situation of transitional communities is not identical to that of paradigm stable democracies. One difference is the implicit or explicit orienting presumption about the justifiability of responses to wrongdoing among both members of transitional societies and scholars evaluating responses to wrongdoing by such societies. A recurring worry about *any* response to wrongdoing, including criminal trials, in transitional contexts is that it will fail to be an instrument of justice, and fail to be viewed as such by members of the community in question. As Pablo de Greiff nicely puts it, criminal trials risk being seen as mere "victor's justice" or scapegoating; reparations risk being perceived as attempts to "buy off" victims and blood money; and truth commissions risk being seen as "a form of whitewash in which the truth emerges but no one pays any price."[34] The form skepticism takes in any particular society may vary in terms of breadth and depth in a given population. Skepticism may be wide (shared by the majority of a population) or narrow (shared only by a minority). The degree to which a given population is skeptical about such responses may also differ.[35] Skepticism about the justice of any response to wrongdoing seems intuitively plausible in such contexts, and in particular cases may in fact be justified.

For example, writing in 2014, Ali Mamouri articulates skepticism about transitional justice in Iraq following the fall of Saddam Hussein. He references the case of Nada. Imprisoned with her mother and sister when she was three years old, Nada spent three years in prison. Four years after

---

[34] De Greiff, "Theorizing Transitional Justice," 38.

[35] In cases where skepticism is not widely shared, a minority population may be so deeply skeptical of a criminal justice system that the attempt to apply that system would lead to genuine political instability. That is, the minority population would simply give up any pretense that they would continue to abide by the authority of the state. If the minority population is small enough then skepticism may not be widespread but still deep enough to be problematic. I thank Linda Radzik for drawing this point to my attention.

applying for compensation, she still has received no payment. Mamouri cites, as well, the numerous cases where criminal files were opened but investigations faltered. Recommendations from international organizations such as the International Center for Transitional Justice (ICTJ) have been ignored by the Iraqi government in his view. At the same time, ongoing sectarian violence combined with an altering of the ethnic group enjoying the locus of political power has further complicated notions of who is a victim and perpetrator. Mamouri summarizes his skeptical view of the actual justice of any transitional justice efforts in Iraq in these words:

> Sectarian tension in the country has caused some state institutions to act in bad faith with regard to transitional justice, which led to further violence in the past years. ... transitional justice in Iraq is not seen as a project to transition from dictatorship to a fair democratic system. It has been, rather, dealt with with a very selective approach. The focus has been on trial and punishment, while other basic elements were left out, leaving room for further crimes to be committed in the name of justice.[36]

Against this background, a central theoretical task is to explain how measures can in fact be measures of *justice* in a context in which they are not likely to be seen in this way and in which these perceptions are often justified. Such explanations stand to have significant practical consequences and affect the meaning that individuals within transitional communities attach to particular measures. By contrast, the same skepticism is not characteristically present among members of stable democratic societies or among scholars theorizing about responses to wrongdoing in such contexts. No criminal justice system is perfect, and many criticisms have been raised about criminal justice systems in stable democracies.[37] However, there is no general presumption by scholars or by members of democratic communities that punishment involves the mere exercise of power by a stronger party over a weaker, or that civil damages amount to blood money, nor consequently an assumption among scholars that there are tangible practical consequences that a theoretical justification of a response like punishment or truth commissions will have.

---

[36] Mamouri, Ali, "Transitional Justice Fails in Iraq," *Al-Monitor: The Pulse of the Middle East,* www .al-monitor.com/pulse/originals/2014/06/iraq-transitional-justice-failed.html#ixzz3rT75qXef (accessed November 14, 2015).

[37] In the United States, for example, there are advocates of restorative justice who argue that the system of criminal justice should be replaced, and there are critics of particular features of specific criminal justice systems, such as the system of the United States, who advocate for their reform. There are recurring concerns about racial bias in the administration of criminal justice in the United States.

One source of these varying presumptions is the different moral needs present in each context. In transitional societies the basic importance of human rights and their efficacy in governing conduct often need to be established. The new political order that commits to such rights protections needs to be legitimized, and the previous political order that officially and publicly sanctioned violence rejected.[38] There is thus a need to draw a line between what communities sanctioned in the past and what will be sanctioned in the future. Yet these large tasks are pursued in the midst of a "justice gap": "the radical disparity between justice needs and resources available to transitional regimes."[39] As I discuss in detail in Chapter 2, these moral needs (e.g., establishing the currency of human rights generally and their significance for communities, not just for individuals) are different from the moral needs that theories of retributive and corrective justice typically address. Such theories are oriented around individuals, and are concerned with responding to the needs that arise when particular individuals violate norms of conduct that result in wrongs or harms to others. The background efficacy of human rights norms and the legitimacy of the legal order are assumed to be present.

Nuanced compromise views adapt theories of particular kinds of justice to respond to problems and address moral needs different than those they were originally designed to address. In moving to accommodate these needs, theorists often sever the link between a particular kind of justice and its widely recognized constitutive principles. For example, a central principle of retributivism is "that those who commit certain kinds of wrongful acts, paradigmatically serious crimes, morally deserve to suffer a proportionate punishment."[40] In explaining the justifiability of the South African Truth and Reconciliation Commission, however, Allais argues, "There are ways other than punishment of responding to the moral concerns underlying retributivism."[41] Allais makes the case for the retributive character of a truth commission by appealing to the moral concerns that ground or are connected to the core retributive principles, such as respecting the value of human beings or upholding the law.[42] Focusing on the moral concerns at this level of generality also allows Allais to demonstrate the ways in which other mechanisms satisfy the core concerns

---

[38] See de Greiff, "Theorizing Transitional Justice"; Teitel, *Transitional Justice*; and Gray, "Extraordinary Justice," 91–92.

[39] Gray, "Extraordinary Justice," 24.   [40] Walen, "Retributive Justice."

[41] Allais, "Restorative Justice," 338. Allais argues that theories of restorative and retributive justice answer different questions rather than providing competing answers to the same question.

[42] Ibid., 342–43.

underpinning standard kinds of justice, despite fulfilling those concerns in a nonstandard way (e.g., without punishment).

However, separating retributive justice from its orienting problem and substantive normative principles undermines the basis for distinguishing it from other kinds of justice. Discussions of justice operate at many different levels and have different meanings at each level. Justice can be a virtue of individuals as well as a characteristic of laws. As philosophers since Aristotle have recognized, there are different kinds of justice.[43] Aristotle distinguished between distributive and corrective justice. Contemporary philosophers examine retributive justice, corrective justice, distributive justice, international justice, procedural justice, and justice in war.[44]

In book 5 of the *Nicomachean Ethics*, Aristotle notes that the different ways something can be just must be distinguished, and in particular a description of different kinds of justice is needed.[45] Aristotle does not explain why it is important for justice to be divided, but here is one explanation for its importance. Justice is fundamentally normative, concerned with action. We theorize about justice so as to understand what we should do as individuals and as communities.[46] Communities confront a variety of problems that call for normative guidance. Kinds of justice focus on specific problems and offer normative guidance on how to deal with a particular issue. Retributive justice focuses on perpetrators of wrongdoing, and asks what should be done in response to their actions. Corrective justice focuses on the injuries individuals can suffer, and what should be done to repair wrongful injuries or losses. Theories of distributive justice answer the question: what principles must be satisfied by a set of social arrangements that assigns rights and duties, and determines the distribution of the benefits and burdens of social cooperation?[47] As the descriptions of the problems indicate, kinds of justice differ in the basic subject of

---

[43] Aristotle, *Nicomachean Ethics*, trans. Terence Irwin, 2nd ed. (Indianapolis: Hackett Publishing, 1999). See especially book 5.34 (30).

[44] One indication of the widely recognized character of these kinds is that each has a separate entry in the *Stanford Encyclopedia of Philosophy*. Corrective justice falls under the "Theories of Tort Law" entry.

[45] Aristotle, *Nicomachean Ethics*, 5.34 (30), 122.

[46] Stating that justice is normative, not purely evaluative, is taking a particular stand on one particular debate within ideal/non-ideal theory. See Valentini, Laura, "Ideal vs. Non-Ideal Theory: A Conceptual Map," *Philosophy Compass* 7, no. 9 (2012): 654–64.

[47] This is one way of reading the fundamental question in Rawls, John, *Theory of Justice* (Cambridge, MA: Harvard University Press, 1971). Another way of framing the question is articulated by Samuel Freeman, who links distributive justice with "fairly designing the system of basic legal institutions and social norms that make production, exchange, distribution, and consumption possible,"

interest (e.g., perpetrators of wrongdoing, victims of wrongdoing, and/or the basic economic institutions of a community). Principles of justice specify what counts as doing justice, and different kinds of justice propose different injunctions. Examples include the retributive principle that justice requires punishment of wrongdoers or Rawls's difference principle, according to which departures from strict equality in the distribution of primary goods is just so long as the inequalities are to the benefit of the least advantaged. Thinking of justice discretely in terms of particular kinds allows us to keep clear which problem we are dealing with, and to come up with specific principles for responding to a given problem that will be action guiding. I assume that the separation among kinds of justice is a valid one. In any given case, the separation among kinds of justice should be preserved unless there are overriding reasons not to in any given case.

All kinds of justice share features that count as aspects of justice rather than another moral value. A basic concern with respect for human dignity is arguably one such feature. Respecting human dignity is thus a very general and basic moral concern of justice, which can be expressed in action in a range of ways. Distributing goods according to a specific set of principles or inflicting suffering on perpetrators of wrongdoing may be two such ways. Demonstrating that responses such as truth commissions respect human dignity is not sufficient to show that truth commissions respond to *retributive* justice. Thus the fact that responses like truth commissions respect human dignity may count in favor of them respecting justice in general, but is not enough to show that they respect retributive justice specifically.

The preceding discussion suggests some desiderata for an adequate account of transitional justice. First, an account should recognize that fulfillment of the demands of justice comes in degrees. This makes it possible to judge that a given response to wrongdoing is more or less just, or just or unjust, to different extents. Second, an analysis should not violate or undermine the distinctions between different kinds of justice. Third, there is a distinct practical need for a theory of transitional justice, and an account of transitional justice should be such that it responds to this need. This requires an account to be normative in the sense of action-guiding, specifying principles that can actually help actors involved make choices about how a given community in transition will deal with its legacy of violence.

see Abizadeh, Arash, "Cooperation, Pervasive Impact, and Coercion: On the Scope (Not Site) of Distributive Justice," *Philosophy & Public Affairs* 35, no. 4 (2007): 335.

A Different Kind of Justice?

A second kind of account of transitional justice focuses specifically on one moral value, justice, and explains why and under what conditions alternative responses fulfill the requirements of this particular value. Responses are "just" in such accounts insofar as they satisfy these requirements. Standards or principles of justice I take to reflect especially stringent deontological constraints on action designed to recognize the basic, irrevocable, and equal dignity of individuals. Such constraints ground claims that individuals have on other individuals, institutions, or agents, claims that give rise to the obligations or duties of justice of such individuals, institutions, or agents. Such duties are legally and socially enforceable by society.[48] Scholars who adopt this strategy focus on either *restorative justice* or *transitional justice*. Advocates of restorative justice generally view the requirements of justice as context insensitive. Advocates of transitional justice generally view justice claims in a context-sensitive manner. According to context-sensitive views, the moral principles or standards that need to be satisfied in order for a response to wrongdoing to be justified vary across contexts. Here context influences which moral demands are salient in a given case.[49] I discuss each of these kinds of justice in turn.

Restorative justice conceptualizes crime as a problem in the relationship among the offender, the victim, and the local community.[50] In the view of advocates of restorative justice, the core justice intuition at stake in addressing wrongdoing is "the notion that a social equality or equilibrium has been disrupted (or further disrupted) by the offense and that it must be

---

[48] For a similar conceptualization of the demandingness constraint shared by principles of justice, see Risse, Mathias, *Global Justice* (Princeton, NJ: Princeton University Press, 2012). He writes, "It is commonly agreed, though, that obligations of justice are not the only sorts of moral obligation, and that among moral obligations, obligations of justice are especially stringent" (5). In a similar vein, Valentini writes, "'Justice' has a privileged position in the history of political ideas. Principles of justice are typically seen as particularly stringent, and as giving rise to rights. To say that something is a matter of justice is to make a particularly weighty normative assertion" ("Ideal vs. Non-Ideal Theory," 658).

[49] The position I defend with respect to claims of justice has similarities with epistemic contextualism. According to epistemic contextualism, the truth of a proposition expressed in a knowledge claim ("S knows that P") depends on features of the "conversational-practical situation" of the knowledge attributor(s). Consequently, the truth value of knowledge claims may be different in different contexts. Similarly, I claim that the truth value of a justice claim is context dependent. See Rysiew, Patrick, "Epistemic Contextualism," *Stanford Encyclopedia of Philosophy*, ed. Edward N. Zalta (2011), http://plato.stanford.edu/archives/win2011/entries/contextualism-epistemology/.

[50] For a summary of the key commitments of restorative justice, see Walker, Margaret Urban, "Restorative Justice and Reparations," *Journal of Social Philosophy* 37, no. 3 (2006): 383.

restored through social action."[51] According to this framework, a chief goal of the criminal justice system should be to restore the relationships among the criminal, the victim, and/or the community in the aftermath of crime.

Restorative justice theorists generally regard it as a mistake to equate justice with retributive justice. The proper aim of the state in the aftermath of crime is not to secure retribution or deter crime but to restore the proper relationships among citizens, and between the citizens and the state. Forgiveness is characteristically a key aim of restorative justice. Restorative justice processes have been adopted in a number of democratic contexts. Such processes focus on rebuilding or building bonds rather than isolating or alienating the perpetrator, and turn to measures such as restitution payments and face-to-face dialogue in order to restore that relationship.[52] When used in criminal sentencing, victims play an important participatory role, shaping what the offender must do to make amends.[53] Such participation, proponents claim, increases the likelihood that victims will be satisfied with the process of dealing with crime, will be in a position to overcome resentment or anger, and will regain their status as recognized members with value within the community.[54] The role of offenders is characteristically active, as well, which, advocates claim, enables offenders to regain their sense of self-worth.[55]

The insight at the core of restorative justice – that relationships and their repair is a central concern of justice – is important. Indeed, relational repair is at the core of the account of transitional justice I develop in Chapter 3. However, in my view, the justice that is salient in transitions should not be understood as restorative justice. For one thing, the idea of restorative justice is still underdeveloped. The core commitments of restorative justice are still being clarified. Moreover, fundamental areas of disagreement remain. Importantly, restorative justice theorists disagree about whether punishment is compatible with restorative justice. For some, the idea that punishment is needed to restore equilibrium is

[51] Llewellyn, Jennifer and Robert Howse, "Institutions for Restorative Justice: The South African Truth and Reconciliation Commission," *University of Toronto Law Journal* 49, no. 3 (1999): 357.
[52] Braithwaite, John, *Restorative Justice and Responsive Regulation* (Oxford: Oxford University Press, 2002); van Ness, Daniel W. and Karen Heetderks Strong, *Restoring Justice*, 2nd ed. (Cincinnati: Anderson Publishing, 2002); Kiss, Elizabeth, "Moral Ambition within and beyond Political Constraints: Reflections on Restorative Justice," in *Truth v. Justice: The Morality of Truth Commissions*, ed. Robert I. Rotberg and Dennis Thompson, 68–98 (Princeton: Princeton University Press, 2000).
[53] Johnstone, Gerry, *Restorative Justice: Ideas, Values, Debates* (Cullompton, UK: Willan Publishing, 2002).
[54] Ibid.
[55] Zehr, Howard, *Changing Lenses: A New Focus for Crime and Justice* (Scottsdale, PA: Herald Press, 1990); Braithwaite, *Restorative Justice*.

"arbitrary and historically contingent,"[56] while other theorists of restorative justice include punishment as a process of restorative justice.[57]

One reaction might be to further develop an account of restorative justice. However, two further limitations suggest this is not the most fruitful course for understanding transitional justice. The first limitation stems from the key role that forgiveness plays in most accounts of restorative justice.[58] *Forgiveness* is generally defined as the overcoming or forswearing of negative emotions such as resentment, anger, or hatred.[59] Here relational repair depends fundamentally on a change of reactive attitude or emotion among those wronged. However, in my view, forgiveness should not be a requirement for relational repair in transitional contexts.[60]

The morally laudatory role of forgiveness in interpersonal relationships is most powerful when considering wrongdoing that is the exception but not the rule. When exceptional, wrongdoing occurs in the context of an otherwise healthy or normal relationship predicated on, for example, mutual respect. A willingness to forgive in this context can reflect recognition by the forgiver of her imperfection and fallibility. Just as she hopes the other will forgive her for her transgressions, she is willing to now forgive. Moreover, she is willing to overcome resentment or anger at the wrong she suffered for the sake of maintaining the relationship recognizing that simmering resentment and anger can obstruct and even end relationships. In these ways, a willingness to forgive can be essential to maintaining a valuable relationship that is predicated on reciprocity.

However, in transitions the background relational context is not one of a mutually respectful and reciprocal relationship in which wrongdoing is the exception and not the rule. In contexts where relationships are not mutually respectful and reciprocal, urging forgiveness risks maintaining oppression and injustice since the focus of forgiveness is not on fundamentally altering the terms of interaction but rather on overcoming obstacles to ongoing or continuing interaction. Indeed, there is a certain passivity in forgiving attitudes; encouraging or requiring forgiveness can

---

[56] Llewellyn and Howse, "Institutions for Restorative Justice," 357.

[57] Philpott, Daniel, *Just and Unjust Peace: An Ethic of Political Reconciliation* (New York: Oxford University Press, 2012).

[58] Ibid.

[59] This basic definition was first articulated by Bishop Butler and later expanded on by theorists, including Richards, Norman, "Forgiveness," *Ethics* 99, no. 1 (1988): 77–97; Hughes, Paul M., "What Is Involved in Forgiving?" *Philosophia* 25 (1997): 33–49; Hieronymi, Pamela, "Articulating an Uncompromising Forgiveness," *Philosophy and Phenomenological Research* 62, no. 3 (2001): 529–55.

[60] The full argument for this claim was originally made in Murphy, Colleen, *A Moral Theory of Political Reconciliation* (New York: Cambridge University Press, 2010). See in particular the Introduction.

thus motivate precisely the form of submission to unjust terms for interaction that recent violence was trying to achieve.

In addition, the imperative to forgive places the burden for relational
repair squarely on victims, which in transitional contexts is deeply morally
problematic. In contexts of widespread wrongdoing urging forgiveness can
reflect a failure to fully acknowledge or take seriously the wrongdoing to
which victims were subject. Placing the burden of relational repair on
victims can reflect a failure to recognize that victims are justified in feeling
resentment and anger in response. The failure to feel resentment can itself
reflect an insufficient sense of self-respect or self-worth among victims,
leading them to think wrongs done were permissible or unobjectionable.
Emphasizing or calling for forgiveness can reflect denial among perpetrators and those complicit in wrongdoing of their responsibility for wrongs
that occurred, and the corresponding obligations they now have as a result.

The first limitation points to the second limitation of restorative justice:
it is insufficiently context sensitive. Restorative justice theories do not
consider the context in which the wrongs being dealt with occurred.
Inattention to contextual differences obscures the fact that the reasonableness and plausibility of placing forgiveness at the core of an account of
relational repair depends on certain background conditions being in place.
Altering the background conditions affects the reasonableness of the moral
imperative to forgive; it can turn a reasonable demand into a presumptively
morally troubling one.

Accounts of transitional justice generally take seriously the idea that
transitional justice is not reducible to forms of justice with which we are
already familiar. They also generally take seriously the idea that claims of
justice are context sensitive. As noted earlier in this chapter, numerous
social scientific studies of the social impact of mechanisms for dealing with
past wrongs are predicated on the assumption that the impact will not be
identical to the impact one finds in stable democratic contexts. However,
until recently very little attention focused on whether there is a conceptual
and normative difference in justice, and what that difference might entail.
In addition, normative discussions of transitional justice generally concentrate on the moral evaluation of the various means of pursuing justice (e.g.,
reparations or criminal trials), and not on the idea of transitional justice
itself. As Paige Arthur puts it, "So far, there is no single theory of
transitional justice, and the term does not have a fixed meaning."[61] Pablo

---

[61] Arthur, Paige, "How 'Transitions' Reshaped Human Rights: A Conceptual History of Transitional
Justice," *Human Rights Quarterly* 31 (2009): 359.

de Greiff makes the same point even more forcefully when he writes, "The field remains tremendously undertheorized. It is not just that the consensus around any given understanding of transitional justice and its components is far from complete; the consensus is, moreover thin."[62] Below I briefly survey the few conceptual accounts of transitional justice currently present in the literature.

In her seminal book *Transitional Justice*, Ruti Teitel articulated one of the first accounts of transitional justice. Teitel argues that justice is ultimately *instrumental*: a just response to wrongdoing is one that will promote the transformation of a community into a liberal democratic order.[63] Transitional justice is also pragmatic in the sense that just responses to wrongdoing will offer a pragmatic resolution to the dilemmas inherent in transitional contexts. Importantly, for Teitel what is needed to transform a particular community is contingent on the particular character of the injustice in the past, and so there is no general prescription of what a just response to wrongdoing must do. Indeed, Ruti Teitel explicitly eschews general standards of justice for transitional contexts, arguing that what counts as just in any particular case "is contingent and informed by prior injustice."[64]

However, defining what counts as justice on a strictly-case-by-case basis is at odds with a basic intuition about justice: there is a general set of principles of justice applicable across a range of cases.[65] Moreover, there is a pressing need for criteria by which responses to a legacy of wrongdoing in the midst of a transition can be judged (il)legitimate and (un)just. Defining justice on a case-by-case basis does not provide useful criteria for distinguishing among or critically evaluating the choices communities make.

A few scholars have attempted to articulate the core or orienting principles of transitional justice. Such analyses characteristically begin with an explanation of what is morally distinctive about transitions. There is no consensus on this issue, although there are recurring themes in the literature. One recurring motif is that *law* is different in transitional contexts, and this difference has moral implications. Law, it is frequently claimed, has a "Janus-faced" character in transitions.[66] For example, criminal law is concerned not just about backward-looking considerations of desert but

---

[62] De Greiff, "Theorizing Transitional Justice," 32.
[63] Teitel, *Transitional Justice*, 6; Teitel, "Transitional Jurisprudence," 2011.
[64] Teitel, Transitional Jurisprudence," 2014.   [65] De Greiff, "Theorizing Transitional Justice," 60.
[66] Teitel, *Transitional Justice*; Gray "Extraordinary Justice."

also forward-looking transformation of a community.[67] Another illustration offered concerns the rule of law. In stable democratic contexts, the rule of law provides "order and stability" by guaranteeing a forward-looking prospective character to legal rules.[68] By contrast, in transitional contexts law must provide order and, at the same time, facilitate transformation by renouncing in a backward-looking manner what was previously endorsed or previously defined the legal order.[69] However, scholars have convincingly refuted the claim that law is uniquely Janus-faced in transitional contexts; backward- and forward-looking concerns govern law even in democratic contexts.[70]

A second motif is that transitional contexts are distinctive because of the specific moral needs that past wrongdoing generates.[71] For example, any goal commonly attributed to such processes for dealing with past wrongdoing, such as recognition of victims, cannot be achieved by dealing with victims and perpetrators in isolation. Frank Haldemann argues that recognition is the key goal of transitional justice, "giving due recognition to the pain and humiliation experienced by victims of collective violence." However, he argues that such recognition requires communities to overcome the characteristic institutional and broader societal denial regarding the occurrence of and responsibility for wrongs of the past.[72] Similarly, David Gray argues that "the central transitional task is to achieve between former victims and former abusers an acceptable level of status parity," but such parity can only be established in part by reshaping the social and political significance of certain identities. Gray starts from the observation that mass violence only becomes possible with the support of a community. He then defines an "abusive paradigm" as a "combination of social norms, law, and institutional practice that utilizes a bipolar logic to justify targeted violence. . . . Once dominant, abusive paradigms rationalize and enforce a pathological status inequality that excludes those in an oppressed group from cross-secting identities, allowing abusers to regard them as appropriate targets for exclusion and abuse."[73] In other words, violating norms that prohibit violence against members of certain targeted groups becomes

---

[67] Teitel, *Transitional Justice*; Gray "Extraordinary Justice."   [68] Teitel, *Transitional Justice*, 6.
[69] Ibid., 7.
[70] See Posner and Vermeule, "Transitional Justice"; de Greiff, "Theorizing Transitional Justice."
[71] See de Greiff, "Theorizing Transitional Justice"; Gray, "Extraordinary Justice," 58.
[72] Haldemann, Frank, "Another Kind of Justice: Transitional Justice as Recognition," *Cornell Journal of International Law* 41 (2008): 678.
[73] Gray, "Extraordinary Justice," 55–56.

justifiable.[74] Thus identities need to be redrawn in a way that precludes justification of violence in the future. At the same time, the experience of victims cannot be ignored, and part of that experience is being targeted because of a particular identity. Members of a formerly targeted group have a unique place in the community, which must also be recognized. In Gray's words, "The project of seeking justice for victims in transitions is one not only of seeking equality but also of recognizing difference without reifying any particular line of opposition and association."[75]

These accounts have a key insight: the wrongs to which transitional communities must respond had concrete victims. Recognizing the equal moral status of such victims and recognizing the moral demands that being a victim generates is, as noted by Gray and Haldemann, a fundamental part of what transitional justice demands. However, this recognition is necessary but not sufficient for justice. Dealing with structural factors that enabled violence in the past is also important, and not only or even primarily because it is necessary to give victims the recognition needed, though it is important for that reason. What the accounts of Gray and Haldemann do not fully acknowledge is that recognition for victims is only part of the task of justice in the aftermath of wrongdoing. Dealing with structural and institutional reform is also intrinsically part of what justice demands in transitions.

Pablo de Greiff recognizes the structural dimensions of transitional justice, arguing that what is morally required in transitions is the rehabilitation of the force of basic norms prohibiting violence; mass wrongdoing is possible only when this normative erosion occurs. De Greiff identifies this breakdown as a constitutive feature of what he calls very imperfect worlds. Imperfect worlds are defined by "huge and predictable costs associated with the very effort to enforce compliance. At the limit, in such a world, that effort puts at risk the very existence of the system that is trying to enforce its own norms."[76] That is, adhering to or enforcing norms prohibiting violence becomes too risky. De Greiff's account is compatible with a population (or a portion of a population) within a given transitional context continuing to recognize the impermissibility of violations of basic norms, but such recognition does not have much effect in constraining action. For the force of norms prohibiting violence to become

---

[74] Gray recognizes that such regimes require overwhelming support, which is compatible with the presence of some resisters and others who act under duress but do not actively support unjust objectives being pursued. Gray, David, "An Excuse-Centered Approach to Transitional Justice," *Fordham Law Review* 74 (2005–2006): 2630.

[75] Gray, "Extraordinary Justice," 97.   [76] De Greiff, "Theorizing Transitional Justice," 35.

rehabilitated, an expanded range of goals must be facilitated by transitional justice measures. In addition to recognition of victims, another intermediate goal of such measures is the cultivation of civic trust. Recognition of victims and cultivation of trust will in turn promote (legal) justice. De Greiff notes that the operation of legal systems depends on trust, and trust increases when legal systems function well.[77] The final ends of such measures are reconciliation and democracy.[78]

De Greiff points to objectives commonly invoked in transitional contexts and within the literature on transitional justice, such as trust, reconciliation, and democracy, and shows how they are related in transitional justice processes. However, the precise relationship between these objectives and justice is not clear. More specifically, it is not clear whether objectives such as trust and democracy should be viewed as important independent moral values to be promoted by transitional justice processes or as components demanded by the specific moral value of justice. One source of the ambiguity lies in the definition of justice de Greiff provides. Eschewing talk of a distinctive set of principles of justice, de Greiff argues that general principles of justice are applied in a distinctive manner in the context of a very imperfect world. He does not elaborate on what such general principles of justice are. Clarification on the relationship between the intermediate and final objectives of transitional processes and the demands of justice is needed, especially in light of conceptual challenges being raised regarding the necessity of democracy for transitional justice.

Whether democracy as an aspiration is in fact necessary to transitional justice is one of a number of increasingly pronounced conceptual questions that arise in discussions of the range of cases that should properly fall under the scope of transitional justice. The last part of this section provides an overview of these conceptual questions, and then explains the significance of these debates for theorizing about transitional justice.[79] In her intellectual history of transitional justice Paige Arthur articulates the paradigm transition case informing early discussions of transitional justice, exemplified by Argentina in its transition from rule by a military junta and the

---

[77] This is a point I argue for at length in Murphy, *Moral Theory*, chap. 1.

[78] Following Aristotle, final goals are those for the sake of which all is done. Mediate goals are those that can be promoted (though perhaps not completely) by such measures.

[79] For helpful overviews of these debates, see Roht-Arriaza, Naomi, "The New Landscape of Transitional Justice," in *Transitional Justice in the Twenty-First Century*, ed. Naomi Roht-Arriaza and Javier Mariezcurrena (Cambridge: Cambridge University Press, 2006), 1–16; Bell, Christine, "Transitional Justice, Interdisciplinarity and the State of the 'Field' or 'Non-Field,'" *International Journal of Transitional Justice* 3, no. 1 (2009): 5–27.

Dirty War in the 1980s.[80] In this paradigm, past abuses were defined as violations of civil and political rights such as rape, execution, kidnapping, and torture. The range of legal measures available for dealing with such wrongs consisted primarily of programs of lustration, reparations, truth commissions and/or prosecutions – measures well suited to dealing with victims and perpetrators of violations of civil and political rights. Four general features characterized the political context within which wrongs were addressed. First, the society was in transition from one political regime to another. Second, the transition was to democracy, where democracy entailed changes in law and of political institutions. Third, the choices of elites determined the trajectory of a given transition. Fourth, the transition occurred in a context in which no party to a conflict was completely vanquished; the threat remained that parties previously in power would try to undermine the success of the transition and reassume power. In this context, the core challenge in dealing with past wrongs was to identify the appropriate legal tool to deal with past wrongs without threatening the transition to democracy.

Each feature of this paradigm has been called into question as necessary for cases that fall under the scope of transitional justice. In terms of wrongdoing, scholars problematize the exclusive emphasis on violations of civil and political liberties. For example, Louise Arbour argues that an emphasis on civil and political rights is self-defeating. The long-term prospects for peace and democracy depend on addressing grievances that could fuel future conflict, and such grievances include violations of economic rights. Examples of violations of economic and social rights include unequal or discriminatory access to land, to work, and to housing or resources. In Arbour's words, "Violations of civil and political rights are intrinsically linked to violations of economic, social, and cultural rights, whether they are causes or consequences of the latter."[81] Moreover, in practice an expanded set of rights has been covered by responses to wrongdoing. Dustin Sharp notes that economic violence has been included in the mandate of truth commissions in Chad, East Timor, Ghana, Kenya, Liberia, and Sierra Leone.[82] Other scholars question the extent to which a focus on civil and political liberties

---

[80] Arthur, "How 'Transitions' Reshaped Human Rights."

[81] Arbour, Louise, "Economic and Social Justice for Societies in Transition," *International Law and Politics* 40, no. 1 (2007): 8.

[82] Sharp, Dustin N., "Emancipating Transitional Justice from the Bonds of the Paradigmatic Transition," *International Journal of Transitional Justice* 9 (2015): 150–169. See also Laplante, Lisa, "Transitional Justice and Peace Building: Diagnosing and Addressing the Socioeconomic Roots of

adequately addresses gender-based harms.[83] Unsurprisingly, the call for an expansion of the rights violations dealt with by transitional justice mechanisms has coincided with critiques of the exclusive focus on kinds of legal responses to wrongdoing considered in the paradigm articulated above. Reform of existing processes and an expanded menu of responses, such as programs of land restitution or rights of return for refugees, have been proposed.[84]

The assumption that the trajectory of transitions is shaped by decisions made by state (and international) elites, as well as the moral implications of that assumption if true have also been challenged.[85] Increasingly, scholars of transitional justice call for an expansion of the participatory role of citizens and greater emphasis on bottom-up decision making about how to deal with the past.[86] They also highlight concern with the lack of accountability of transitional justice responses to local citizens. The notion of hybridity has been proposed, which "calls on us to consider the ways in which peacebuilding initiatives are made and remade through a complex cocktail of local resistance, cooptation and appropriation. Thus, it suggests that peacebuilding does not involve a dynamic of external actors introducing new ideas and practices to static local societies, but is in practice a 'glocal' phenomenon. . . . Hybridity helps to shift the focus in peacebuilding from efficiency to the need to generate a sense of local legitimacy that has often been sorely lacking."[87] Underpinning the demand for greater local participation are concerns about the effectiveness and justifiability of responses to wrongdoing. Responses to wrongdoing are claimed to be more effective in achieving certain outcomes if there is local buy-in to them. There is also recognition of the noninstrumental moral importance of respecting and recognizing the agency of the individuals in local transitional communities.

Violence through a Human Rights Framework," *International Journal of Transitional Justice* 2, no. 3 (2008): 331–55.

[83] Ní Aoláin, Fionnuala and Eilish Rooney, "Underenforcement and Intersectionality: Gendered Aspects of Transition for Women," *International Journal of Transitional Justice* 1, no. 3 (2007): 338–54.

[84] See Rubio-Marin, Ruth, ed., *What Happened to the Women? Gender and Reparations for Human Rights Violations* (New York: Social Science Research Council, 2006).

[85] See McEvoy, Kieran, "Beyond Legalism: Towards a Thicker Understanding of Transitional Justice," *Journal of Law and Society* 34, no. 4 (2007): 411–40; and Sharp, Dustin N., "Interrogating the Peripheries: The Preoccupations of Fourth Generation Transitional Justice," *Harvard Human Rights Journal* 26 (2013): 149–78.

[86] See, for example, Orentlicher, Diane F., "'Settling Accounts' Revisited: Reconciling Global Norms with Local Agency," *International Journal of Transitional Justice* 1, no. 1 (2007): 10–22.

[87] Sharp, "Emancipating Transitional Justice," 16.

The relationship between democracy and transitional justice is the subject of ongoing debate. The necessity of including democracy as a constitutive normative aim of transitional justice has been called into question. Scholars point to the fact that not all societies considered to be transitional share the normative aim of democracy. Transitional justice scholarship includes countries in transition but not moving in a liberal political direction such as Chad and Uganda. Research is also conducted on countries that have not had a political transition but have experienced a reduction in conflict. Moreover, scholars point out that it is a mistake to assume that a democratic aim or aspiration will translate into the achievement of democracy.[88] As Sharp notes, "The mechanisms of transitional justice are not a one-way ratchet of liberal betterment, but can in fact be used to reinforce illiberal ideologies and to consolidate the power of illiberal regimes, just as they can be invoked in regimes that are decidedly liberal but which may be undergoing normative transitions with respect to historical injustices."[89] Even if democracy is included as a necessary feature of transitional justice, there is disagreement about what democracy and the process of democratization entail. Democracy may be conceptualized in terms of liberal democracy, where principles of constitutionalism, the rule of law, and respect for human rights are at the core. As conceptualized by UN peacebuilding efforts, democracy also includes free markets.[90]

Finally, skepticism about the necessity of "transition" in transitional justice exists. The countries dealing with past wrongs that have been the focus of transitional justice scholarship and practice include a broader set of cases, including, importantly, consolidated democracies that are not "in transition" to democracy but are already democratic. Australia, Canada, and the United States fall into this category. Scholars also argue that even if transition is necessary, it is inadequately conceptualized. It is a mistake to assume that transition refers to a process that will succeed in reaching a predetermined end and to think the process is a temporary or short-lived one. Assuming that a transition follows a predetermined trajectory blinds theorists to the complex power dynamics that shape what happens in a

---

[88] Carothers, Thomas and Oren Samet-Marram, "The New Global Marketplace of Political Change," *Carnegie Endowment for International Peace*, April 20, 2015, http://carnegieendowment.org/2015/04/20/new-global-marketplace-of-political-change/i7fw?mkt_tok=3RkMMJWWfF9wsRoisq%2FBZKXonjHpfsX57OwrXKag38431UFwdcjKPmjrtYcGTsJoaPyQAgobGp5I5FEIQ7XYTLB2t6oMWAemXSjrtqDIZoxAZZ13gZI3.

[89] Sharp, "Emancipating Transitional Justice," 7.

[90] Ibid., citing the United Nations, *United Nations Peacekeeping Operations: Principles and Guidelines* (2008).

given case.[91] In addition, "transitions," it is claimed, never actually involve a sharp break between a past in which repressive policies and practices took place and a future predicated on consolidated democracy.[92] Many countries remain in a situation between democratic and repressive rule for extended periods of time. In light of this, Thomas Carothers argues that political analysis should "start by assuming that what is often thought of as an uneasy, precarious middle ground between full-fledged democracy and outright dictatorship is actually the most common political condition today of the countries in the developing world and the post-communist world. It is not an exceptional category ... it is a state of normality for many societies."[93]

In this section I discussed two broad ways of thinking about transitional justice as a discrete kind of justice. Both restorative justice and transitional justice remain theoretically underdeveloped, but the transitional justice alternative is in my view the most promising to pursue. To be adequate, however, any account of transitional justice that is developed must answer conceptual questions about transitional justice discussed at the end of this section.

A New Alternative

Desiderata for an adequate conception of transitional justice emerged from the discussion in Sections 2 and 3. In brief, an adequate account of transitional justice should clarify the principles of justice constitutive of transitional justice. In this articulation, the relationship between transitional justice and other types of justice (retributive justice, restorative justice, distributive justice) should be clarified. The scalar character of the demands of justice should also be recognized so that we see how it is possible to judge that a given response to wrongdoing is more or less just, or just or unjust, to different extents. The principles should also be such that they satisfy the pressing practical need for a normative theory of transitional justice. That is, principles of transitional justice should be such that they can be action guiding. An account should also be context sensitive in the sense of explaining why a given set of principles is salient in the specific context of transition. Finally, an account must answer the

---

[91] Hansen, Thomas Obel, "Transitional Justice: Toward a Differentiated Theory," *Oregon Review of International Law* 13, no. 1 (2011): 1–54.

[92] Dyzenhaus, "Judicial Independence."

[93] Carothers, Thomas, "The End of the Transition Paradigm," *Journal of Democracy* 13, no. 1 (2002): 17–18.

conceptual questions raised about, for example, the necessity of transition and democracy and the range of wrongs that fall under the scope of transitional justice.

The chapters that follow develop in detail my positive account of transitional justice that, I argue, meets these desiderata. This introduction concludes with an overview of the position I defend. My argument takes as a basic starting point a methodological insight from eighteenth-century philosopher David Hume: actions or institutions are labeled just or unjust against a background set of circumstances. Such circumstances trigger a question of justice that criteria of justice are needed to answer.[94] Principles of justice provide guidelines for how to respond to a given problem. In Hume's own account, the basic problem of justice is instability of possessions. Creating this problem are specific circumstances of justice, including the limited scarcity of goods and the limited benevolence of people.[95] Conventions of justice thus specify rules regulating property, which when followed stabilize property claims.

Hume's approach to justice suggests that in order to identify the concrete standards of justice that legal responses to wrongdoing must satisfy – and therefore to implement legal and other procedures that promote justice in transitional communities – we must first pinpoint the central moral challenge or problem confronting transitional communities. To isolate the central moral problem, I begin by identifying in Chapter 1 four circumstances of transitional justice: pervasive structural inequality, normalized collective and political wrongdoing, serious existential uncertainty, and fundamental uncertainty about authority. First, *pervasive structural inequality* is such that the institutional structure itself is illegitimate and revolution is permissible. Second, with *normalized collective and political wrongdoing*, wrongful acts are political as well as criminal acts. Moreover, it is often groups – characteristically targeting other groups – that perpetrate wrongdoing. Such wrongs are normalized in the sense that they become a basic fact of life around which individuals must orient their conduct. Third, transitional societies face *serious existential uncertainty*, which is empirical uncertainty surrounding the probability that a normatively desired transition will actually obtain. Transitions to democracy frequently falter, and in many cases authoritarian regimes return and

---

[94] This account is based on Hume, David, *A Treatise of Human Nature*, ed. L. A. Selby-Bigge, 2nd ed. (Oxford: Oxford University Press, 1978); Hume, David, *An Enquiry Concerning the Principles of Morals*, ed. Tom L. Beauchamp (Oxford: Oxford University Press, 1998).

[95] I elaborate on Hume's argument in detail in Chapter 1.

conflict resumes. Fourth, there is *fundamental uncertainty about authority* because the state is complicit in wrongdoing and a democratic structure of authority has yet to fully emerge. I contrast these characteristics with the analogous features of stable democratic contexts: what I call limited structural inequality, deviant individual and personal wrongdoing, minor existential uncertainty, and narrow uncertainty about authority.

Drawing on the circumstances of transitional justice, I then argue in Chapter 2 that the problem of justice in transitional circumstances is not reducible to the problem of other familiar kinds of justice, such as retributive justice, distributive justice, or corrective justice. Instead transitional justice queries: *What constitutes a just pursuit of societal transformation?* This was the central question facing Germany after the defeat of the Nazi regime, Eastern Europe after the collapse of state communism, and South Africa following the end of apartheid. The fundamental challenge of transitional justice is not giving perpetrators what they deserve; rather, it is how to pursue and achieve societal transformation in a just manner.

Chapter 3 develops my conception of the tasks involved in societal transformation. I define *transformation* relationally, specifically as the transformation of relationships among citizens into relationships premised on reciprocal respect for agency. As such, relationships are governed by the rule of law; characterized by reasonable, limited trust; and ensure genuine opportunities to shape the terms for interaction in the political, economic, and social arenas. Critical to these opportunities is the basic capability of individuals to avoid poverty. Fostering relational transformation is the overarching objective of legal responses to wrongdoing in transitions. I articulate in this chapter the general criteria that need to be satisfied for a process of transitional justice to contribute to relational transformation so defined.

Chapter 4 discusses the "just pursuit" of relational transformation. It is widely recognized within moral philosophy that there are backward-looking reasons to acknowledge serious moral wrongs done and to reassert the moral standing of victims.[96] The "just pursuit" of transformation signals the impermissibility of dealing with past wrongs in a strictly instrumental manner, that is, in a manner that considers only contributions to broader societal transformation and is insensitive to the backward-looking claims vis-à-vis perpetrators and victims that wrongdoing generates. Just responses to wrongdoing hold perpetrators and those complicit accountable in a

[96] Radzik, Linda and Colleen Murphy, "Reconciliation," in *Stanford Encyclopedia of Philosophy*, ed. Edward N. Zalta (2015), http://plato.stanford.edu/archives/sum2015/entries/reconciliation/.

morally appropriate or fitting way given their roles in collective and political wrongdoing, and respond to victims in a way that is appropriate given what they have experienced. This chapter fills out the general characteristics of appropriate and fitting responses to victims and perpetrators in the circumstances of transitional justice.[97]

The theoretical puzzle is: how should we understand the relationship between the requirements of societal transformation and the demands associated with its just pursuit? I argue that traditional versions of just war theory provide a useful structural model for answering this question. Traditional just war theory evaluates the justice of a war on the basis of two general considerations: the justice of the recourse to war (*jus ad bellum*) and the justice of the conduct in war (*jus in bello*). Wars can fail to be just because they are pursued for impermissible objectives and/or because pursued in an impermissible manner.[98] Thus the most efficient pursuit of morally permissible objectives may be unjust if it entails a violation of *jus in bello* requirements. Similarly, I suggest, the pursuit of transitional justice can fail to be just in one of two ways: by failing to pursue a morally permissible objective (societal transformation) and/or by pursuing a morally permissible end in an impermissible manner.

By way of conclusion, let me foreshadow how my analysis of transitional answers the conceptual questions raised at the end of Section 3. First, in the account I develop there is no reason to limit the wrongdoing with which transitional societies deal to violations of civil and political rights. Social and economic wrongdoing can and should be included in any adequate account of transitional justice. Second, the emphasis on respect for moral agency at the core of my account of societal transformation provides theoretical support for the importance of local participation in decision making on how transformation is pursued.

Third, democracy is a necessary feature of transitional justice in my view. It is empirically true that communities can transition in a number of different directions, from one form of repression to another or from repression to conflict. However, this empirical fact does not settle the question of the place of democracy in a normative account of transitional justice. For processes to be processes of *justice*, the aims they seek to

---

[97] For a very early articulation of a number of the objectives I include as part of transitional justice, see Crocker, David, "Reckoning with Past Wrongs: A Normative Framework," *Ethics & International Affairs* 13, no. 1, (1999): 43–64.

[98] The criteria of *jus ad bellum* include more than simply the reason for which a war is being waged. They also include, for example, a requirement that the turn to war is a last resort. Thus when discussing *jus ad bellum* I am using a broad definition of the "objective" for which a war is waged.

cultivate must be morally defensible. For the aim of social transformation to be morally defensible, the way a society is transformed must be. Responding to past wrongs in a manner that further entrenches oppression thus would not qualify as an instance of transitional *justice* because what is entrenched is injustice. Democracy is a form of governance predicated on the equality all citizens at important points in the process of collective decision making. As a form of governance, it is both morally defensible and a necessary constitutive part (though only a part) of the account of societal transformation I defend.

Fourth, transition is also necessary for a theory of transitional justice. However, transition matters in a normative and not in a descriptive sense.[99] As a matter of empirical fact, few attempts of transition to democracy succeed. One form of authoritarian government is often replaced by another repressive regime; conflict may mitigate and then resume; or repression may be replaced by conflict. One reason for the burgeoning literature on transitional justice is that we do not yet fully understand all of the factors that explain why transitions falter, and conversely, what makes a transition succeed. It is precisely because of this empirical fact that serious existential uncertainty exists as a circumstance of transitional justice in my account.

To say that transition matters in a normative sense is to say the following: the fact that a community has as a normative aspiration trans-forming itself from a repressive or conflict-ridden form of government to a democratic one, *but has not yet achieved and is in fact not certain to achieve that aspiration* matters morally. As I detail in the chapters that follow, the fact that we are dealing with communities aspiring to transition in a context in which achieving this aspiration is itself precarious shapes the kinds of considerations that should inform our moral analysis of the way a community in flux deals with its past. My analysis thus includes within its scope societies that are not actually going to in fact transition; rather, it includes societies that may plausibly be attributed with the aim or aspir-ation of ending conflict and replacing repression with a democratic form of governance.

Before concluding my introduction, I want to consider one initial worry. In my analysis, transitional justice is not reducible to other kinds of justice with which we are familiar and to which philosophers usually focus their attention (e.g., retributive justice or distributive justice). How-ever, introduction of new types of justice is prima facie concerning for

---

[99] I am grateful to Mark Drumbl for pressing me on this point.

many theorists. De Greiff articulates some reasons for concern very nicely. Specifically, de Greiff worries that the proliferation of categories of justice and the introduction of distinctions not only among categories of justice but also among contexts of justice will undermine the function that theories of justice are supposed to serve. Instead of providing general normative guidance across a range of cases, theories of justice will become too specific.

Such concerns are not warranted. What the chapters that follow draw attention to is the fact that circumstances of justice *always* shape normative theorizing. To generate a set of normative principles that are adequate for dealing with a particular problem, it is necessary to identify what facts give rise to the problem in the first place.[100] Principles of justice are not always salient in every possible context. In any given context, not every problem of justice is at issue. The circumstances of justice help us identify and understand which questions of justice are the salient ones to ask given that context. Circumstances help delimit which cases fall under the domain of a given subject of justice by drawing attention to the conditions that give rise to a particular question of justice in the first place. Circumstances help us identify where the theoretical spotlight should be focused.

---

[100] In framing the point this way, I am referencing debates in the literature on ideal/nonideal theory about the fact-sensitive character of principles of justice. As is clear from the above, I reject G. A. Cohen's strong view that principles of justice are fact independent. My view is more in keeping with that of John Rawls, who aimed to "design principles for this and nearby possible worlds, inhabited by beings like us, in circumstances similar enough to those in which we live" (Valentini, "Ideal vs. Non-Ideal Theory," 658).

CHAPTER I

Circumstances of Transitional Justice

This chapter discusses the circumstances of transitional justice. My discussion provides the necessary background for Chapter 2, in which I ask: What is the problem of justice that arises in transitions? After identifying this problem, I go on in Chapters 3 and 4 to articulate principles of transitional justice that are responsive to this problem.

Eighteenth-century philosopher David Hume provides the classic articulation of circumstances of justice.[1] Understanding Hume's basic idea is thus important before turning to my positive account. In Hume's view, circumstances of justice identify the conditions that must be in place for justice to be useful. According to Hume, justice is useful when there is a problem of justice that it is both necessary and possible for a society to address.[2] Circumstances of justice thus specify when there is an intelligible need for criteria of justice; they, in Hume's words, outline the context in which "justice conventions are likely to be invented or maintained by normal human beings."[3] They also delimit the conditions under which criteria of justice have some reasonable chance of being respected in practice. As I discuss in more detail in the following, circumstances of justice do not capture features that are necessarily unique to a particular context. Rather, circumstances specify when a given feature or condition triggers a concern for justice.

To illustrate, consider Hume's own account of justice. For Hume, the basic problem of justice is instability of possessions. Conventions of justice

---

[1] Some contemporary philosophers also discuss the idea of circumstances of justice. See, for example, Rawls, *Theory of Justice*; Nussbaum, Martha, *Frontiers of Justice* (Cambridge, MA: Belknap Press, 2006); Barry, Brian, *Theories of Justice* (Hemel-Hempstead: Harvester-Wheatsheaf, 1989).

[2] This account of Hume on the circumstances of justice is based on Hume, *A Treatise of Human Nature*, 3.2.2.18; Hume, *An Enquiry Concerning the Principles of Morals*, 3.12; Hope, Simon, "The Circumstances of Justice," *Hume Studies* 36, no. 2 (2010): 125–48; Vanderschraaf, Peter, "The Circumstances of Justice," *Politics, Philosophy and Economics* 5, no. 3 (2006): 321–51; Ridge, Michael, "David Hume, Paternalist," *Hume Studies* 36, no. 2 (2010): 149–70.

[3] Ridge, "David Hume," 154.

specify rules that regulate property, the following of which will solidify the stability of goods. Justice is for Hume "the disposition to honour and respect rules of property."[4] In Hume's view, a set of circumstances must obtain for possessions to be unstable in a manner that is both necessary and possible for a society to deal with, and thus for principles of justice to be salient.[5]

One circumstance of justice generating the need to specify standards for the distribution of property and property rights is limited scarcity of goods.[6] Hume recognizes that goods exist in all communities. Goods exist within a society along a spectrum, from being abundantly present to extremely scarce. Only when there is limited scarcity do goods create a problem of justice that is possible and necessary to address.

To explain why, Hume considers the utopian and dystopian versions of the amount of goods that are available in a society.[7] The dystopian circumstance is extreme scarcity of goods, "such want of all common necessities, that the utmost frugality and industry cannot preserve the greater number from perishing."[8] In this circumstance, justice is impossible in the sense that demands of "justice would inevitably give way to 'the stronger motives of necessity and self-preservation.'"[9] Rules of justice are futile because they will not constrain action. Consequently, for Hume there is no just or unjust way to distribute goods in this circumstance. By contrast, the utopian circumstance is extreme plenty or superabundance of resources. Here justice is not necessary. In Hume's words, "Why call this object mine, when upon the seizing of it by another, I need but stretch my hand to possess myself of what is equally valuable?"[10] In this context, stabilizing the possession of goods serves no important purpose.

---

[4] Hope, "Circumstances of Justice," 128.

[5] John Rawls's own discussion of the circumstances of justice suggests that circumstances make a given question of justice necessary and possible to answer. He writes, "The circumstances of justice may be described as the normal conditions under which human cooperation is both possible and necessary ... although a society is a cooperative venture for mutual advantage, it is typically marked by a conflict as well as an identity of interests. ... Thus principles are needed for choosing among the various social arrangements that determine this division of advantages and for underwriting an agreement on the proper distributive shares. These requirements define the role of justice. The background conditions that give rise to these necessities are the circumstances of justice" (*Theory of Justice*, 126). At another point he writes, "The circumstances of justice obtain whenever mutually disinterested persons put forward conflicting claims to the division of social advantages under conditions of moderate scarcity. Unless these circumstances existed there would be no occasion for the virtue of justice, just as in the absence of threats of injury to life and limb there would be no occasion for physical courage" (ibid., 128).

[6] Another example of a circumstance is limited benevolence.

[7] Hope, "Circumstances of Justice," 128.   [8] Ibid., 128, citing Hume.

[9] Ridge, "David Hume," 156.   [10] Hope, "Circumstances of Justice," 127.

Consequently, for Hume, there are no standards for a just or unjust distribution that are salient. In sum, in the circumstance of extreme scarcity property rights are futile because they will not constrain action. In the circumstance of extreme abundance, it is not necessary to assign specific property rights.

It is important to make three points of clarification about the relationship of my account of the circumstances of transitional justice to Hume's own account of the circumstances of justice. First, Hume's focus was on justice in general, not with a particular kind of justice. By contrast, my interest is a particular kind of justice. My restricted focus on one kind of justice is in keeping with the focus of much contemporary scholarship on justice. Few contemporary scholars theorize about justice in general; theories of justice in contemporary political philosophy are theories of a particular kind of justice. Theorists standardly recognize different kinds of justice, such as distributive justice, corrective justice, and criminal justice. Scholars, such as Rawls, also refer to circumstances of justice. Thus the adoption of the idea of circumstances of justice to discuss a particular type of justice has precedent.

Second, Hume's circumstances of justice aim to capture enduring features of the human condition, rather than features facing some human beings in some situations. By contrast, any account of the circumstances of transitional justice will by definition not represent enduring features of the human condition.[11] In my view, there is no conceptual necessity in circumstances of justice being defined as enduring features of the human condition. Moreover, it is not clear that Hume's own circumstances do in fact reflect enduring features of the human condition. Part of what makes transitional societies so important for theorists to take into account is the fact that they draw attention to conditions and features that may be taken by theorists to be enduring features, but in fact reflect contingent circumstances that human beings are in a position to alter and that ongoing effort is required to maintain.[12]

Finally, I take Hume's fundamental insight to be methodological in nature, concerned with how to theorize about justice. Hume offers a

---

[11] I am grateful to Leslie Francis for drawing my attention to this point.

[12] Climate change similarly poses challenges to the notion that the circumstances of justice Hume identifies are in fact enduring features of the human condition. It has implications in particular for the condition of limited scarcity. In light of this possible impact of climate change, Tim Mulgan's book *Ethics for a Broken World* (McGill-Queen's University Press, 2011) discusses ethics in a condition where resources are insufficient to meet everyone's needs and future generations are worse off than at present.

structure of argumentation for claims about justice, and it is this structure of argumentation I adopt. Hume's methodological point is that instead of theorizing about justice in the abstract as Plato did, we should approach the question of what is just in a given case by identifying the problem of justice that is at issue in a set of circumstances. Behind this methodological point is a critical insight: actions or institutions can only sensibly be called just or unjust against a certain background set of conditions. These conditions explain why justice is an issue in the first place, that is, why a problem of justice exists and what the contours of that problem are. Principles of justice in turn are problem responsive, providing guidelines for the way that a problem should be dealt with. The adequacy of any specific principles of justice is a function of how well they respond to that problem. Accepting Hume's core methodological point is compatible with disagreeing with Hume's substantive claims. Indeed, there are substantive differences between Hume's account and mine. For example, Hume identified the fundamental concern of justice to be with property and its instability. By contrast, as will become clearer in Chapter 2, I do not take transitional justice to be fundamentally concerned with property and the stability of property rights.

In Section 1, I argue that there are four circumstances of transitional justice. These are widely recognized as characteristic of paradigm transitional societies: *pervasive structural inequality, normalized collective and political wrongdoing, serious existential uncertainty,* and *fundamental uncertainty about authority.* Societies are transitional when these four circumstances of justice obtain. By contrast, the circumstances of justice obtaining in stable democracies are *limited structural inequality, deviant individual and personal wrongdoing, minor existential uncertainty,* and *narrow uncertainty about authority.* I discuss each circumstance of transitional justice in turn in Section 1, contrasting with the analogous circumstance for paradigmatic stable democratic contexts.[13]

Before turning to this discussion, I want to clarify the basis for my claim that these are the circumstances of transitional justice and of stable democratic societies. These circumstances of transitional justice reflect characteristics of transitional communities that are widely recognized in

---

[13] I offer a brief discussion of these circumstances in my chapter Murphy, Colleen, "Transitional Justice, Retributive Justice and Accountability for Wrongdoing," in *Theorizing Transitional Justice,* ed. Claudio Corradetti, Nir Eisikovits, and Jack Rotondi, 59–68 (Burlington, VT: Ashgate Publishing, 2015). However, I have slightly modified the title for three of the circumstances in light of valuable feedback received since that went into press.

the literature on transitional justice. Thus in arguing for each of these circumstances, my claim is not that I am the first to recognize each feature. Instead what I offer is an interpretation of the moral salience of features that are widely recognized. The circumstances that I attribute to stable democratic communities are drawn from the literature in political philosophy that deals with questions of retributive justice, corrective justice, and/or distributive justice. Specifically, I articulate the orienting assumptions of the characteristic features of the communities around which theorists develop their accounts of justice. The circumstances also capture widely recognized characteristics of reasonably just, stable democracies.[14]

As will become clear in Section 1, transitional and stable democratic societies are not distinguished by the presence or absence of certain features characterized at a certain level of generality or abstraction; rather, it is the way in which a given feature is present – in particular where it figures along a continuum – that distinguishes the two societies. This is in keeping with Hume's own analysis of the circumstances of justice.[15] It also reflects the following assumption: the presence or absence to different degrees of a given feature can be morally salient or significant. Morally significant differences are not always differences in kind, but also sometimes differences in degree.

Finally, when evaluating any actual political society it may be difficult to determine if that society has the transitional or stable democratic version of a circumstance of justice. Such borderline cases should not be taken to undermine either the analytic or practical value of the categories themselves. Just as the existence of a particular individual whose hair loss is such that it is not clear whether to categorize him as bald does not challenge the analytic or practical value of categories of baldness or nonbaldness, so too the existence of a society in which, for example, structural inequality does not obviously fall into the pervasive or limited category should not challenge the usefulness of the distinction between pervasive and limited structural inequality. My aim is in analytic clarification, not in determining the appropriate empirical characterization of any specific political society.

---

[14] In what follows I call such societies simply "stable democracies."

[15] As noted earlier, Hume recognizes that goods are present in all communities. What distinguishes the existence of goods as a circumstance of justice is the degree to which they are present in a society; only when goods neither pass the threshold of extreme abundance nor the threshold of extreme scarcity do they constitute a circumstance of justice.

Pervasive Structural Inequality

The first circumstance of transitional justice is pervasive structural inequality.[16] The subject matter of this circumstance is the basic terms shaping the general interaction among citizens and between citizens and officials. Terms of interaction among citizens and between citizens and officials are defined by institutional rules and norms. Such institutions shape interaction directly by specifying what actions are required, permitted, or prohibited by whom and toward whom in a society. The institutions of interest are broad, including, economic, political, social, cultural, and legal institutions.

Here are some examples of the ways institutions shape interaction. Political rules that are legally codified specify who is eligible to serve in political office and the process by which political offices will be filled, such as by appointment or by election. They also outline who is eligible to participate in either process of appointment. Institutional norms among participants in the political process also influence the relationship between legally codified rules and actual political practice. If the norm among political officials is to disregard restrictions placed on them by declared legal rules, then that will alter the form of the interaction in a political society. Disregard of legal rules can occur when, for example, rules that stipulate the holding of elections over a certain period of time are ignored, and officials continue to maintain their position.[17] In this case the terms for interaction are dictated by the whims of particular individuals and not by declared legal rules. Social norms can also shape interaction by tangibly constraining possibilities within institutions. For example, although not formally barred from participating in elections or holding certain appointments, it may be the norm within a political society that a member of a certain group is chosen or that member(s) of certain group(s) is (are) not chosen. The implicit norms shaping the outcome of institutional processes

---

[16] Authors who discuss what I call pervasive structural inequality include de Greiff, "Theorizing Transitional Justice"; Gray, "Extraordinary Justice"; Fletcher et al., "Context, Timing and the Dynamics of Transitional Justice"; Ní Aoláin, Fionnuala and Colm Campbell, "The Paradox of Transition in Conflicted Democracies," *Human Rights Quarterly* 27 (2005): 172–213. I am very grateful to Paul Morrow for extensive comments on this section, which prompted substantial changes and revisions.

[17] On this point, see Nino, Carlos Santiago, *Radical Evil on Trial* (New Haven, CT: Yale University Press, 1998). For a discussion of the general importance of congruity between declared rules and the practice of law officials, see Fuller, Lon, *The Morality of Law*, rev. ed. (New Haven, CT: Yale University Press, 1969). For a general discussion of the ways congruence is undermined during conflict and repression, see Murphy, Colleen, "Lon Fuller and the Moral Value of the Rule of Law," *Law and Philosophy* 24, no. 3 (2005): 239–62; and Murphy, *Moral Theory*, chap. 1.

are revealed when the "unexpected" occurs; a member of a marginalized group gains a high-level government position for the first time and this is labeled a watershed moment for a society.

Legal institutions shape interactions in myriad ways. They stipulate the official language(s) in which certain kinds of transaction must be conducted. Economic institutions specify who is legally permitted to own land and have title, and thus who is permitted to control land and who must get access to land through the permission of another. Informal cultural and social norms, importantly including gender norms, influence the extent to which legal title is respected in practice in many contexts. Educational institutions play a key role in constructing civic identity by outlining what must be taught in schools about the history of a given society and which groups are taken to be part of that history. This list is not exhaustive but rather provides some sense of the range of ways in which institutional rules and norms shape the terms for interaction among citizens and between citizens and officials.

I use the word *structural* in this circumstance to capture the fact that institutions jointly regulate and shape interaction among citizens and officials in political societies. Structural draws on Rawls's notion of the basic structure of a society, which he describes in terms of institutions. Rawls writes:

> For us the primary subject of justice is the basic structure of society, or more exactly, the way in which the major social institutions distribute fundamental rights and duties and determine the division of advantages from social cooperation. ... Taken together as one scheme, the major institutions define men's rights and duties and influence their life-prospects, what they can expect to be and how well they can hope to do. The basic structure is the primary subject of justice because its effects are so profound and present from the start. The intuitive notion here is that this structure contains various social positions and that men born into different positions have different expectations of life determined, in part, by the political system as well as by economic and social circumstances. In this way the institutions of society favor certain starting places over others.[18]

---

[18] Rawls, *Theory of Justice*, 8. I say part of the subject matter because Rawls qualifies his discussion in a way that does not pertain to structural inequality. He draws a sharp distinction between institutions and institutional rules, and rules of private associations, writing that the principles of justice he proposes "may not work for the rules and practices of private associations or for those of less comprehensive social groups. They may be irrelevant for the various informal conventions and customs of everyday life; they may not elucidate the justice, or perhaps better, the fairness of voluntary cooperative arrangements or procedures for making contractual arrangements" (ibid.). In articulating structural inequality I do not make such distinctions. Rules and norms of institutions as I understand them can include those of private associations. Moreover, part of the norms in which

In his discussion of the importance of the basic structure of society, Rawls points to how terms for interaction fundamentally shape life prospects. What the basic structure draws attention to is the ways in which life prospects for individuals are fundamentally shaped by the institutional rules and norms that govern a society and that shape and constrain individual action.

I take "life prospects" to be a function of the range of things an individual can feasibly do or become throughout her lifetime. The genuine opportunities open to an individual are a measure of the freedom or capability she enjoys.[19] There are two aspects to freedom of interest to this circumstance of transitional justice. The first aspect is what Amartya Sen calls a *process* aspect of freedom.[20] It concerns individuals' opportunity to shape the structurally defined terms of interaction. Such an opportunity exists in part by having the right to participate in formal processes through which institutional rules come into being or are changed. It also requires freedom of choice in the actions, objectives, and relationships individuals will pursue or participate in. The second aspect of freedom concerns the *genuine opportunities* themselves afforded to individuals given the institutional rules and norms.[21] *Opportunities* refer to specific doings and beings that individuals have a feasible chance of achieving, such as becoming a lawyer or avoiding or escaping poverty. Opportunities can be fundamentally relational; genuine opportunities to be recognized as a member of one's political community or be respected are two such examples.[22]

I am interested are norms that are informal, precisely because of the way such norms influence interaction among citizens and between citizens and officials, in ways that can profoundly affect the freedom or genuine opportunity of individuals.

[19] This definition of inequality and freedom draws on the idea of capabilities as developed in Sen, Amartya, *Development as Freedom* (New York: Knopf, 1999); Nussbaum, Martha, *Women and International Development* (Cambridge: Cambridge University Press, 2001); Wolff, Jonathan and Avner de-Shalit, *Disadvantage* (New York: Oxford University Press, 2007).

[20] Sen, Amartya, "Elements of a Theory of Human Rights," *Philosophy and Public Affairs* 32, no. 4 (2004): 315–56.

[21] Sen distinguishes between the two kinds of freedom with the following example: "Now consider the threat of a violation of this freedom if some authoritarian guardians of society decide that she must not go out in the evening ("it is most unseemly"), and if they force her, in one way or another, to stay indoors. To see that there are two distinct issues involved in this one violation, consider an alternative case in which the authoritarian bosses decide that she must – absolutely must – go out ("you are expelled for the evening: just obey"). There is clearly a violation of freedom here even though Rima is being forced to do exactly what she would have chosen to do anyway, and this is readily seen when we compare the two alternatives "choosing freely to go out" and "being forced to go out." The latter involves an immediate violation of the process aspect of Rima's freedom, since an action is being forced on her (even though it is an action she would have freely chosen also)" ("Elements," 331).

[22] For an extended discussion of relational capabilities, see Murphy, *Moral Theory*, chap. 3.

The two dimensions of freedom are often mutually reinforcing. For example, restricted ability to participate in processes defining terms of interaction can result in restricted opportunities.

Institutional rules, norms, and practices can be profoundly harmful or beneficial to individuals and/or groups within a society depending on how they limit, foreclose, or make possible these two aspects of freedom. In the circumstance of pervasive structural inequality, differential institutional restrictions exist on the process and/or genuine opportunity dimensions of freedom. Individuals are differentially able to shape their relationships with others and differentially limited in the range of opportunities they can feasibly achieve. Another way of putting this point is that individuals are subject to differential constraints. Constraints can arise as a result of legal restrictions, as well as from "stereotypical expectations, wealth, income, social status, conventions, norms, and practices."[23] Constraints can serve as both up-front obstacles to pursuing certain courses of action or as predictable negative consequences for pursuing certain courses, such as social isolation or punishment. Such consequences do not accompany the same choice made by an individual not subject to the same constraints.

Structural inequality reflects a failure to grant or recognize the equal status of (some) individuals or groups. Thus the differential opportunities and constraints of interest are not fundamentally a function of individual choices. Two individuals similarly situated can make different choices that result in differential outcomes, outcomes that in turn further constrain future possibilities and opportunities. One individual may choose to spend all of her income on commodities, while another invests a portion of her income. Over time, the wealth of the second individual becomes greater than that of the first. This kind of result is not the kind of inequality of interest in structural injustice. Rather, the interest is in differences of wealth that are explained not by different choices made by different individuals similarly situated, but by, for example, differential constraints shaping choices. To illustrate, one way of maintaining the relative poverty of members of particular groups is through employment or wage discrimination. Segregation, the legal or informal clustering of certain groups in particular residential areas, jobs, or schools, is another.[24] Disproportionate results can be produced through the differential constraints that institutional rules impose on members of different social groups.

---

[23] Cudd, Ann, *Analyzing Oppression* (New York: Oxford University Press, 2006), 50.
[24] An emphasis on differential institutional constraints is at the core of Cudd's analysis of oppression in *Analyzing Oppression*.

Structural inequality is pervasive when many different kinds of institutions are defined by terms that are unequal (the horizontal dimension), and the inequality permeates each institution (the vertical dimension). The groups subject to differential constraints in a community vary across societies. Sometimes inequality tracks particular identities, such as racial, ethnic, or religious identities. At other times it is a function of ideological commitments. It may track distinctions between those who are members of the ruling elite and their supporters versus all other citizens. When structural inequality is pervasive, people have reason to adopt certain kinds of measures to overthrow an existing institutional system. The institutional order is not legitimate in the sense of there exists a right to rebel.[25] In some cases it is appropriate to characterize the institutional structure, and not simply individual infractions of legal norms, as criminal.

To illustrate this circumstance, consider apartheid South Africa, a paradigm case of pervasive structural inequality.[26] Racial segregation extended to every major aspect of life; segregation was imposed for "taxis, ambulances, hearses, buses, trains, elevators, benches, lavatories, parks, church halls, town halls, cinemas, theaters, cafes, restaurants, and hotels, as well as schools and universities."[27] Segregation was coupled with lower public funding and inferior amenities for, as well as formal and informal discrimination against, nonwhite South Africans.[28] Black South Africans in particular were clustered in lower-paying, lower-status forms of employment than white South Africans, and they also faced significant wage discrimination.[29] The unequal status of nonwhite South Africans relative to white South Africans was at the core of apartheid. Segregation, discrimination, and marginalization of black South Africans in every area of life was justified by and in turn reinforced the view that they were not equal members or participants in South African society.

---

[25] I am grateful to John Tasioulas for discussions about different notions of legitimacy. The notion of legitimacy on which I am drawing is from Philip Pettit. See his "Legitimacy and Justice in Republican Perspective," *Current Legal Problems* 65 (2012): 59–82. He writes, "Legitimacy imposes a *pro tanto* moral obligation, then, if you oppose certain laws or measures related to the laws, to oppose them in ways consistent with the system's surviving: to stop short of revolution or rebellion or, in an older word, resistance" (ibid., 62).

[26] It is also an institutional order deemed criminal; apartheid is a crime in international law. I also discuss the economic dimensions of apartheid at length in Murphy, *Moral Theory*, chap. 3.

[27] Thompson, Leonard, *A History of South Africa* (New Haven, CT: Yale University Press, 2000), 197. Generally the government privileged coloreds and Indians over Africans (ibid., 201).

[28] Areas were racially designated for each of these groups. Africans suffered the most under the system of apartheid.

[29] Ibid. By 1982 this gap had lessened, but it still existed.

Blacks living in the designated Homelands characteristically lacked running water and electricity, problems white South Africans did not face. Poverty and poor health services led to high levels of undernutrition, disease, and infant mortality rates among Africans.[30] There were also few employment opportunities available within the Homelands. At the same time, pass laws, employment segregation, and wage discrimination combined to severely reduce their opportunities for employment. Legal restrictions on movement made the pursuit of employment outside of the Homelands, where most employment options were, burdensome, arduous, and risky. Tens of thousands were arrested each year for violations of pass laws, which required certain documentation from black South Africans moving outside the Homelands.[31] Unsurprisingly, as a consequence there were higher rates of unemployment among black South Africans.[32] Those successfully gaining employment outside the Homelands did so at the cost of spending extended time away from family. This led to one form of isolation and was a source of stress and anxiety for many. Another source of isolation stemmed from the necessity for many of remaining as socially invisible as possible to avoid arrest for violation of pass laws. In its final report, the South African TRC characterized apartheid as "a grim reality for every black South African. . . . Dumped in the 'national states' without jobs, communities experienced powerlessness, vulnerability, fear and inequality. . . . One did not need to be a political activist to become a victim of apartheid; it was sufficient to be black, alive and seeking the basic necessities of life that whites took for granted and enjoyed by right."[33]

Apartheid was an intentionally designed and implemented program. However, pervasive structural inequality can also exist in a less targeted manner. In his analysis of Sierra Leone, William Reno describes what he calls the "Shadow State," which refers to "the emergence of rulers drawing authority from their abilities to control markets and their material rewards."[34] Through their relationships with international businessmen and private networks, politicians and warlords manage to control markets and resources in ways that lead to personal enrichment and expansion of

---

[30] Ibid., 195.   [31] Ibid., 193.

[32] Ibid., 195; unemployment increased substantially during the 1970s, and by 1977 an estimated 26 percent of Africans were unemployed.

[33] TRC, *Truth and Reconciliation Commission of South Africa Report* (London: Macmillan Publishers, 1999), 1:34.

[34] Reno, William, *Corruption and State Politics in Sierra Leone* (Cambridge: Cambridge University Press, 1995), 3. In his book *Blood Oil: Tyrants, Violence and the Rules That Run the World* (New York: Oxford University Press, 2016), Leif Wenar similarly examines the role of control of natural resources in the oppression and repression of individuals.

power and control over a population. That power is coupled with the repression and impoverishment of the general population.

Every political society is characterized by some degree of structural inequality. What distinguishes structural inequality as a circumstance of *transitional* justice is the degree to which it is present.[35] If structural inequality is sufficiently pervasive, it passes a threshold beyond which the legitimacy of the institutional order is in doubt in the sense that people have reason to adopt certain kind of measures to overthrow that order. By contrast, political theorists and philosophers conceptualize the presence of structural inequality in stable democracies as not sufficiently pervasive to pass this threshold.[36] Structural inequality is moreover conceptualized as *localized and limited.* Structural inequality is present in some but not necessarily all institutions, and its presence within such institutions is not ubiquitous. Because of the presence of structural inequality, institutions are taken to be flawed and imperfect. Extant structural inequality generates a moral imperative to enact structural changes or reform, the successful implementation of which will be a tangible improvement from the perspective of justice. However, while reform is needed, revolutionary action is not. The overall institutional system works sufficiently well from a moral point of view; there is no reason to act so as to overthrow the existing institutional order.

Normalized Collective and Political Wrongdoing

The second circumstance of transitional justice is *normalized collective and political wrongdoing.*[37] By *wrongdoing* I refer to the actions or omissions of particular human beings that result in violations of human

---

[35] This is in keeping with Hume's basic idea of circumstances of justice as features present at a certain point along a continuum.

[36] For example, we see this in discussions of civil disobedience in democracies. See, e.g., Rawls, *Theory of Justice*; Kimberley Brownlee, "Civil Disobedience," *Stanford Encyclopedia of Philosophy*, ed. Edward N. Zalta (2013), http://plato.stanford.edu/archives/win2013/entries/civil-disobedience/ .

[37] Some of the many scholars who discuss this circumstance include de Greiff, "Theorizing Transitional Justice"; Drumbl, Mark, *Atrocity, Punishment, and International Law* (New York: Cambridge University Press, 2007); Gray, "Extraordinary Justice"; Bronwyn Leebaw, *Judging State-Sponsored Violence, Imagining Political Change* (New York: Cambridge University Press, 2011); Danner, Allison Marston and Jenny S. Martinez, "Guilty Associations: Joint Criminal Enterprise, Command Responsibility, and the Development of International Criminal Law," *California Law Review* 93, no. 1 (2005): 75–196; Lang, Anthony F., "Crime and Punishment: Holding States Accountable," *Ethics and International Affairs* 21, no. 2 (2007): 239–57; May, Larry, *Genocide: A Normative Account* (New York: Cambridge University Press, 2010); May, Larry, *Crimes against Humanity: A Normative Account* (New York: Cambridge University Press, 2005); Osiel, Mark, *Making Sense of Mass Atrocity* (New York: Cambridge University Press, 2009); Teitel, *Transitional Justice.*

rights.[38] Conceptualizing wrongdoing in terms of human rights violations is common in the literature on transitional justice. As Lieselotte Viaene and Eva Brems put it, "Transitional justice is strongly linked to human rights, as it concerns the way a society deals with gross human rights violations of the past."[39]

Linking wrongdoing with human rights violations is also justified. Violations of human rights constitute an especially serious kind of moral wrong. All human beings possess human rights "simply in virtue of their humanity."[40] Human rights reflect the basic claims individuals can make on others to certain forms of treatment. Human rights capture core demands of justice.[41] Thus the specific wrongs committed when human rights are violated are those that constitute injustices.[42] Their association with justice reflects the special strength and weight of human rights claims. Human rights generate duties on other individuals to act or refrain from acting in particular ways. Thus, when obligations are violated there is always a victim with the standing to complain as a result. The duties imposed by human rights exist independently of whether the duty holder has consented to be bound by such duties or desires to be so bound. The duties corresponding to particular human rights are not absolute but are such that they exclude from consideration certain kinds of reason for acting otherwise than as required by a given duty. For example, the mere fact that social utility would be maximized by the violation of a human right is not by itself a reason that should be weighed against the reason to fulfill the duty not to torture. Social utility is not a reason that should figure in deliberation.[43] Given the nature of the moral claim at the core of

---

[38] By claiming that the wrongs of interest are violations of human rights, I am not at all implying that human rights have no place in an evaluation of the institutional structure regulating a community. Indeed, as I argue in Chapter 3, the relational transformation at which processes of transitional justice ultimately aim requires the institutional recognition and protection of key human rights.

[39] Viaene, Lieselotte and Eva Brems, "Transitional Justice and Cultural Contexts: Learning from the Universality Debate," *Netherlands Quarterly of Human Rights* 28, no. 2 (2010): 202. Naomi Roht-Arriaza similarly writes that transitional justice is 'aimed directly at confronting and dealing with past violations of human rights and humanitarian law'"; see Roht-Arriaza, Naomi, "The New Landscape of Transitional Justice," in *Transitional Justice in the Twenty-First Century: Beyond Truth versus Justice*, ed. Naomi Roht-Arriaza and Javier Mariezcurrena (Cambridge: Cambridge University Press, 2006), 2.

[40] This conception of human rights is based on Tasioulas, John, "On the Nature of Human Rights," in *The Philosophy of Human Rights: Contemporary Controversies*, ed. G. Ernst and J.C. Heilinger (Berlin: Walter de Gruyter, 2012), 26.

[41] Ibid., 28.   [42] I am grateful to John Tasioulas for crucial feedback on this circumstance.

[43] At least up to a certain threshold level. On this point, see Alexander, Larry and Michael Moore, "Deontological Ethics," *Stanford Encyclopedia of Philosophy*, ed. Edward N. Zalta (2015), http://plato.stanford.edu/archives/spr2015/entries/ethics-deontological/.

human rights and its association with justice, it is plausible to claim that violating a human right is sufficiently egregious as to meet any threshold of moral importance that must be satisfied for a wrong to warrant a response.

There is consensus in the literature on transitional justice on the importance of responding to violations of civil and political rights; wrongs stemming from the violation of these rights are wrongs with which processes of transitional justice should deal. Paradigm examples of such wrongs include torture, killing, abduction, and rape. However, as I noted in the Introduction, one subject of disagreement in the literature on transitional justice centers on the inclusion of social, economic, and cultural rights violations. Some examples of the violations of these duties by state actors or nonstate actors at times acting with the sanction of the state include state-sponsored displacement of individuals, dispossession or burning of homes, destruction of crops, contamination of water sources, as well as the deliberate destruction of infrastructure such as schools and hospitals that are needed for the enjoyment of rights.[44]

In my view, it is important that social, economic, and cultural rights be included in the wrongs for which redress is sought because omitting such rights excludes an important source of concern in many transitional contexts.[45] The emphasis placed on social and economic rights is powerfully illustrated by the complaints articulated by ordinary citizens in many countries in what has been called the Arab Spring.[46] More broadly, in developing countries the impact of economic and social rights violations are at the forefront of discussions about how to redress the past.[47] Victims seeking land or compensation for land taken, or more generally relief from severe poverty characterized by limited opportunities to be adequately nourished, are focused on violations of economic and social rights.

Part of the motivation for excluding such violations from the scope of transitional justice is often the sense that inclusion would require a radical revision of transitional justice or that it is beyond the practical ability of states to respond to such violations. However, such concerns are

[44] Ibid., 367 and 373–74.   [45] Arbour, "Economic and Social Justice."

[46] Schmid, Evelyne and Aoife Nolan, "'Do No Harm'? Exploring the Scope of Economic and Social Rights in Transitional Justice," *International Journal of Transitional Justice* 8 (2014): 362–82; UN Special Rappateur Pablo de Greiff makes a similar point in "Report of the Special Rapporteur on the Promotion of Truth, Justice, Reparation and Guarantees of Non-Recurrence," UN Doc. A/HRC/21/46 (August 9, 2012), para. 17.

[47] For a discussion of South Africa and Zimbabwe, see, for example, Moyo, Khanyisela, "Mimicry, Transitional Justice and the Land Question in Racially Divided Former Settler Colonies," *International Journal of Transitional Justice* 9 (2015): 70–89.

unfounded.[48] Evelyne Schmid and Aoife Nolan demonstrate that the legal obligations that correspond to economic and social rights are articulated with some degree of specificity in international law.[49] Legal obligations fall into three general categories, characterized as duties to "respect, protect, and fulfill."[50] Duties of respect are generally defined negatively, entailing refraining from engaging in actions that would interfere with the enjoyment of currently respected rights. Duties to protect require states to take actions to ensure that others do not interfere with the economic and social rights of others, for example, by "adopting and enforcing legislation to protect against abuses in the workplace by private companies."[51] Duties to fulfill are obligations to establish the conditions that would enable individuals to enjoy social and economic rights by removing the obstacles to such rights. Moreover, by focusing even more narrowly on minimum core obligations with respect to these rights, we can further delimit feasible obligations. Minimum core obligations are "those that must be fully secured with immediate effect by all states."[52]

Normalized collective and political wrongdoing deals with violations of human rights that are a result of the specific actions and omissions of particular human beings, and the failure of particular individuals to fulfill the obligations owed to others. Individuals implicated are perpetrators of or complicit in such wrongs. The commission of wrongdoing is characteristically political, carried out by the state (or with the permission of the state) or by actors fighting the de facto authorities to further political objectives.[53] Thus even when private actors commit abuses in contexts of repressive regimes, political actors are typically involved. Teitel captures the involvement of political actors in contexts of repression when she writes, "Repressive regimes are often defined by criminal behavior, such as torture, arbitrary detention, disappearances, extrajudicial executions, all substantially state sponsored . . . even when past evil is perpetrated by private actors, the state is often, nevertheless, still implicated, whether in policies of persecution, by acts of omission in failing to protect its citizens, or, finally, in the cover-up of criminal acts and impunity."[54] Similarly, abuses committed

---

[48] Schmid and Nolan, "Do No Harm."
[49] Sources of such rights are various but include international human rights treaties such as the International Covenant on Economic, Social, and Cultural Rights (ICESCR) and domestic constitution; see ibid., 365.
[50] Ibid., 366.   [51] Ibid.
[52] Tasioulas, John, *Minimum Core Obligations: Human Rights in the Here and Now* (Washington, DC: World Bank, forthcoming), 23.
[53] On this point, see Teitel, *Transitional Justice*; Gray, "Extraordinary Justice."
[54] Teitel, *Transitional Justice*, 28.

during the course of civil war are carried out by competing factions that are vying for political control of a specific state or territory within a state.

Wrongs are political in another sense. The reason that actors engage in violations of human rights norms is not primarily for personal gain or out of personal animosity toward victims; rather, it is done for the sake of furthering political goals or policies that often articulate and reflect views about how a given political society should be structured. In Gray's words, "As is the case in most transitional contexts, the abuses of the past that demand attention are political in nature. By definition, political crimes are not the result of purely individual action. They are rooted in some collective conviction about the way that the country should be run."[55] This is not to say that political ideology or commitments are the only or exclusive reason individuals commit atrocities. Duress, fear, ignorance, indifference, greed, and desperation may also be part of the explanation for why specific individuals participate in collective wrongdoing; however, in cases of political wrongdoing political motivations and objectives provide the lens through which individuals interpret, justify, and explain their actions to others. In some cases the espoused political beliefs may provide cover for more individual or personal motivations.

Wrongdoing is moreover collective. At a very basic level, wrongdoing is collective in the sense that it is characteristically organized and perpetrated by groups, and often targets groups of citizens. The groups targeted and the groups perpetrating vary across conflicts and repressive regimes. Groups within a state may be targeted on the basis of an ethnic identity, religious identity, political ideology, occupation, class, or race. Wrongdoing is also collective in that the wrong itself has a collective character. That is, an accurate description of the wrong committed is characteristically not just a product of aggregation. To illustrate, consider genocide. Brian Lawson notes, "The wrongness of genocide seems morally distinct from the aggregation of individual murders that make up the genocide."[56] Genocide is not identified or characterized by summing the number of intentional murders committed by a group of individuals targeting a group of individuals over a specified period. Genocide also entails a particular intention: to destroy a targeted group. Thus two instances in which ten thousand individuals are murdered are not morally equivalent if in one of those scenarios the killings were done for the sake of destroying a group of which those individuals were members.

---

[55] Llewellyn and Howse, "Institutions for Restorative Justice," 381.
[56] Lawson, Brian, "Individual Complicity in Collective Wrongdoing," *Ethical Theory and Moral Practice* 16 (2013): 227–243, 227.

The case of genocide illustrates another common feature of wrongs that have a collective dimension: specific individual actions are frequently causally insufficient and/or causally unnecessary to bring about wrong-doing.[57] To return to the genocide example, one individual cannot commit genocide,[58] nor can many individuals acting together. It is only when working as a group that genocide can happen. In most cases the decision of one individual to not participate in a genocidal campaign does not alter the outcome of the campaign itself. Even if no one steps in, the overall contribution of any particular individual is not decisive in determining the success or failure of achieving a particular political objective through the violation of human rights. Often in cases of collective wrongdoing, another individual will simply replace the individual who opts out. Wrongdoing in this way becomes overdetermined.[59]

The collective character of wrongdoing complicates the moral categories appropriate to use when trying to make moral sense of the wrongs done. As important as examining direct perpetrators or victims is examining those complicit in wrongdoing. By *complicity* I mean very broadly "responsibility for the commissions and omissions that allow harm to occur but that are not necessarily causally efficacious in a straightforward way."[60] For purposes of understanding the circumstances of transitional justice, in this chapter I focus on the broader category of moral complicity.[61]

---

[57] Ibid., 3. The characterization of necessary and sufficient comes from ibid. On this general point, see Kutz, Christopher, *Complicity: Ethics and Law for a Collective Age* (New York: Cambridge University Press, 2007). In collective wrongdoing, Kutz writes that the harms inflicted by wrongdoing are overdetermined in the sense that the failure of any one given individual to participate in wrongdoing does not or would not significantly alter the resulting harm. Individual contributions are marginal and do not make a significant causal difference to the outcome. In other cases, individual actions considered in isolation seem morally neutral. Individual polluters do nothing obviously wrong when driving a vehicle, if considered in isolation. It is only when their action is conjoined with the action of millions of others that problematic CO_2 emissions occur. On this kind of case, see Ashford, Elizabeth, "The Inadequacy of Our Traditional Conception of the Duties Imposed by Human Rights," *Canadian Journal of Law and Jurisprudence* 29, no. 2 (2006): 217–35.

[58] See, e.g., May, *Genocide.* "The *actus reus* of the crime of genocide may involve many individual acts, but it seems they must be coordinated somehow. And the *mens rea* of the crime of genocide may also involve many guilty minds, but seemingly there must be a sense in which they were directed as well. For without the coordination and direction, it looks like what we have is merely killing based on persecution. . . . Individuals can intend to destroy a protected group, although normally without planning or without many others having the same intent, the group intention is empty" (205–6). For a minority dissenting view on this point, see Luban, David, "A Theory of Crimes against Humanity," *Yale International Law Journal* 85 (2004): 98.

[59] The language of overdetermination is from Kutz, *Complicity.*

[60] May, Larry, "Complicity and the Rwandan Genocide," *Res Publica* 16 (2010): 137.

[61] I do not take up the narrower category of legal complicity and the question of the legal standard for complicity that might make one eligible for some form of legal response.

Characteristically, many individuals are complicit in collective and political wrongdoing.[62] It has been argued that more than one million individuals, or one-third of the population, were complicit in the 1994 Rwandan genocide.[63] The actions or omissions taken by individuals complicit in wrongdoing vary along a wide range. Examples include watching a neighbor be kidnapped by a plainclothes police office and doing nothing, standing by and guarding a door while a military or rebel force rapes an individual, giving security or rebel forces information about the location of an individual targeted for killing, or providing machetes or arms used for torture and killing. Individuals can become complicit by virtue of their failure to fulfill role-related responsibilities; police officers who turn a blind eye to killing committed by private citizens would be one such example. Gray draws attention to the often-critical role of public support for atrocities when he writes, "The grueling labor of atrocities are carried out by cadres of 'willing executioners' with the knowledge, support, and assistance of public personalities, such as the military, police, political leaders, and members of the media."[64]

Collective and political wrongdoing is *normalized* in a descriptive, empirical sense. Wrongdoing such as rape, disappearing, or torture is or becomes a basic fact of life for individuals in the midst of conflict or repression, a fact around which individuals must orient their conduct. Becoming a victim of wrongdoing, witnessing wrongdoing, or being called on to participate in or perpetrate wrongdoing is something that individuals anticipate could happen to them in a predictive sense. What should be unthinkable is or becomes thinkable. Because such wrongdoing comes to be taken as a basic fact of life for individuals in the society in question, it is or becomes seen as unexceptional.

This empirical normalization does not entail that at the micro level every individual or even most individuals view the wrongs or atrocities being committed as morally acceptable. Some individuals, and in some

---

[62] In contexts of normalized collective and political wrongdoing, bystanders risk becoming complicit in such wrongs. Bystanders are third parties to wrongdoing, witnessing or coming to be knowledgeable of wrongdoing. See Fletcher, Laurel, "From Indifference to Engagement: Bystanders and International Criminal Justice," *Michigan Journal of International Law* 26 (2004–2005): 1013–95. Elaborating on this general definition, Fletcher writes, "In the context of mass violence, bystanders are those who did not participate in crimes but nonetheless did not intervene to stop the carnage. They may have been silent supporters or opponents of the political and military forces that waged the war, but their role in events is defined by their *inaction* and *passivity*. As their country and community became engulfed in war, regardless of their private opinions about the political fissures, they remained onlookers, quiescent or acquiescent witnesses to the social breakdown of their communities" (ibid., 1027).

[63] May, "Complicity," citing Drumbl, *Atrocity.*   [64] Gray, "Extraordinary Justice," 71.

contexts most individuals, may view wrongdoing as morally acceptable. This may be a result of either processes of norm inversion or norm breakdown.[65] Other individuals may deny the full reality of what is occurring, redescribing forced expulsions as "transfers" and systematic torture as a few instances of "excesses," or justifying what is recognized as torture by appealing to an external threat in the face of which such action is warranted.[66] People may think it is wrong but just the way things are, and not give the moral acceptability of such conduct much thought. Individuals who think wrongdoing is occurring may also think of it as too entrenched a problem to be outraged over. Absent or limited outrage at what has become normalized may also be a function of individuals distancing themselves from responsibility for what is happening, because they did not directly participate in killing, because killing was done on the orders of another, or because their contribution was marginal. When normalized, wrongdoing thus does not express a particular denial of a recognized equality or moral demand; it occurs in a social context in which the basic equality of individuals is systematically denied in practice.

Collective and political wrongdoing takes a wide range of forms during conflict and repression, implicating and targeting various individuals and groups. There are different dimensions along which this structure of collective and political wrongdoing varies that are of particular moral relevance: (1) the extent of coordination and organization involved in wrongdoing, (2) the scope of actors implicated in commission of wrongdoing (how far out the periphery of complicity extends), and (3) the extent of overlap in the categories of victim and perpetrators.[67] I illustrate some of the different dimensions of collective and political wrongdoing in the following to get at some of the numerous forms it may take, with historical and contemporary examples.

---

[65] See Morrow, Paul, "The Thesis of Norm Transformation in the Theory of Mass Atrocity," *Genocide Studies and Prevention: An International Journal* 9, no. 1 (2015): 66–82. In norm inversion people appear to come to think that participation in or support for genocidal acts or policies is "right" or "proper." What was previously regarded as correct standards are no longer seen as such, and what was previously regarded as prohibited conduct becomes acceptable or required. In norm breakdown people are left without firm convictions of what is right or proper behavior in their political and social circumstances because previously accepted standards for conduct no longer apply.

[66] On denial, see Cohen, Stanley, *States of Denial: Knowing about Atrocities and Suffering* (Cambridge: Polity Press, 2001); Waller, James, *Becoming Evil* (New York: Oxford University Press, 2005), especially 188–89; Morrow, Paul, "Mass Atrocity and Manipulation of Social Norms," *Social Theory and Practice* 40, no. 2 (2014): 255–80.

[67] I thank Pat Keenan for very helpful discussions of the different forms that collective and political wrongdoing can take.

Some cases of collective and political wrongdoing are instances of *centralized repression*.[68] Here violations of human rights and atrocities are perpetrated by a political regime exercising entrenched control over a society. In some cases the regime enjoys the support of a segment of that society and commits wrongdoing with the tacit knowledge and support of that segment. Nazi Germany would be an example of this kind of regime.[69] The portion of a population implicated varies depending on the size of the segment of the population supporting the regime.[70] In other cases, a state is in a sense hijacked by a group exercising absolute political control, and state agents committing atrocities do so with the endorsement of political leaders but not necessarily the broader society. The Khmer Rouge regime in Cambodia during the 1970s would be an instance of this form. During their four-year reign of terror, more than one million Cambodians died as a result of starvation as well as direct torture and execution.

Other cases of collective and political wrongdoing occur during the course of *symmetrical violence*. Symmetrical violence typically occurs in the context of a contestation for state power in civil war. In these contexts conflict characteristically pits a state military or security force against a nonstate group vying for political control. Competing groups enjoy support from different portions of a population. The civil wars in Mozambique and El Salvador throughout the 1980s and early 1990s, and the Syrian war ongoing as of the date of writing, are exemplars of this form. In such contexts both sides characteristically commit atrocities, though there is not necessarily proportionality in the atrocities committed by both groups. In such cases large portions of a population often become implicated in wrongdoing.

Yet other collective and political wrongdoing may be a product of *unstructured violence*.[71] At the limit, collective and political wrongdoing, especially in contexts of state failure or weakened states, may become a product of "the unconcerted actions of many individuals."[72] Mob violence

---

[68] I am grateful to Linda Radzik for suggesting the label "centralized repression."

[69] Daniel Johah Goldhagen makes this argument in *Hitler's Willing Executioners: Ordinary Germans and the Holocaust* (New York: Vintage Books, 1997).

[70] For a detailed illustration of how such repression can vary, see Periera, Anthony W., *Political (In)justice: Authoritarianism and the Rule of Law in Brazil, Chile and Argentina* (Pittsburgh: University of Pittsburgh Press, 2005).

[71] "Unstructured violence" references Kutz's notion of unstructured collective harm.

[72] Quote is from Kutz, *Complicity*, 113. For a description of this phenomenon, see Gerlach, Christian, *Extremely Violent Societies: Mass Violence in the Twentieth-Century World* (New York: Cambridge University Press, 2010).

would be an example of such unstructured violence. Especially in the case of weak or failed states, wrongdoing can become widespread in the sense that all citizens become potential targets. Perpetrators are many. Categories of victim and perpetrator are muddled and overlapping, as individuals subject to abuse then become abusers. Large segments become vulnerable to abuses as a result of a failure by the state to provide sufficient protection against abuse. Human rights abuses are committed in a context in which a vacuum of authority exists. Atrocities may be carried out by multiple, competing groups with limited coordination and organization from a central base, either of a rebel group or of the state. Contemporary conflicts that demonstrate a similar form include the current conflict in the Democratic Republic of the Congo and the recent civil war in Sierra Leone. The following description of the civil war in Sierra Leone illustrates this form:

> The government army hardly existed. Two years ago it had briefly over-thrown the president; now many of its soldiers fought in volatile tandem with the rebels, and many of the rest, by long-standing tradition, took any random opportunity for terror and looting. Plenty of the men and boys sweeping through Lamin's area were government troops, and though their stated objective was better government, their prime enemy seemed to be anyone without a gun, anyone not raping and making mayhem alongside them. All was anarchy. The government of President Tejan Kabbah, such as it was, was defended mostly by a proxy force of Nigerians, dispatched by a dictator with his own reasons, and by a loose alliance of Sierra Leonean hunting societies. ... And while the Nigerian army and the inoculated gunman fought the opposition inside Freetown—tying, flogging, beating, and often executing anyone suspected of rebel sympathy along the way— the rebel and government troops went into an ever-increasing frenzy on the outskirts of the city.[73]

As this should make clear, the precise form collective and political wrongdoing takes can – and does – vary across transitional contexts along multiple dimensions. It varies in the political objectives or goals being pursued (e.g., secession, revolution, or maintenance of an established political regime); the identities of the group targeted and perpetrating wrongdoing (e.g., ideologically based or ethnically based); how official the wrongdoers are; and the form that wrongdoing takes (e.g., rape, torture, or mass displacement); as well as the scale on which it occurs and the degree to which it is well organized. Wrongdoing varies in the numbers of individuals complicit in wrongdoing and the victims of

---

[73] Bergner, Daniel, *In the Land of Magic Soldiers: A Story of White and Black in West Africa* (New York: Picador, 2003), 17.

wrongdoing, and in how broadly known the acts of wrongdoing are. Understanding collective and political wrongdoing in any specific transitional context, then, requires attending to these various dimensions. There is also variation in the overall collective or organizational structure of wrongdoing. The specific form collective and political wrongdoing takes in any given context has important ramifications for the form accountability should take and the potential subjects of accountability responses.

One final point about normalized collective and political wrongdoing is important to emphasize. Individuals make up the collective groups that jointly commit wrongdoing. Such individuals remain agents even when acting with a group. Individuals exercise their agency in multiple and varied ways in the midst of widespread and often systematic atrocity, and this is true even in genocidal campaigns or ethnic cleansing. Specific individuals raped and tortured particular prisoners during the Dirty War in Argentina. Many particular individuals wielded machetes that killed neighbors during Rwanda, yet some particular individuals chose to hide their neighbors in the hope of protecting them from the killing. Just as there is variation in the actions themselves, so, too, there is variation among individuals in the reasons behind the same actions. As Mark Drumbl notes when specifically discussing child soldiers:

> Children may be offered up – like chattel – by family members or local leaders. ... That said ... many children, notably older adolescents, come forward intentionally to join armed forces or groups. Environmental factors and situational constraints – which include poverty, insecurity, lack of education, socialization into violence, and broken families – certainly inform decisions to enlist. ... In joining armed forces or groups, children may simply be pursuing paths of economic advancement, inclusion in occupational networks, pursuit of political or ideological reform, and professional development.[74]

Individual choices are thus not predetermined, even when choices are constrained or circumscribed in profound and important ways by the context in which choices are being made.[75]

The circumstance in stable democracies that contrasts with normalized collective and political wrongdoing is *deviant individual and personal wrongdoing*.[76] Wrongdoing is personal in the sense that it is motivated

---

[74] Drumbl, Mark, *Reimagining Child Soldiers in International Law and Policy* (New York: Oxford University Press, 2012), 14.
[75] On the idea of circumscribed action see ibid., 15.
[76] The term *deviant* comes from Drumbl, *Atrocity*.

and explained by private factors. For example, one individual kills another out of malice, jealousy, or recklessness. Wrongdoing is moreover personal in the sense that it is not characteristically orchestrated and carried out by individuals acting with the sanction or backing of the state to fulfill political objectives. Wrongdoing is individual in the sense that it is not characteristically carried out by groups and does not typically target groups. Liberal political theorizing about the appropriate way to respond to wrongdoing typically assumes that wrongs are individual and personal.[77] In such contexts, the commission of crime is the structurally condemned exception and not the rule. That is, crime and criminal activity represent deviations from behavior that is the norm.[78]

I have discussed two circumstances of transitional justice so far: pervasive structural inequality, and normalized collective and political wrongdoing. Before turning to the third circumstance of transitional justice, I want to clarify the distinction between pervasive structural inequality and normalized collective and political wrongdoing. The core distinction lies in the subject matter of each. Structural inequality looks at the wide-ranging institutional rules, norms, and practices that set the general parameters for interaction among members of a political society and officials: they specify who may interact with whom on what matters and in what manner. Such rules and norms also specify rewards and benefits for conforming and nonconforming behavior. Attending to such institutional rules, norms, and practices matters because of how they can profoundly harm or benefit individuals and/or groups within communities by limiting, foreclosing, or making possible opportunities for individuals and groups to pursue their objectives and become and do what they value.

By contrast, the primary subject of collective and political wrongdoing is not general parameters for interaction institutionally specified or sanctioned; rather it is particular interactions among specific individuals acting in concert with other particular individuals that result in tangible harms – and in particular violations of human rights – to particular people, who are often members of targeted groups. Collective and political wrongdoing focuses attention on what happens to certain human beings as a direct result of the actions or omissions of others. Such actions may be predictable given the institutional structure itself,

---

[77] Ashford, "Inadequacy."

[78] A few exceptions to this general picture may exist in a given society. For example, in the United States purchasing alcohol while underage is criminal behavior that is the norm rather than the exception.

without those actions being identical to the institutional rules themselves or even required by such rules.

Although conceptually distinct, pervasive structural inequality and normalized collective and political wrongdoing are empirically correlated and mutually reinforcing conditions. Pervasive structural inequality can serve to justify differential treatment and by extension denials and violations of human rights. In looking at the conditions that facilitate atrocity, Gray writes: "The role of background social norms and institutional practice in the production of willing agents is well documented. The ability of public expectations and bureaucratic structures to turn normal people into agents of destruction is at the center of Hannah Arendt's famous account of the 'banality of evil.'"[79] The practical possibility of normalized collective and political wrongdoing taking place in the circumstance of pervasive structural equality or limited structural inequality is remote.

The systematic erosion of capabilities to be respected; recognized as a member of a political community; participate in economic, political, and social institutions; and avoid poverty renders individuals and groups more vulnerable to rights violations. Studies demonstrate the vulnerability to abuse and rights violations increases when there is an absence of a minimum level of respect and recognition of the humanity of members of a certain group.[80] Failure to recognize the humanity of others can impact the capacities required for interpersonal interaction that can act as a check on wrongdoing. Reflecting this point, during the trial of Daniel Holtzclaw, convicted of committing rapes and sexual assaults while on duty as a police officer in Oklahoma, prosecutor Lori McConnell stated in her closing argument, "He didn't choose CEOs or soccer moms; he chose women he could count on not telling what he was doing. . . . He counted on the fact no one would believe them and no one would care."[81]

Such lack of recognition and respect is reflected in and justified by what Gray calls an "abusive paradigm," which as I noted in the Introduction refers to "the complex of cultural norms, social practices, institutional regimes, black letter law, official policies, institutional practices, social norms, cultural ideology, and historical teleology that together provide

---

[79] Gray, "Extraordinary Justice," 71.
[80] Gray, "Extraordinary Justice"; Fletcher and Weinstein, "Violence and Social Repair"; Brooks, Thom, "Getting Reparations Right – A Response to Posner and Vermeule," *Notre Dame Law Review* 80 (2004): 251–88.
[81] Larimer, Sarah, "Disgraced Ex-Cop Daniel Holtzclaw Sentenced to 263 Years for On-Duty Rapes, Sexual Assaults," *Washington Post*, www.washingtonpost.com/news/post-nation/wp/2016/01/21/disgraced-ex-officer-daniel-holtzclaw-to-be-sentenced-after-sex-crimes-conviction/.

the organizing ontology and justificatory ethic of abusive regimes and which ratify, induce, and sustain programs of mass violence."[82] Distrust of groups of citizens can be a key part of this dynamic, where an appeal to the intrinsic ill will of members of a targeted group who are seen as a threat is part of the rationale for collective and political wrongdoing itself.[83] Marginalized groups face greater barriers to the recognition, respect, and enforcement of human rights.

The causal interaction can come from the opposite direction, as well. Normalized collective and political wrongdoing can have as one of its functions maintaining pervasive structural inequality. Multiple capabilities can be undermined at once through certain forms of normalized collective and political wrongdoing. During its civil war, limb amputation became a strategy used by the Revolutionary United Front (RUF) in Sierra Leone. In its report the commission documents sixteen hundred survivors but does not know the total number of amputees, including those who died from their wounds.[84] Amputation was fundamentally disrespectful of the basic dignity of those targeted, was done for the sake of creating an incentive among citizens to forgo participating in political elections, and made amputees more vulnerable to poverty by imposing greater obstacles to employment and higher medical costs. The Sierra Leone Truth Commission addresses many of these consequences in the following passage from its report:

> Amputation was a deliberate strategy on the part of the RUF, designed to sow terror in the hearts and minds of civilians. The Commission has found that this deliberate strategy was on occasion aimed at preventing civilians from voting. Many amputees testified that the RUF ordered them, after amputating their hands, to take the amputated hand to the elected President of Sierra Leone, Ahmad Tejan Kabbah. The RUF had adopted the strategy of "Peace before Elections" and the call of the President-in-waiting for "Elections before Peace" had infuriated the RUF leadership. Thus the RUF resorted to targeting civilians and amputating their limbs. During the campaign of amputations known as "Operation Stop Elections" in 1996, the right hand of victims, being the hand symbolic of voting, was cut off and handed back to the victim with the direction that it should be delivered to Tejan Kabbah. ... The Commission finds the act of amputation to be a particularly inhuman act amounting to the mutilation and physical and psychological torture of those upon whom it was inflicted.

---

[82] Gray, "Extraordinary Justice," 70.   [83] Ibid.; Goldhagen, *Hitler's Willing Executioners*.
[84] Sierra Leone Truth & Reconciliation Commission, *Witness to Truth: Report of the Sierra Leone Truth & Reconciliation Commission* (Accra, Ghana: Graphic Packaging LTD, 2004): vol. 1, 156.

The Commission finds the RUF and the AFRC to have pursued a deliberate strategy of amputations with the intention of torturing them and sowing terror throughout the civilian population.[85]

In a study of the civil wars in the former Yugoslavia, Colette Donadio reports similar impacts on the estimated twenty thousand to fifty thousand women raped, and notes that Serbian soldiers targeted Muslims. Donadio writes:

> The survivors are not granted support, shelter and assistance, and find themselves facing stigmatising situations. Reports from FIDH, Amnesty and Impunity Watch describe traumatized victims who refuse to go back to their households as they are denied access to health services and rejected by their local communities ... The following extract from the Impunity Watch Report on "War Victims and Gender-Sensitive Truth, Justice, Reparations and Non-Recurrence in Bosnia And Herzegovina" is highly significant: "Victims of war crimes suffer physical, psychological and social consequences. There are severe, permanent and serious effects both on their economic and social circumstances, as well as on a psychological level."[86]

Bonadia's description presents the severely diminished opportunities for interaction, social or otherwise, subsequent poverty, and ostracization from communities that result from wrongdoing. Those living under the threat of violence because they share a targeted identity can have their opportunities to participate in political and economic processes constrained, even if they do not suffer the direct forms of disrespect constitutive of violence. I take up these consequences of some forms of normalized collective and political wrongdoing in Chapter 4

Normalized collective and political wrongdoing generates and strengthens distrust both among victims and among members of a targeted group. The experience of wrongdoing is traumatizing and can impact the ability of victims and members of a targeted group to assume that fellow citizens or officials are basically decent or lack ill will. Such wrongdoing can erode faith in the law since such rules fail to protect individuals from egregious rights violations. Moreover, normalized collective and political wrongdoing, as the example from Argentina below illustrates, can itself constitute a systematic violation of the requirements of the rule of law.

---

[85] Ibid., 156–57.
[86] Donadio, Colette, "Gender Based Violence: Justice and Reparation in Bosnia and Herzegovina," *Mediterranean Journal of Social Sciences* 5, no. 16 (July 2014): 697–99. For a powerful account from a different context, Uganda, see Hollander, Theo and Bani Gill, "Every Day the War Continues in My Body: Examining the Marked Body in Postconflict Northern Uganda," *International Journal of Transitional Justice* 8 (2014): 217–34.

Situations of conflict and repression are messy and complicated, and language is not perfect to analytically carve out their various features. Unsurprisingly, given their close connection in practice, the identification of the two circumstances of normalized collective and political wrongdoing and pervasive structural inequality may be fuzzy and overlapping in actual cases. To illustrate, let me return to an example that I took up in *A Moral Theory of Political Reconciliation*, namely, the systematic disappearing of tens of thousands of citizens during the Dirty War in Argentina from 1976 to 1983 by agents of the state or individuals acting on the behest of the state.[87] Disappeared individuals were kidnapped, characteristically tortured, and often raped in secret locales, and in most cases ultimately killed. "Disappeared" is the description given to such cases because kidnapped individuals were literally removed from their social world and no evidence or explanation of their removal was available to family members or friends. Government officials characteristically denied responsibility for their disappearance as well as more general knowledge of what had happened to them. Disappearing of this general kind occurs in many contexts of conflict and repression.

We may view the moral significance of systematic disappearing through two lenses. The first lens, provided by the circumstance of normalized collective and political wrongdoing, concentrates on the disappeared. The focus here is on detailing the nature of morally egregious violations and the harm suffered by those specific individuals who were kidnapped, tortured, drugged, and tossed from airplanes into the sea because of their suspected political beliefs or actions. Such violations were manifold and in many cases horrific, entailing severe violations of rights of bodily integrity, life, and movement. Secondary victims of such violations include family members left without knowledge of the whereabouts and fate of a parent, child, or spouse and left living with the anxiety and stress such uncertainty creates; for those who learn or assume the worst there is the pain stemming from an inability to properly lay to rest the body of the loved one, which for many is seen as a significant obligation. From the perspective of normalized collective and political wrongdoing, identifying the particular individuals implicated in and responsible for each of the disappearances is morally important. When state sponsored, the circle of those implicated is quite large, including, uncontroversially, the particular agents responsible for the abduction itself, the direct infliction of torture, and ultimately the

---

[87] For a comprehensive overview of disappearing in Argentina, see Feitlowitz, Marguerite, *A Lexicon of Terror: Argentina and the Legacies of Torture* (Oxford: Oxford University Press, 1998).

murder of the disappeared individual. Also included in those complicit in wrongdoing are individuals who aided in transporting the abducted victim, guards at the place where prisoners were kept, those present during torture sessions, senior officials ordering disappearances or knowledgeable about the political objectives being furthered through the disappearing of dissidents, and police or local officials interacting with family members inquiring about missing members.

By contrast, pervasive structural inequality highlights the impact of the campaign of disappearing citizens on the general structure of interaction among citizens, and among citizens and officials.[88] Here the group impacted is not exclusively or even primarily the particular disappeared individuals; rather, individuals living in a particular society generally are impacted. State-sponsored disappearing of citizens was designed to incentivize citizens to be submissive to the policies of the military junta, and to incentivize them by undermining the stability of the political and social environment in which they interacted. The kidnapping, torture, and murder of citizens constitutive of disappearing were not legally sanctioned; indeed, disappearing is illegal under international law.[89] Thus in conducting tens of thousands of disappearances, government officials were consistently acting in ways contrary to what was officially sanctioned by declared legal rules. Officials responded to citizens deemed subversive in ways that bypassed any demonstration of such citizens' guilt through the criminal process. In denying that disappearings were occurring and/or that government officials were responsible for the fate of those disappeared, government officials avoided publicly articulating that for which such citizens were deemed guilty. Citizens were thus put into a situation in which they could not turn to declared rules to anticipate what official expectations of their conduct were, or what the official response to their actions would be. The resulting "terror and uncertainty create a chilling effect on political activity in general."[90] Such uncertainty in turn profoundly constrains the freedom of action and interaction among citizens, as legal subjects are not in a position to be able to form reliable expectations of how fellow citizens or officials will respond to their actions. Moreover, officials by denying their actions became unanswerable to the laws that would have applied to ordinary citizens if they engaged in comparable activities. Through the lens

---

[88] It was the institutional, interactional dimensions of disappearing that were the focus of the discussion in Murphy, *Moral Theory*, chap. 2.

[89] Roht-Arriaza, Naomi, "State Responsibility to Investigate and Prosecute Grave Human Rights Violations in International Law," *California Law Review* 78 (1990): 456.

[90] Ibid., 451–55.

of pervasive structural inequality, we identify the harm done by the practice of disappearing in which officials systematically disregard limitations placed on their conduct by declared legal rules to political relationships among citizens and officials and specifically to citizens' ability to exercise their agency in a society.

Serious Existential Uncertainty

The third circumstance of transitional justice is *serious existential uncertainty*, by which I refer to the deeply unclear empirical trajectory of a political society. Transitions to democracy frequently falter; in many cases authoritarian regimes return and conflict resumes. Indeed, part of the reason for the intense social scientific interest in transitional justice is that successful and lasting transitions to a democratic order are not the rule. In this context, determining what factors influence particular social outcomes becomes imperative.

Characteristically, there is both subjective and objective deep ambiguity surrounding the very possibility of a democratic transition.[91] To give some sense of the objective uncertainty, consider the following. Out of the approximately 100 countries classified as transitional, "in recent years, only a relatively small number – probably fewer than 20 – are clearly en route to becoming successful, well-functioning democracies or at least have made some democratic progress and still enjoy a positive dynamic of democratization."[92] In postcommunist countries in Eastern Europe and Eurasia, there are "a handful of successful transitions and easy consolidations, several incomplete transitions, a few transitions followed by reversion to authoritarian politics, even some transitions that never really began at all."[93] Political scientists use the terms *bouncer* and *cyclers* to describe societies that fluctuate between autocracy and democracy numerous times.[94] An examination of the 1990s reveals that 43 percent of conflicts

---

[91] I use "objective" to refer to uncertainty that is based on statistical trends and social scientific studies. I use "subjective" to refer to individuals' perspective about their own situation or the situation of others.

[92] Carothers, "End of the Transition Paradigm," 9.

[93] King, Charles, "Review Article: Post-Postcommunism: Transition, Comparison, and the End of 'Eastern Europe,'" *World Politics* 53, no. 1 (2000): 143–72.

[94] Epstein, David L., Robert Bates, Jack Goldstone, Ida Kristensen, and Sharyn O'Halloran, "Democratic Transitions," *American Journal of Political Science* 50 (2006): 556. On this point the authors cite Jack A. Goldstone and Adriana Kocornik-Mina, "Democracy and Development: New Insights from Dynagraphs," George Mason University, Center for Global Policy, Working Paper #1, Fairfax, VA (2005).

that ended via a negotiated peace settlement saw a return to civil conflict within five years of the agreement.[95]

What these figures suggest, and what the condition of serious existential uncertainty draws attention to, is that in any given transitional context there is enormous empirical uncertainty about what the actual political trajectory of a transitional society is and will be. In some cases there may be empirical uncertainty about whether a single political society will continue to exist. Whether or not there is doubt about where the boundaries of a political society will (continue to) fall, there is empirical uncertainty about whether there will in fact be a transition to democracy.[96] It remains often deeply unclear whether there will be substantive change and reform within a given society and whether change represents a stable and lasting achievement. Perhaps there will be a return to sustained conflict. Perhaps elections will be held. If elections are held, perhaps they will be credible. Perhaps all parties to the elections will respect the results. Perhaps politicians will act in ways that are significantly different from the actions of politicians past, or perhaps they will seek to amend the constitution to broaden the powers they enjoy. A shift in the political order might occur without having the character that advocates of transitional justice desire. Deep inequalities could persist or be entrenched in new ways in the new political order. Schisms may develop within communities that were not present before. There is a real risk that peace will not stick and violence will return. In sum, there is substantial uncertainty surrounding whether the trajectory presupposed by accounts of transitional justice will be achieved and, if achieved, whether it will represent a stable and lasting achievement.

Yussef Auf's analysis of the situation in Egypt as of February 2015, four years after the fall of Hosni Mubarak, captures this uncertainty:

> According to a timeframe put in place by the High Elections Commission (HEC) in January, a new Egyptian parliament should be elected and convened by mid-May 2015, at the latest. However, a study of the current situation, particularly in legal and constitutional terms—irrespective of the political context and electoral alliances that may be formed—indicates that the parliament will face a number of major obstacles. These obstacles may threaten the very existence of the parliament itself, whether through the

---

[95] Mack, Andrew, "Global Political Violence: Explaining the Post-Cold War Decline," in *Strategies for Peace: Contributions of International Organizations, States and Non-State Actors*, ed. Volker Rittberger and Martina Fischer (Opladen, Germany: Barbara Budrich Publishers, 2008), 83.

[96] Unsurprisingly, there is widespread interest and disagreement among political scientists in regard to factors that influence the likelihood of success for transitions and what undermines the prospects for success.

postponement of elections entirely or the dissolution of the parliament after it is formed. As such, Egypt could witness a parliamentary absence that may last indefinitely, leading to a continuation of the current political vacuum.[97]

Auf goes on to note that since the fall of Mubarak and the dissolution in February 2011 of the Mubarak-era elected houses of parliament (the People's Assembly and Shura Council) by the Supreme Council of the Armed Forces in a constitutional declaration, there has been no parliament with the exception of a five-month period in 2012 following elections.

Serious subjective existential uncertainty about the future of one's own society is characteristically broad and shared by citizens and officials alike in a society in transition.[98] Transitions are often labeled as such by outside observers. However, to those who live through them, it is often quite unclear whether a particular moment is the temporary turbulence of the ancient regime or really a break that might lead somewhere new. For those within the system it is hard to distinguish in real time between a brief interlude in a system that will remain deeply unaffected by it or a real opening to something different. What this means at the individual level is that it becomes difficult for individuals to exercise their agency. Individuals are not in a position to determine with any degree of confidence what the impact of choices they make will be. Acting on the basis of any particular projection about the future is a gamble. How to organize your behavior so as to achieve certain objectives, such as maintaining the safety of self and family, is profoundly unclear. If choices are made oriented around an assumption that there will be democracy, the basis for such choices often represents a leap of faith.

Although transitions are conceptualized and described in a teleological fashion, ordered linearly from an illiberal to a liberal political order, this teleology is not always – or even usually – representative of the reality in a given transitional society.[99] A teleologically ordered transition from conflict or repression to democracy is in most cases profoundly aspirational, reflecting the normative aspiration and deep hope that a given transition will be successful. However, it does not capture the actual empirical political trajectory it is reasonable to expect in any particular case, nor the subjective perspective of members of a given transitional society.

---

[97] Auf, Yussef, "The Egyptian Parliament: After a Lengthy Absence, an Uncertain Future," *Atlantic Council*, February 26, 2015, www.atlanticcouncil.org/blogs/egyptsource/the-egyptian-parliament-after-a-lengthy-absence-an-uncertain-future.

[98] I thank Kim Lane Scheppele for very helpful comments on what I am calling "subjective existential uncertainty."

[99] Teitel, "Transitional Jurisprudence"; Teitel, *Transitional Justice*.

Serious existential uncertainty can be contrasted with minor existential uncertainty and critical existential uncertainty. In contexts of minor existential uncertainty the political trajectory of a society is relatively stable. Democracies tend to be objectively subject to minor existential uncertainty. In a study of the world democratization trends from 1960 to 2000, Epstein et al. found that 98.2 percent of democracies remain democratic over a given year, while partial democracies are "four times less stable." Over a five-year span only 7 percent of full democracies changed, compared with 40 percent of partial democracies.[100] When minor subjective existential uncertainty is characteristic among citizens, there is an assumption orienting action that elections will take place as scheduled and that the winner will assume power on the specified date.

In contexts of minor existential uncertainty, even controversial shifts in policy and rights do not typically pose a threat to the stability of the political order, nor are they seen as posing such a threat. While there may be resistance to the enforcement of new rights or to shifts in policies, characteristically there is no robust threat that a shift will undermine or destabilize a liberal political order. This is not to suggest that changes in policy or attempts at structural reform are always welcome; they are not, and they are often vigorously and sometimes violently resisted. In many cases there may be a long road between the initiation of limited structural change and its successful entrenchment; however, characteristically there is an underlying confidence in the eventual success of a given reform and the trajectory of a political society.[101] In contexts of critical existential uncertainty there is no political trajectory of which we can speak.

In terms of its relationship to the first two circumstances of transitional justice, pervasive structural inequality is a necessary but not sufficient condition for serious existential uncertainty to obtain. This is because uncertainty surrounds whether a society can transition from a condition of pervasive structural inequality to a condition of limited structural inequality, the circumstance constitutive of stable democratic societies. However, pervasive structural inequality is not sufficient for serious

---

[100] Epstein et al., "Democratic Transitions," 555.

[101] Political philosophers such as Rawls take seriously stability as a concern. Stability is understood normatively in terms of the stability of the justification of a set of policies, as well as empirically. Normative stability is seen to support empirical or descriptive stability. See Rawls, *Theory of Justice*; Weithman, Paul, *Why Political Liberalism? On John Rawls's Political Turn* (New York: Oxford University Press, 2011); Vallier, Kevin and Fred D'Agostino, "Public Justification," *Stanford Encyclopedia of Philosophy*, ed. Edward N. Zalta (2014), http://plato.stanford.edu/archives/spr2014/entries/justification-public/.

existential uncertainty to obtain. Also required are credible attempts to disrupt the status quo overhauling pervasive structural inequality. Only then is it appropriate to speak of a society in "transition," however remote the prospect for achieving the normative aim of the transition may be. It may be normatively desirable to end to repressive regimes and long-standing conflicts, but a society is only transitional when there are efforts taken to realize this end.

Fundamental Uncertainty about Authority

Political philosophers have a long-standing interest in understanding the nature of authority, including where authority comes from and the nature and limits of its legitimate exercise. Political authority is a particular subject of ongoing debate. Although the precise way to define political authority is disputed, for my purposes I assume that authority refers to the right to rule, that is, the right to make and coercively enforce rules regarding the behavior of subjects. Paradigm transitional societies are characterized by *fundamental uncertainty about authority*.

To see what is fundamentally uncertain about authority in the circumstances of transitional justice, it is helpful to begin with a summary of how political philosophers and political theorists conceptualize political authority as a theoretical issue. The sources of uncertainty about political authority at issue in transitional contexts are different than the sources of uncertainty as typically conceptualized by political philosophers. As a result, the project of establishing the authority of the state in transitional contexts is different from the project of establishing the authority of the state in stable democratic contexts or in previous historical transitions. The theoretical issues and concerns driving each project are distinct.

In standard philosophical analyses of authority, the general theoretical aim is to justify an authority that is currently in power or to explain the conditions under which revolution would be justified.[102] The possibility of justified political authority is a general theoretical concern because of the potential tension between authority, on the one hand, and autonomy and equality, on the other. In brief: If individuals are equal and autonomous, why would it ever be justified for one individual or group to order another individual to do something? For theorists of the seventeenth and eighteenth centuries who focused on the right of revolution such as John Locke,

---

[102] See, e.g., Hobbes, Thomas, *The Leviathan*, intro. by C. B. MacPherson (New York: Penguin Classics, 1982).

another central theoretical concern was understanding and articulating the limits of political authority.[103] Given the existence of a government in power, what could that government do lawfully? Was it entitled to tax or take the property of citizens without their consent, for example? It is in the context of articulating the limits on the lawful action of the state that we can situate many theories of punishment. Punishment involves the intentional infliction of suffering on an individual by the state; theories of punishment strive to help us understand why this is something it would ever be permissible for a political authority to do.

The question of authority has in fact arisen as a political and theoretical issue in historical transitions to democracy, such as transitions to democracy in ancient Greece stemming from opposition to tyrannical rule, and transitions following important revolutions like the French Revolution and American Revolution. There are important differences among these different historical transitions, including in the character of the democratic institutions established, who was included (as well as excluded) from full democratic citizenship, and the means by which democratic government was pursued. Despite such differences, such transitions have been theoretically conceptualized in similar terms. Importantly, the question of the authority of a new government is framed as a question about the origins of government authority *de nova*, or with no past. In state-of-nature accounts, political authority is conceptualized as being established in a social and political vacuum, thus the regime established has no relationship with past regimes. There is also no consideration of wrongs done in the past. In reality, transitions are and have historically been characteristically bloody, with wrongs done in the process of establishing a new form of government. However, for theorists the wrongs are not taken as having a bearing on the authority of the new government that is established and play no role in the state-of-nature narratives of political theorists.

Scholars of transitional justice conceptualize contemporary transitions in different terms.[104] Transitions are thought of as bridges, not complete

---

[103] Locke, John, *Second Treatise of Government*, ed. C. B. MacPherson (Indianapolis: Hackett Publishing, 1980).

[104] In this section I am interested in how transitions are conceptualized by scholars. Such theoretical characterizations may not map onto the experience of how people actually living in the wake of transitions conceptualize their situation. The people actually living in the wake of the French and American Revolutions and the American Civil War all probably had the experience of a "bridge" and not a "break." Moreover, there was, for example, a question of whether to pursue the murderers of the architects of the Reign of Terror (who were also murderers). The United States and England both had to deal with legacies of people considered traitors. The theory is changing, not necessarily the facts. For very helpful conversation on this point, I thank Linda Radzik.

breaks, between the past and the present.[105] Transitional societies have as part of their recent history collective and political wrongdoing. However, this history of wrongdoing prior to and during the establishment of a new political regime is not idealized away. Wrongs that have been committed are no longer "in the past."

This change in conceptualization has two important implications that give rise to *fundamental uncertainty about authority.* "Uncertainty about authority" references ambiguity about the standing of a political regime to rule and enforce rules. By "political regime" I refer to the specific form of government in control of a given state. The first implication of the change in conceptualization is narrow and concerns the authority of a regime to address wrongdoing within a political society. As noted in the Introduction, at the core of a generally accepted definition of transitional justice is the process of dealing with past wrongs. Yet justifying the standing of a transitional regime to respond to wrongdoing is especially morally difficult and contentious, given that the prior political regime, R1, was complicit in or perpetrators of the past wrongdoing that must now be addressed by the transitional political regime, R2. A central theoretical task is to explain how R2's authority to address past wrongdoing can be forged in a context in which the R1 in power prior to a transition is implicated in that wrongdoing.[106] Further complicating this question is the fact that a number of state agents and agents from R1 who were perpetrators of or complicit in the wrongs being dealt with may continue to hold official positions in R2. This is often out of practical necessity, as in many the removal of all state agents from R1 would remove the group of individuals qualified for and knowledgeable about such positions.

The second implication of the change in conceptualization is broader and concerns the basic framework of justification for the general authority of R2.[107] There are characteristically de facto multiple competing norms of authority present, and there is also no theory for the authority of such mixed orders. By definition, in transitional contexts a democratic structure of authority has yet to fully emerge. Transitional regimes are mixed

---

[105] This was explicitly the case in the language used by the South African TRC. It is also the language found in scholarly work. See, for example, Dyzenhaus, "Judicial Independence."

[106] It could be objected that there is no problem since the regime is new and not the same as the regime implicated in past wrongdoing. However, while there has been a regime change, there remains a question of to what extent the new regime really is "new." As serious existential uncertainty highlights, it is not clear that the new regime will be substantively different than what came before, let alone democratic.

[107] As noted earlier, general authority concerns the basic right to rule and enforce rules.

political orders; elements of liberal democratic political orders coexist with, for example, aspects of authoritarian legacies. During the transitional period there is not, and practically speaking cannot be, an immediate and comprehensive overhaul of all existing institutions and practices. Thus, for example, "postauthoritarian constitutions may leave in place (i.e., unreformed) certain aspects of the *ancien regime*, notably those that have low salience at the moment of transition or that are not considered among the gravest problems of the immediately preceding regime."[108] Carothers argues that most transitional societies "have some attributes of democratic political life, including at least limited political space for opposition parties and independent civil society, as well as regular elections and democratic constitutions. Yet they suffer from serious democratic deficits, often including ... frequent abuse of the law by government officials, elections of uncertain legitimacy, very low levels of public confidence in state institutions."[109]

Consequently, de facto in transitional societies multiple standards of authority may operate at the same time. Some standards may derive from the authoritarian past, either as an authoritarian standard of authority or as authority based on resistance to the authoritarian period; other standards may derive from democratic reforms. Yet other standards may derive from the capacity to control violence or maintain peace.[110] At times these standards may conflict. For example, the authority of many politicians in transitional contexts is taken to stem from the role that they played in resisting oppression and repression during the authoritarian period. The authority of officeholders in a liberal democratic order characteristically stems from procedural criteria, such as being elected or appointed by someone who was duly elected according to specified procedures. However, in transitional contexts little weight may be given in practice to the fact that such politicians were elected, or little attention paid to the character of such elections. Rather, weight may be placed on their role in enabling a change in the political order, and so politicians who lack this kind of authority may not be viewed as authoritative simply by virtue of being elected.

Theoretical justifications of the authority of political regimes are based on pure regime types. Such theories provide limited guidance for contexts

---

[108] Prempeh, H. Kwasi, "*Marbury* in Africa: Judicial Review and the Challenge of Constitutionalism in Contemporary Africa," *Tulane Law Review* 80, no. 1 (2006): 53.

[109] Carothers, "End of the Transition Paradigm," 9–10.

[110] The authority of temporary occupiers has been justified on these grounds within just war theory.

in which a pure regime is not in place, but such an account is needed, especially in light of disputes that predictably arise. In a context in which competing standards for authority coexist, an additional source of dispute can arise over who has the standing to determine how past wrongdoing will be addressed.

For example, consider cases of grudge informers, individuals who report those against whom they have a personal grudge to authorities ruling repressive regimes. In a famous case of a particular grudge informer in Nazi Germany, there was deep disagreement about whether the judiciary or legislative branch were authorized to retroactively declare certain statutes from the Nazi era unconstitutional.[111] As this case indicates, there can be a genuinely open question about who has the standing to deal with past wrongs. There can also be questions about whether, if claimed, that standing will in fact be recognized and acknowledged by the transitional community. Often citizens and sometimes officials in transitional circumstances do not assume, and indeed in some cases openly question and challenge, the authority of the new government both as a general matter and in regard to dealing with past wrongs. Understanding and clarifying the grounds and limits of the regime's authority has a particular force and meaning in transitions.

Normalized collective and political wrongdoing and serious existential uncertainty generate fundamental uncertainty about authority. Normalized collective and political wrongdoing implicates the state, and so calls into question the standing of the state to deal with wrongs in which it is so implicated. Serious existential uncertainty reflects the absence of a stable institutional framework for analyzing and justifying the authority of the state more generally.

By contrast, in circumstances of *narrow uncertainty about authority* one particular representative or agent of the political regime may be complicit in wrongdoing, challenging his or her individual authority to respond to wrongdoing in a particular instance. Alternatively, there may be some confusion or debate about how to interpret the generally accepted norms that determine who is authorized to respond to wrongdoing in a given case. Insofar as uncertainty about authority arises in stable democratic contexts, it is typically this narrow kind. The general questions of what constitutes a legitimate exercise of authority and who constitutes the legitimate authority are, in these stable communities, settled. Standards for authority derived from a democratic constitutional framework are well

---

[111] Dyzenhaus, "Judicial Independence."

entrenched and without substantial challenge from competing sources of authority. The social and institutional conditions required for such standards to be satisfied in practice by and large obtain. Furthermore, there is widespread social acceptance of the authority of branches of government, including the judiciary. The framework of authority for deciding contested questions and dilemmas is not up for grabs in the way that it is in transitional contexts. To illustrate, although substantial disagreement exists among judges, members of the legal community, and ordinary citizens about the principles that should guide judicial interpretation, few in stable democracies contest the authority of judges to decide what the law is, and so the basic principle of judicial review. The recognition of this authority is reflected in the fact that judicial decisions are viewed by members of the legal community and the community as a whole as legally binding, even when individuals may view a particular decision as incorrectly decided. The framework of authority for deciding contested political questions and resolving pressing political dilemmas is not in dispute.[112]

Objections

My account of the circumstances of transitional justice identifies features constitutive of transitional societies. Societies are properly categorized as transitional, that is, when the four circumstances discussed above – pervasive structural inequality, normalized collective and political wrongdoing, serious existential uncertainty, and fundamental uncertainty about authority – obtain.[113] The contrasting circumstances are constitutive of paradigm stable democracies: limited structural inequality, individual and personal wrongdoing, minor existential uncertainty, and narrow uncertainty about authority.

[112] As contemporary theorists interested in the authority of the state, such as Joseph Raz and A. John Simmons, would likely readily admit, today there are few immediate or important political consequences that follow from the theoretical issues such scholars take up. While there are a number of philosophical anarchists and they occupy a place of respect within philosophical debates, there are few political anarchists. Moreover, those political anarchists who do exist generally tend to be on the fringe of reasonably just and stable democratic political communities.

[113] I thus understand these circumstances of transitional justice as existence conditions. The issue of transitional justice arises when these four circumstances obtain. The circumstances of transitional justice are thus not constitutive conditions, requiring these conditions to obtain as part of the intrinsic demands of justice, nor are they properly understood as instrumental conditions, conditions that are conducive to justice. On the different role of circumstances of justice as existence, constitutive, or instrumental conditions, see Abizadeh, "Cooperation, Pervasive Impact, and Coercion."

Before examining the problem of justice that arises in the circumstances of transition, the subject of Chapter 2, I want to consider two objections to the analysis presented so far. According to the first objection, the circumstances of transitional justice are not distinctive to transitional societies but in fact obtain more broadly, including, importantly, in democracies. The second objection is the inverse of the first. According to the second objection, the circumstances of transitional justice I identify obtain more narrowly and do not in fact characterize all transitional societies.

Let me articulate the first objection, which provides a number of reasons to challenge the restriction of the circumstances of transitional justice to transitional societies. The circumstances of pervasive structural inequality and collective and political wrongdoing are especially salient for the objection. The core concern in the objection is that a restricted scope of application fails to recognize the serious moral problems facing actual contemporary democracies, such as the United States and Canada, non-transitional and nondemocratic societies, and post-transitional societies. In these countries as well as many other stable democracies, the objection points out, structural inequality exists. In the United States, for example, existing institutions reflect the legacy of slavery and the Jim Crow era. Indeed, Michelle Alexander argues that the prison industrial complex of the United States represents the new Jim Crow.[114] Normalized collective and political wrongdoing has also occurred. The United States has a history of collective and political wrongdoing; the practices of lynching and of contemporary biased policing drive home this point. Canada's recent release of the Truth and Reconciliation of Canada report highlights the collective and political wrongdoing carried out by the Canadian government against indigenous peoples and is framed by many as a case of transitional justice.[115] Similarly, the objection points out, nontransitional, nondemocratic countries frequently have pervasive structural inequality; more to the point, in such contexts structural inequality may be even more pervasive than in societies in transition.[116] Moreover, post-transitional societies are not necessarily better off in terms of structural inequality; some post-transitional societies may in fact have more structural inequality following a transition than during their period of transition. Excluding post-transitional cases from the circumstances of

---

[114] Alexander, Michelle, *The New Jim Crow: Mass Incarceration in the Age of Colorblindness* (New York: New Press, 2012).

[115] See www.trc.ca/websites/trcinstitution/index.php?p=3 (accessed June 4, 2015).

[116] I thank an anonymous reviewer of an earlier draft of this chapter for this point.

transitional justice blinds us to this fact. More generally, by restricting structural inequality to the circumstances of transition, my account fails to account for the facts just noted.

In response to this objection, I want to make one point of clarification about the circumstance of pervasive structural inequality specifically and then one point of clarification about the circumstances of justice more generally. First, my account of the specific circumstance of pervasive structural inequality does not preclude the possibility that nontransitional, nondemocratic societies are pervasively structurally unjust, nor the possibility that such societies are even more pervasively unjust than transitional societies.[117] Post-transitional societies that are no longer in transition but failed to transition to democracy may be similarly pervasively structurally unjust as well. Moreover, there can and will be variation among societies that satisfy a threshold level of pervasiveness to be characterized as pervasively structurally unjust. There is important variation both in terms of the form structural inequality takes and the pervasiveness of its presence. The same observations hold for the circumstance of normalized collective and political wrongdoing.

What is distinctive about transitional societies versus nontransitional, nondemocratic or post-transitional societies is not simply the presence of pervasive structural inequality; it is the presence of this in combination with the other three circumstances of transitional justice.[118] Absent in nontransitional, nondemocratic societies and post-transitional societies are two other circumstances: serious existential uncertainty, stemming from the lack of clarity in the empirical political trajectory of a society from both objective and subjective perspectives, and fundamental uncertainty about authority, stemming from ambiguity about who has the standing to deal with past wrongs and the mixed character of the political regime.

When considering stable democracies, my account of the circumstances of justice for such societies also includes structural inequality. I attribute to paradigm democracies not the absence of structural inequality as such, but

---

[117] On the idea of post-transitional countries, see Collins, Cath, *Post-Transitional Justice: Human Rights Trials in Chile and El Salvador* (State College: Penn State University Press, 2011). For the purpose of the objection, I understand post-transitional societies broadly to encompass communities that have transitioned from one political regime to another without necessarily having transitioned specifically to democracy. This understanding is in keeping with the spirit of the objector's concern. In my view, however, post-transitional societies that strictly speaking fall into this category would have transitioned to democracy, in which case pervasive structural inequality would no longer hold.

[118] This is similar to the circumstances of justice discussed by Hume. Such circumstances include not only limited scarcity but also limited benevolence.

rather the absence of pervasive structural inequality. Structural inequality is limited and localized. The key theoretical distinction is that pervasive structural inequality is such that the legitimacy of the institutional order is not in doubt and inequality is not systemic.

So far I have concentrated in my reply on theoretical distinctions. When it comes to evaluating actual societies, my analysis does not preclude the possibility that actual societies thought or claimed to be democratic have in fact pervasive structural inequality. Any country, the United States or Canada included, may be or become pervasively structurally unjust. Countries can change in normatively desirable or undesirable directions. No country that is currently pervasively structurally unjust is destined to stay in that condition in any deterministic manner. Similarly, just institutions may be stable, but maintaining such institutions requires the active work of individuals holding specific institutional roles. No such institutions are completely invulnerable to corruption. The role of the circumstances of transitional justice is to provide the theoretical resources needed to categorize a given society. The circumstances of transitional justice outline conditions that would need to be established to argue that a particular society such as the United States, typically assumed by many scholars or its citizens to have limited structural inequality, is in fact characterized by pervasive structural inequality. Establishing this claim would in turn call into doubt the legitimacy of the institutional order of that society, and demonstrate that that society is not in fact a paradigmatic democracy. This conclusion is compatible with many of the most penetrating critiques of countries like the United States. The point of many critics is not to challenge the assumption that democracies are characterized by limited and localized structural inequality; rather, it is to challenge the assumption that a given society actually warrants being labeled democratic.[119] Circumstances also provide resources for critique of specific categorizations proposed for particular communities. As the illustration of the United States shows, the circumstances of transitional and democratic societies provide theoretical resources for radical critique of easy assumptions made by citizens, scholars, or politicians on how it is justified to categorize a particular society.

---

[119] See, e.g., Curry, Tommy, "Please Don't Make Me Touch 'Em: Toward a Critical Race Fanonianism as a Possible Justification for Violence against Whiteness," *Radical Philosophy Today* 5 (2007): 133–58; Curry, Tommy J., "The Fortune of Wells: Ida B. Wells-Barnett's Use of T. Thomas Fortune Philosophy of Social Agitation as a Prolegomenon to Militant Civil Rights Activism," *Transactions of the Charles S. Pierce Society* 48, no. 8 (2012): 456–82; Curry, Tommy and Max Kelleher, "Robert F. Williams and Militant Civil Rights: The Legacy and Philosophy of Preemptive Self-Defense," *Radical Philosophy Review* 18, no. 1 (forthcoming).

When evaluating actual political communities, determining what circumstance it is appropriate to attribute may be a subject of disagreement. Concluding that a specific society is pervasively structurally unjust is not always straightforward. There may be disagreement in particular cases and among particular groups within the same political society. The appropriate categorization of a specific political society may also be unclear in particular cases. This is unsurprising given that actual societies exhibit structural inequality (as well as other characteristics) on a continuum. The closer communities come to the threshold that distinguishes pervasive structural inequality from more limited forms, the less clear the appropriate label to use may be. There is nothing especially troubling about this fact. With a concept like adolescence there may be disagreement about when youth ends or adulthood begins in particular cases. However, despite ambiguity and disagreement about how to categorize certain moments of a given society, we can recognize clear conditions under which such a society would be appropriately characterized as pervasively unequal and others under which it would be appropriately characterized as unequal in a more limited and localized manner. The same is true for the other circumstances. There will be specific moments in which the political trajectory is deeply unclear and in flux. Similarly, there will be specific moments in which it is clear that a society is no longer in flux or that an old regime had been displaced.

The second objection challenges my account of the circumstances of transitional justice from the opposite direction. In the view of the objector, there is a wide range of cases in which it is appropriate to invoke the label "transitional justice." This objection calls for modesty in my claim about the circumstances of transitional justice. According to the second objection, it is a mistake to think that one can identify general features found across all transitional contexts. There is in fact no single set of features that can properly characterize all societies properly thought of as transitional. For example, it is a mistake to think that transitions from repression and transitions from conflict share the same circumstances.[120] Stable democracies deal with legacies of wrongdoing without facing fundamental uncertainty about authority or serious existential uncertainty. With the circumstances outlined in the preceding, I may have identified some characteristics found in some transitional contexts, but I have not identified circumstances common to all transitional societies.

In responding to skepticism about the validity of the general features I have identified as characterizing all transitional contexts, I want first to

---

[120] On this point, see Ní Aoláin and Campbell, "Paradox of Transition."

note that the four circumstances of transitional justice I identify are characterized at a very abstract level of generality. Importantly, there will be significant variation across transitional contexts regarding what these general features look like in detail. For example, the form that structural inequality takes will vary significantly across contexts, as well as the depth of its pervasiveness. In some communities structural inequality will be exhibited most prominently in the economic arena, while in others disadvantage in the political and legal arena will be most pressing. Similarly, the form that collective and political wrongdoing takes differs. The state is complicit in wrongdoing to different extents and in different ways. Nor will the form of wrongdoing be constant. In some contexts there will be land appropriation; in others there are programs of rape and mutilation; yet other contexts will feature targeted killing and torture. In some transitional contexts all these forms may be present. Not only will there be variation in how each feature is present; there will also be variation in the relative importance of each feature for a community. Normalized collective and political wrongdoing may be more pronounced and pressing to deal with than pervasive structural inequality, or serious existential uncertainty considered as an issue of more immediate concern.

In characterizing these circumstances of transitional justice at a level of abstraction and generality, I am not suggesting that the particular histories of specific communities are unimportant or irrelevant for transitional justice – quite the contrary. Understanding what specifically must be done to satisfy the general demands of transitional justice in any particular society will require a fine-grained social scientific analysis and understanding of that context. Deep knowledge of the particular history of a specific transitional context is absolutely critical for identifying the form that transitional justice responses should take. If structural inequality does not stem primarily from inconsistent application of legal rules or corruption in the judiciary, then responses focused on reform of the legal system are not apt. Knowledge of context is essential for identifying exactly who was complicit in wrongdoing, which in turn impacts the scope of individuals who should be held accountable in some manner for wrongdoing.

Despite not capturing – and not aiming to capture – the detailed variation across transitional contexts, there is value in having a general characterization of four shared features or circumstances of transitional justice. The abstract circumstances of transitional justice outlined in Section 1 draw attention to the fact that, despite their significant differences, transitional societies share broad features that give rise to a common moral problem if characterized at an appropriate level of generality. Just as it is a mistake to fail to recognize the significant variation among societies, so too is it a mistake to think there is nothing common across societies characterized as transitional. Radical contextualism can be just as problematic as an unnuanced universalism. At its limit and in its moral form, radical contextualism can undermine the very possibility of normative categories.[121]

My second response to the objection that I have failed to identify features common to all transitional societies is to deny that all the cases claimed to be instances of transitional justice in fact fall under the scope of transitional justice. There is a proliferation of the use of the term *transitional justice* to label a wide range of communities and to characterize a wide range of attempts to deal with past wrongs. My account is not designed to capture all the cases that fall under this broadening "transitional justice" rubric. For example, as suggested in my previous reply, my account of the circumstances of transitional justice is not intended to accurately represent or capture stable democracies with legacies of inequality and collective and political wrongdoing. Rather, my account of the circumstances of transitional justice is intended to capture features of widely recognized core or paradigm cases of transitional justice.

Why reject a broader characterization of transitional societies? One reason for rejecting the move to include a wide range of cases as cases of transition is that it obscures the moral problem at issue in different circumstances. As I argue in detail in Chapters 2 and 3, in transitional societies the pursuit of societal transformation becomes morally bound up with the process of responding to past wrongs because of the presence of serious existential uncertainty. As I demonstrate in Chapter 2, when a society is no longer characterized by the circumstances of transitional justice, this has implications for the question of justice it is salient to ask. For example, in post-transitional contexts, which are characterized by reduced existential uncertainty, responding to past wrongdoing need not be linked with the pursuit of societal transformation. Moreover, when a post-transitional society has reduced pervasive structural inequality, societal transformation, the radical overhaul of basic terms of interaction among citizens and between citizens and officials, may no longer be necessary. Rather, societal reform or change on a more limited scale may be required. Such change and responding to past wrongs can justifiably be pursued as separate objectives. The implications of a particular response to wrongdoing for the prospect of societal transformation need not be considered in any moral justification of a given response to past wrongs.

---

[121] On this point, see de Greiff, "Theorizing Transitional Justice."

Spain is an example of a formerly transitional and currently post-transitional society in my analysis. While in Spain the question of how to deal with past wrongs is still pressing, it is pressing primarily because of the need to fulfill the independent moral demands that collective and political wrongdoing create. I spell out such demands in detail in Chapter 4, but they include acknowledgment and repudiation of past wrongdoing, accountability for those responsible for such wrongs, recognition of the status of victims as moral agents who are rights bearers as well as members of a political community, and reparation. A final overarching objective is nonrecurrence. These objectives are conceptually distinct from the objectives involved in pursuing the repair of political relationships. It is these objectives too that are being appealed to in recent discussions of dealing with the legacy of the Spanish civil war and General Francisco Franco's regime. As Dr. Pelai Pagès, professor of contemporary history at the University of Barcelona, puts it, "The civil war was the most important event in the history of 20th-century Spain. It was the prologue of the second world war; it generated a dictatorship that lasted almost 40 years and its effects continue into our times. Creating a museum is a means to preserve the historical memory of an event that should never be repeated."[122]

Thus in my view the taxonomy for political communities includes transitional, nontransitional, semitransitional, and post-transitional circumstances. When the four circumstances outlined in Section 1 obtain, a society is transitional. Further theoretical work would clarify and sharpen the distinctions among these cases. The circumstances of transitional justice as I have defined them provide theoretical resources for filling out this taxonomy, identifying when a given society has moved from a transitional to a post-transitional context, by focusing on what circumstance(s) change in this move. One benefit of locating actual societies within the taxonomy of transitional, post-transitional, and nontransitional circumstances is that we can evaluate them against a set of paradigm cases, identifying them as cases that are paradigmatic or as cases that exhibit stronger or weaker resemblances to these paradigms. Another benefit is that we can begin to understand more clearly the various kinds of moral questions that arise for communities. As becomes clearer in Chapter 2, we can also identify the analogies and disanalogies among the moral questions that are operative in different sets of circumstances.

[122] Coman, Julian, "Eighty Years On, Spain May at Last Be Able to Confront the Ghosts of Civil War," *Guardian*, May 29, 2016, www.theguardian.com/world/2016/may/29/national-museum-spanish-civil-war-barcelona?CMP=twt_gu.

The Problem of Transitional Justice

This chapter focuses on the problem of justice that is salient in the circumstances of transitional justice. I argue that the problem of justice is not the same as the problem with which theories of retributive justice, corrective justice, or distributive justice are generally concerned, and that the contrasting circumstances of transitional justice and of stable democracies outlined in Chapter 1 provide the requisite theoretical resources for understanding and explaining why this is the case. As my discussion in this chapter highlights, theorizing about justice is always informed by background circumstances. It is these circumstances that generate problems of justice with which theories of different kinds of justice deal. Changing the circumstances of justice alters the general question or problem of justice that is salient and the issues that must be addressed when answering this question.

My purpose in this chapter is not to critique theories of retributive justice, corrective justice, or distributive justice. I am not claiming that the problems with which theories of each kind of justice deal are not problems of justice. Nor am I casting doubt on the validity of the principles of each kind of justice. Rather, my aim is to explain why the problems of retributive, corrective, and distributive justice are not the problem to which principles of transitional justice are responsive.

In Sections 1, 2, and 3, I analyze retributive justice first, followed by corrective justice and distributive justice. In each case, I begin by summarizing a standard characterization of the moral problem associated with each kind of justice. I then argue that informing both the explanation of why communities face a given problem and the characterization of the problem of justice itself is an implicit assumption of the presence of the circumstances of stable democracies. Next I show that when you assume instead the circumstances of transitional justice the problem of justice and the rationale for a set of principles of justice to deal with that problem become less compelling. In Section 4, I argue that the problem of transitional justice is best characterized as how to justly pursue societal transformation.

The Problem of Retributive Justice[1]

What is the problem of justice in the circumstances of transitional justice? Given wrongdoing, a plausible characterization of the problem is the following: How should a society respond to perpetrators of wrongdoing? Standard theories of retributive justice focus on perpetrators and articulate what constitutes just responses to them. Theories of retributive justice thus answer the following question: *What constitutes just treatment of a perpetrator of a criminal wrong?* The retributive answer to the question of the just treatment of perpetrators is simple: proportional punishment.[2] *Punishment* is generally defined as the intentional imposition of hard treatment (often in the form of a deprivation of something to which a person would otherwise be entitled such as certain liberties, or the imposition of a burden) on someone judged guilty of a (criminal) wrong by an authority. Punishment is generally taken to be communicative, expressing condemnation for the wrong done.[3] Proportionality is taken to be a function of the relationship between the amount of hard treatment inflicted, on the one hand, and the gravity of the offense and culpability of the perpetrator, on the other.[4]

Theories of retributive justice explain why punishment is morally deserved and thus why punishment is an appropriate way to deal with the problem posed by the presence of perpetrators of wrongdoing. Justifications respond to two primary sources of skepticism about the moral appropriateness of punishment. The first is skepticism about the moral appropriateness of ever intentionally inflicting suffering or hard treatment on another human being. For skeptics, the infliction of something unpleasant serves no moral purpose, and the desire for punishment simply masks a brute desire for revenge or retaliation.[5] The commission of a crime does not make one liable to the infliction of something burdensome.

---

[1] The discussion of retributive justice is a revised version of my "Transitional Justice."
[2] As in Chapter 1, I use the term *punishment* here to refer to legal punishment inflicted by the state.
[3] See Tasioulas, "Punishment and Repentance"; Hugo Adam Bedau and Erin Kelly, "Punishment," *Stanford Encyclopedia of Philosophy*, ed. Edward N. Zalta (2010), http://plato.stanford.edu/archives/spr2010/entries/punishment/.
[4] Kutz, *Complicity*, 18–23.
[5] For an articulation of this concern, see Darwall, Stephen, "Justice and Retaliation," *Philosophical Papers* 39, no. 3 (2010): 315–41.

The second source of skepticism is specifically about the permissibility of the *state* inflicting punishment. This is not a global skepticism about the authority of the state. The state is assumed to have political authority in retributive accounts.[6] Rather, skepticism is narrower and is focused on why we should think that punishment falls within the boundaries of the legitimate exercise of authority by a legitimate state. The core concern is that the intentional infliction of something burdensome (often in the form of a loss of liberty) on some citizens is incompatible with the recognition of the moral equality of all citizens.[7] A worry is that an intentionally inflicted loss of liberty renders a citizen who is punished unequal in terms of the standing she enjoys within the state. The question thus arises, "How is punishment consistent with, or even expressive of, the respect that citizens owe to each other?"[8]

In the course of justifying punishment as a just response to perpetrators, theories of retributivism counter these sources of skepticism. For the retributivist, the intentional infliction of hard treatment on a wrongdoer is intrinsically good and appropriate for the state to inflict. Here I want to illustrate how explanations of the intrinsic goodness of punishment implicitly or explicitly assume the circumstances of justice of stable democracies. For purposes of illustration, I consider in detail the influential retributive theory developed by Jean Hampton, noting at the end how my analysis applies to other retributive accounts.[9] My aim is not to challenge Hampton's defense of the core retributive intuition;[10] rather, it is to highlight how the background circumstances of justice play a key role in making Hampton's defense of retributivism compelling. I then show how the plausibility of the retributive analysis diminishes when the assumed circumstances of justice change.

All wrongful actions involve the violation of a moral standard for conduct, and often that violation results in wrongful harm to an individual. However, according to Hampton, only a specific category of wrongful action deserves a retributive response. Wrongful actions that inflict moral injury on victims by damaging their ability to realize their moral value and have that value acknowledged warrant punishment.[11] To explain the moral

---

[6] The nature and limits of the authority of the state are often implicitly assumed. Antony Duff, "Legal Punishment," *Stanford Encyclopedia of Philosophy*, ed. Edward N. Zalta (2013), http://plato.stanford .edu/archives/sum2013/entries/legal-punishment/.

[7] See Hampton, "Correcting Harms"; Morris, "Guilt and Suffering."

[8] Duff, "Legal Punishment."   [9] Hampton, "Correcting Harms."

[10] For a challenge to her defense, see Gert et al., "Hampton on the Expressive Power of Punishment."

[11] Hampton, "Correcting Harms," 1666 and 1679.

injury inflicted by some kinds of wrongdoing, Hampton first assumes a Kantian theory of moral worth, according to which all individuals have equal moral value by virtue of their humanity. This value is not something that other individuals can in fact alter through their actions. However, all individuals are vulnerable to being diminished. An individual is diminished if she is the target of behavior or treatment that falsely communicates her relative inferiority. Human behavior is communicative, and our actions express views about the value of others.[12] In particular, in committing some wrongs a perpetrator falsely declares that he is superior to the victim in value and is permitted to treat the victim in the manner constitutive of the wrong done; the victim is entitled to no better treatment. This message is "read off of" the action.[13] Illustrating with the example of rape, Hampton writes, "The action – in both its commission and in its results – representing the rapist as master and the victim as inferior object ... accounts for its being wrongful."[14]

Although victims are not in fact less valuable than perpetrators and do not in fact lose value through such treatment, according to Hampton, they can be injured by such wrongdoing in two ways. First, such treatment damages the acknowledgment of a victim's value. The act of wrongdoing itself fails to acknowledge the victim's value. It also potentially reinforces an incorrect understanding of an individual's value among others, including the victim. Second, wrongdoing impairs a victim's ability to realize her value. Having a certain value generates entitlements to make claims on others, including claims to be treated in particular ways. To be intentionally treated in a way that violates these claims, often by being subject to certain harm, is to deny an individual's ability to have her value respected through the actions of others. That failure by the perpetrator makes a victim vulnerable to similar treatment by others. In Hampton's words, "Harms anger us not merely because they cause suffering we have to see in others, but also because we see their inflictions as *violative of the victim's entitlements given her value.*"[15]

In Hampton's view, justice demands that the false moral claim expressed in wrongdoing be countered and that the moral equality of perpetrator and victim be reasserted. To repair the injury involved in wrongdoing, she argues, it is necessary to annul the act of diminishment.

---

[12] Ibid., 1670.

[13] Ibid., 1674. In Hampton's view the message implicit in an action is objective; it is not a function or product of the psychological responses of a victim to certain treatment. Individuals with a distorted sense of self-worth (undervalued or exaggerated) may not be bothered by objectively injurious actions or be bothered by actions that are not in fact injurious.

[14] Ibid., 1684.   [15] Ibid., 1678.

Annulling the act and asserting the moral truth cannot be accomplished through words alone. Verbally asserting or communicating the worth of the victim is insufficient because the evidence of the inferiority of the victim remains; the wrong did not simply verbally assert the superiority of the perpetrator and relative inferiority of the victim, but tried to achieve that diminishment through action.[16] To annul wrongdoing the social world must be "remade" such that the situation the perpetrator tried to create with his or her action is repudiated.

According to Hampton, retribution, or retributive suffering, remakes the social world by denying the claimed superiority of the perpetrator and repairing the damage to the acknowledgement of a victim's value and ability to realize her value.[17] Suffering repudiates the superiority of the perpetrator by defeating him or her. The intentional infliction of suffering involves a form of mastery over another individual. By being put in a position where he cannot do what he wishes, the perpetrator experiences the state of no longer being a master of another. This directly counters the wrongdoing in the same language as the wrong itself. By punishing the perpetrator on behalf of the victim, the state affirms the victim's importance, acknowledging her value and affirming the central importance of having her claims on others respected. Given the overarching objective of punishment, the amount of punishment to be inflicted must be proportional to the suffering needed to repudiate the message of superiority implicit in the action, thereby reestablishing the equality of the victim.

Hampton directly addresses concern about the legitimacy of the state inflicting punishment. According to Hampton, punishment is taken to be something that the state is uniquely authorized to inflict on individuals who have violated certain criminal prohibitions. She claims that the state is the moral representative of a society's values; as such, it has the standing to address past wrongs. Hampton writes:

> Some crimes are so serious that we cannot imagine any person or institution sufficing as an adequate agent other than the state. As Hegel appreciated, the modern state is the citizenry's moral representative; in the face of pluralism and religious controversy, it is the only institutional voice of the community's shared moral values. Serious crimes represent serious attacks on those moral views, and in particular, on the conception of worth animating those views, and thus the state is the only institution that can speak and act on behalf of the community against the diminishment accomplished by the crime.[18]

---

[16] Ibid., 1687.   [17] Ibid., 1686.   [18] Ibid., 1694.

It must be the state that inflicts punishment if the diminishment is to be countered effectively. The state is also well positioned to punish the perpetrator proportionally. Hampton assumes the state is impartial with respect to the victim and perpetrator. Because of this neutrality, the state can focus on what is morally relevant in determining how the perpetrator should be treated given his action and basic humanity, and similarly what is needed to reaffirm the victim's value.

Hampton's explanation of why punishment constitutes just treatment of perpetrators assumes the circumstances of justice of stable democracies. Specifically, as noted earlier, the state is assumed to be legitimate and state actors are not perpetrators of or complicit in the wrong that occurred. There is thus no *fundamental uncertainty about authority*. Hampton also implicitly assumes *limited structural inequality*. Citizens are – and are generally recognized to be – moral equals. The state endorses and respects this equality. Wrongful acts are threatening precisely because they disrupt a status quo situation of equality. It is urgent to counter the message in punishment so that the situation of equality can be restored and main-tained. Punishment returns the situation to status quo ante.[19] Wrongdoing is implicitly assumed to be *deviant, individual, and personal*. Wrongdoing represents an isolated action by a single individual that communicates that individual's view of the value of the victim. Thus, for the wrongs with which punishment deals, the perpetrator "can be singled out as solely or primarily responsible for a specific harm suffered by a particular victim. ... The focus is therefore on direct and immediate harms the agent causes to a particular victim, where the harm to that particular victim can be attrib-uted to that particular agent."[20] Inflicting suffering on the perpetrator by the state addresses the source of the violation of and threat to the victim's entitlements.

I now argue that if we shift the underlying assumptions to the circum-stances of transitional justice, the reasoning Hampton offers does not establish that punishment (1) will in any given case constitute just treat-ment of a perpetrator, (2) will be permissible for the state to impose, and (3) will in fact be effective in its function, namely, vindicating the value of the victim. These limitations point to a more fundamental problem with

---

[19] Other accounts that conceptualize punishment as returning the situation to a baseline of inequality include Morris, who conceptualizes crime as disrupting fair distribution of benefits and burdens, and accounts that conceptualize crime as reinforcing the public law.

[20] Ashford, "Inadequacy," 217 and 219. In this quote Ashford was discussing assumptions implicit in the criminal law, but her observations apply to the kind of wrong that Hampton had in mind in her account.

using the retributive understanding of the salient problem of justice: determining just treatment of perpetrators is not the central issue in the circumstances of transitional justice.[21]

The circumstance of normalized collective and political wrongdoing gives rise to the first challenge to the retributive justification of punishment. One important criterion that retributively just punishment must satisfy is the criterion of proportionality – punishment must "fit" the crime. The question of how exactly to determine which punishment is proportional to a given crime if we give up on the guideline of *lex talionis* and so do not literally do to the perpetrator what she did to her victim is the subject of some debate.[22] However, it is generally taken to be possible to identify a proportional punishment for deviant individual and personal wrongdoing.

Satisfying the proportionality requirement is especially fraught when the wrongs to which societies are responding are wrongs that groups – acting on behalf of the state, with the sanction of the state, or in opposition to the state – inflicted on other groups. Responsibility for wrongs that have a collective dimension must be individuated if the proportional punishment required by retributive justice is to be given. However, theories of retributive justice do not provide resources for the appropriate way to determine individual responsibility for collective crimes, and so for the appropriate way to satisfy the proportionality requirement.[23]

More fundamentally, satisfying what intuitively seems to be the appropriate individuation requires giving up on key assumptions guiding

---

[21] Hampton sees the proper solution to this problem as dependent on what she sees as another salient problem: the vindication of the victim. For this reason Hampton transitioned from defending a moral education theory of punishment early in her career to defending a retributivist theory of punishment. She does not think that the aim of morally educating the perpetrator is sufficient because it does not take sufficiently seriously that the wrong violated the rights of the victim; it does not put the victim in a sufficiently central place. However, this point is special to her own version of retributivism rather than retributivism in general. I thank Linda Radzik for discussion on this point.

[22] See, e.g., Shafer-Landau, Russ, "The Failure of Retributivism," *Philosophical Studies* 82 (1996): 289–316; Shafer-Landau, Russ, "Retributivism and Desert," *Pacific Philosophical Quarterly* 81 (2000): 189–214.

[23] Theorists who discuss this particular challenge to retributive punishment include Kutz, *Complicity*; Fletcher, "From Indifference to Engagement"; Osiel, *Making Sense of Mass Atrocity*; and Teitel, *Transitional Justice*. Elster, Jon, "On Doing What One Can: An Argument against Restitution and Retribution as a Means of Overcoming the Communist Legacy," *East European Constitutional Review* 1, no. 2 (1992): 15–17. Within international criminal law, the International Criminal Court (ICC) and the ad hoc tribunals have used the doctrines of joint criminal enterprise (JCE) and joint perpetration to prosecute participants in collective and political wrongdoing. However, the adequacy of these doctrines as a basis for attributing individual culpability for collective crimes remains the subject of dispute. See Tanguay-Renaud, Francois and James Stribopoulos, eds., *Rethinking Criminal Law Theory: New Canadian Perspectives in the Philosophy of Domestic, Transnational, and International Criminal Law* (Oxford: Hart Publishing, 2012).

judgments of proportionality in the context of deviant individual and personal wrongdoing. Specifically, "we are accustomed to holding individuals accountable for the harms that they produce on their own, and this approach leaves us without the tools to hold individuals responsible for the wrongs that they bring about together."[24] In the context of deviant individual and personal wrongdoing, we examine what an individual caused on his or her own, consequences that are assumed to be under his or her control.

However, any intuitively plausible proportionality judgment for normalized collective and political wrongdoing cannot look at individual acts in isolation or consider the consequences that were under a particular individual's control. Strictly speaking, that for which individuals should be held accountable must not be only the consequences of their discrete action. To do so would be to leave no one responsible for collective wrongdoing such as genocide.[25] Instead judgments of proportionality must also take into account the relationship between the act of a specific actor and the other acts with which it is connected. However, it is not obvious whether judgments of proportionality that look beyond the consequences of what an individual perpetrator does are compatible with the underlying premise of giving individuals what they deserve given what they have done.

Even if responsibility can be individuated in a manner that satisfies proportionality, some have questioned whether it is even possible to administer sufficiently grave punishment proportional to atrocities, which are at the limit of grave wrongdoing. The fact that transitional societies are responding to mass atrocity can raise special problems. As Drumbl writes:

> Although retributive theory has many shades, these share in common the precept that the criminal deserves punishment proportionate to the gravity of the offense. Liberal legalist institutions that punish extraordinary

---

[24] Lawson, "Individual Complicity," 3. The point is put forcefully in the following way: "The criminal system (and the retributive model of justice more generally) understands and deals with crime as a purely individual-based phenomenon. Consider, for example, the complexity and difficulty with which the idea of 'conspiracy' is deployed in criminal law or the applicability of the criminal model to the corporation. The nature of the crimes in South Africa does not fit this individualist model. This was vividly displayed in the recent trial of former South African Minister of Defense, General Magnus Malan. Malan was tried criminally for several murders committed during apartheid. Despite overwhelming evidence that he was involved in these deaths, Malan was found not guilty on all counts. The problem was not a tainted jury or incompetent prosecutor but rather the criminal justice process itself. The system could not accommodate the political nature of Malan's crimes. Instead, the chain of command and the lack of personal involvement in the act itself or with those who did the killing served to create a reasonable doubt" (Llewellyn and Howse, "Institutions for Restorative Justice," 381).

[25] On this point, see Kutz, *Complicity.*

international crimes place retribution high on the list of the goals of punishment. The question, then, follows: do the sentences issued to perpetrators of extraordinary international crimes attain their self-avowed retributive goals? Can an architect, or tool, of mass atrocity ever receive just desert? . . . How can a perpetrator like Adolf Eichmann receive his just deserts? Or Athanase Seromba, the Rwandan priest who ordered the demolition of his own church in which 1,500 Tutsi refugees were trapped?[26]

Were it possible to identify a roughly proportional punishment for individuals implicated in mass atrocity, it is likely such punishment would be beyond the limits of what liberal legal institutions can permissibly inflict.

Skepticism about the possibility of satisfying a proportionality requirement is not the only challenge to just punishment of perpetrators in circumstances of transitional justice. Another general concern is that punishment for normalized wrongdoing will be, at least in some cases, ex post facto.[27] A basic premise of all theories of criminal punishment, both the utilitarian and retributive kind, is that punishment should not be ex post facto. That is, an individual should be eligible for legal punishment only when her act violates a legal norm that was in effect at the time of her action. Ex post facto punishment violates the commitment to prospectivity at the core of the rule of law. In Fuller's words, when a government rules by law, "government says to the citizen in effect, 'These are the rules we expect you to follow. If you follow them, you have our assurance that they are the rules that will be applied to your conduct.'"[28] Prohibiting ex post facto punishment is one way to satisfy this core commitment since ex post facto punishment applies different rules to individual conduct than those effective at the time of action.[29]

Satisfying the ban on ex post facto punishment is relatively easy in the circumstances of limited structural inequality and deviant individual and personal wrongdoing. Limited structural inequality implies that the criminal law is largely as it should be in terms of the kinds of conduct it proscribes. The rules governing interaction are those required to maintain the equal status of all citizens; criminalized behavior is wrongful behavior. Thus there is no need to apply rules other than those in effect at the time of action to behavior subject to prosecution. The fact that wrongdoing is

---

[26] Drumbl, Mark "Collective Responsibility and Post-Conflict Justice," *Washington & Lee Public Legal Studies Research Paper Series*, Working Paper No. 2010 (May 7, 2010), http://ssrn.com/abstract=1601506, 6–7.

[27] I say for some crimes because there will be resources within international criminal law for prosecuting some perpetrators, especially high-level operatives.

[28] Fuller, *Morality of Law*, 40.   [29] Gray, "Excuse Centered," 2631–32.

deviant implies first that the behavior proscribed in the criminal law roughly coheres with citizens' views about what sorts of behavior should be prohibited by the state. Moreover, it coheres with the standards of behavior citizens generally respect in practice. As Gray writes, "The rule of law, which shapes the call for trials in transitions, retains a strong commitment to the principle of *non malum sine lege*, or the legality principle. . . . In stable states ... wrongs, as crimes, are the exception, perpetrated in violation of established and regularly enforced legal codes."[30] It is reasonable to assume, as retributivists implicitly do, that in such circumstances the punishment inflicted by the state is punishment for behavior that was illegal at the time of action. Retributive theories do not provide an explanation of when and why ex post facto punishment could be permissible because they are premised on the assumption that punishment is not ex post facto.

However, the same assumption is not always reasonable to make in the circumstances of pervasive structural inequality and normalized collective and political wrongdoing. One consequence of pervasive structural inequality is that many morally egregious acts may not have been legally proscribed by declared rules at the time they occurred. Even if proscribed, prohibitions on conduct may not have been enforced regularly. In some cases officially prohibited actions may have been supported in practice. In cases where the legal rules are not generally enforced, the same underlying moral concern with ex post facto prosecution is salient. The message communicated by officials who do not generally enforce certain rules is that certain rules will not in fact be applied to conduct. To then have previously unenforced rules now suddenly enforced is to hold citizens and officials to a standard of conduct they did not reasonably believe applied at the time of action; this can lead to a sense of unfairness and resentment among citizens. Any justification of punishment in the circumstances of transitional justice, then, must explain why ex post facto retribution could be permissible and count as retribution.[31] As discussions of cases like grudge informers show, this case is not easy or straightforward to make.[32]

---

[30] Ibid., 2636.   [31] Ibid., 2636.

[32] The term *grudge informers* refers to individuals who, during periods of conflict or repression, report personal enemies to authorities in order to get rid of them. A range of arguments have been advanced by legal scholars to justify such punishment, many dealing with the specific case of grudge informers, but none are advanced as theories of criminal justice. See, for example, Fuller, Lon, "Positivism and Fidelity to Law: A Reply to Professor Hart," *Harvard Law Review* 71 (1958): 630–72; Hart, H. L. A., "Positivism and the Separation of Law and Morals," *Harvard Law Review* 71 (1958): 593–629; Dyzenhaus, David, "The Grudge Informer Case Revisited," *New York University Law Review* 83 (2008): 1000–34; Rundle, Kristen, *Forms Liberate: Reclaiming the Jurisprudence of Lon*

Theorists grapple with how to make sense of the justice of punishment that could be argued to be ex post facto.

Retributive justifications of the role of the state in punishment are also unconvincing in the circumstances of transitional justice. As highlighted in my discussion of the circumstance of pervasive structural inequality in Chapter 1, the state is not the moral exemplar of a community's values. The state has not symbolized and endorsed an institutional order predicated on the equal status of all citizens, which wrongdoing challenges. Rather, it is – at least in many aspects – the exemplar of values in need of repudiation. The state is moreover characteristically implicated in the collective and political wrongdoing that is possibly subject to prosecution and punishment. The basic standing of the state to inflict punishment is thus in need of justification, which the circumstances of fundamental uncertainty about authority highlights. Moreover, since the state is implicated in wrongdoing, it is not neutral with respect to wrongdoing as the retributive account assumes. As such, the state is not necessarily in the best position to ensure that the appropriate punishment is given.

Finally, altering the background circumstances to the circumstances of transitional justice calls into question the retributive justification for the core claim that the infliction of suffering is an effective response to wrongdoing. In the circumstance of pervasive structural inequality, a single instance of wrongdoing does not assert a false claim about the value of the victim otherwise rejected. No prior baseline of equal standing exists among all citizens that wrongdoing threatens to disrupt; rather, wrongdoing asserts a false moral claim that is widely accepted and institutionally endorsed. Wrongdoing is institutionally endorsed in the sense that it occurs in a context in which some citizens or group of citizens have a lower institutionally recognized status in the political community. Wrongdoing is widely accepted in the sense that violations of basic norms of conduct are normalized, so that an act of rape is one of many acts of its kind in contexts where sexual violence becomes a tool of warfare. Individual acts of wrongdoing are not isolated violations by deviant individuals of the entitlements of specific citizens, but constitute part of a broad pattern of action among many different individuals that cumulatively attempt to establish and maintain the relative inferiority of certain members in a manner that is sanctioned, committed, and/or ordered by government

Fuller (Oxford: Hart Publishing, 2012); Murphy, Colleen, "Political Reconciliation, Punishment and Grudge Informers," in *In the Wake of Conflict: Justice, Responsibility and Reconciliation*, ed. Alice MacLachlan and C. A. Speight, 117–32 (New York: Springer, 2013).

officials. The message implicit in wrongdoing is thus not just that a single individual perpetrator believes that he or she is superior to the victim; it is that this individual perpetrator, along with those complicit in his or her action and many others within the community, hold such a view.

For cases of normalized collective and political wrongdoing committed in the context of pervasive structural inequality isolated punishment of a single individual is not going to be effective in achieving its putative retributive purpose. That is, addressing the message implicit in an isolated act of wrongdoing will fail to reassert the moral truth about the moral standing of the victim because it does not – and cannot – fully address the source of the challenge to the victim's status. The infliction of punishment on a single perpetrator leaves untouched the actions of others complicit in a particular wrong, or the broader institutional context in which wrong-doing occurred. Insofar as there is a message of the equality of the victim implicit in the suffering of punishment, it is not likely to be powerful enough to counter the broader institutional context in which unequal treatment was and often still is sanctioned and justified.[33]

Moreover, it is not obvious that punishment will communicate a message of equality. Given the complicity of the state in wrongdoing, the message of equality at the core of punishment risks being viewed as insincerely expressed by the state at best. At worst, the message will not be about equality at all, but rather about power. The fact that what used to be ignored is now meeting hard treatment risks merely indicating that the people in charge get to do what they want. It is far from obvious that the conventional social meaning that is at the core of Hampton's account of retributive suffering can plausibly be attributed to suffering inflicted by the state in the circumstances of transitional justice.

My discussion of Hampton has so far demonstrated that it is unclear that punishment in the circumstances of transition will constitute just treatment of a perpetrator, will be permissible for the state to impose, and will in fact be effective in achieving its justificatory function. While my arguments for the first two claims did not appeal to any particular retributive theory, my argument for the claim that punishment will not be effective in achieving its justificatory function appealed specifically to the version of retributivism endorsed by Hampton. It is worth noting that similar concerns apply to other retributive accounts. In Morris's view, punishment reestablishes the just distribution of benefits and burdens that wrongdoing disrupted through the unfair advantage gained by the

---

[33] De Greiff, "Theorizing Transitional Justice."

wrongdoer in renouncing the burden of self-restraint that criminal law demands.[34] However, in the circumstances of transitional justice there is no prior just distribution of benefits and burdens that wrongdoing disrupts, nor is there reason to think punishment will be sufficient to establish such a distribution. Moore argues that retributive practices best cohere with our intuitive judgments but, as noted in the Introduction, part of what makes justice in the circumstances of transitional justice so fraught is that our ordinary expectations will not be satisfied and intuitions in the circumstances of transitional justice are unclear.[35]

Of course, the retributivist can modify his or her account to explain how individual responsibility should be individuated for collective wrongdoing, on what basis the state acquires the standing to punish when it is implicated in the crimes that will be prosecuted, and the reasons why the infliction of punishment is an intrinsically appropriate and fitting response to perpetrators. However, the arguments for these conclusions will be fundamentally different in the circumstances of transitional justice. The explanation for why an individual is liable to punishment cannot simply demonstrate how punishment is compatible with the respect owed to individuals. The rationale for why punishment should be pursued cannot be based on an account of the social function of punishment appropriate for contexts in which structural inequality is limited and criminal wrongdoing is isolated. The account of the standing and efficacy of the state to inflict punishment cannot presuppose that the state is legitimate.

Moreover, even if such an account of retributive justice could be produced, it would be incomplete. It would deal with only the part of the problem of justice that is salient in transitional circumstances. Retributive theories isolate a particular criminal wrong and concentrate on explaining the appropriate way to legally respond to the perpetrator of that wrong. The context within which wrongdoing occurred is in the background. Some scholars argue that background injustice should influence our understanding of what a given criminal defendant deserves,[36] but even for such scholars the issue of changing the background context for interaction is not taken to be the salient subject matter for criminal justice.

However, background injustice *is* the subject matter of transitional justice. The limitations of punishment as an effective response to wrongdoing in

---

[34] Morris, "Guilt and Suffering."   [35] Moore, "Justifying Retributivism."

[36] See, e.g., Green, Stuart P., "Just Deserts in Unjust Societies: A Case-Specific Approach," in *Philosophical Foundations of Criminal Law*, ed. R. A. Duff and Stuart P. Green, 352–76 (Oxford: Oxford University Press, 2011).

the circumstances of transitional justice are symptomatic of a deeper problem that is salient in the circumstances of transitional justice, which concerns the basic framework for interaction. Fundamentally altering the basic framework within which individuals interact and not simply responding to the actions of specific individuals is a core concern of transitional justice. The framework for interaction that is pervasively unequal and resulted in collective and political wrongdoing becoming normalized is in need of overhaul.

The Problem of Corrective Justice

Corrective justice is concerned with wrongful losses and gains that arise as a result of individual actions and transactions.[37] Unlike distributive justice, which I take up in Section 3, corrective justice is not focused fundamentally on patterns of distribution of goods. Rather, principles of corrective justice aim to ensure that transactions and interactions manifest a certain level of respect for others, and, when wrongful losses and gains do occur, that the rights claims at stake are dealt with justly.[38] Corrective justice is most closely associated with tort law, and many assume that corrective justice provides at least part of the underlying moral justification for the presence of tort law within a legal system.[39]

The basic question that theories of corrective justice answer is the following: *What counts as a just response to the wrongful losses suffered by an individual?* Like retributive justice, corrective justice is a backward-looking moral theory. It concerns the moral demands and claims that arise now,

---

[37] This section benefited significantly from numerous conversations with Heidi Hurd and Linda Radzik. For classic articulations of corrective justice theories, see Aristotle, *Nichomachean Ethics*, V2–4; Fletcher, George, "Fairness and Utility in Tort Theory," *Harvard Law Review* 85 (1972): 537–73; Epstein, Richard, "A Theory of Strict Liability," *Journal of Legal Studies* 2 (1973): 151–204; Weinrib, Ernest, *Corrective Justice* (Oxford: Oxford University Press, 2012); Hurd, Heidi, "Correcting Injustice to Corrective Injustice," *Notre Dame Law Review* 67, no. 1 (1991): 51–96; Hurd, Heidi, "Nonreciprocal Risk Imposition, Unjust Enrichment, and the Foundations of Tort Law: A Critical Celebration of George Fletcher's Theory of Tort Law," *Notre Dame Law Review* 78, no. 3 (2003): 711–30.

[38] On the idea that transactions are at the core, see Gardner, John, "What Is Tort Law For? Part 1. The Place of Corrective Justice," *Law and Philosophy* 30, no. 1 (January 2011): 1–50.

[39] Like criminal law, there are several competing accounts of the underlying moral justification of tort law. There are retributive and distributive justifications of tort law, which I set aside in my analysis. For a brief summary of such views, see Coleman, Jules and Gabriel Mendlow, "Theories of Tort Law," in *Stanford Encyclopedia of Philosophy*, ed. Edward N. Zalta (2010), http://plato.stanford.edu/archives/fall2010/entries/tort-theories/. For a recent collection on the moral foundation of torts, see Oberdiek, John, *Philosophical Foundations of the Law of Torts* (New York: Oxford University Press, 2014). Here I focus on the justification based in an appeal to corrective justice. I do so because corrective justice is conceptualized as a distinct kind of justice separate from retributive or distributive justice.

given what individuals did (or failed to do) in the past. However, unlike retributive justice, corrective justice is victim oriented (or plaintiff oriented, if we take legal proceedings into account). The core answer that theories of corrective justice provide is that individuals who suffer wrongful losses should be made whole again or repaired.[40] Individuals are made whole by being paid compensation by the injurer. As Ernest Weinrib puts it, in certain conditions injuring another person can give rise to an obligation to the victim for compensation; the victim has a right to compensation specifically from the injurer.[41] Unlike in retributive justice, the form of liability does not consist in punishment of the injurer but rather in a duty to pay on the part of the injurer. The amount of compensation should be such that the individual injured is brought back to the prior situation he or she was in, or where that is not possible, a morally equivalent position.[42] In John Gardner's words, "Norms of corrective justice ... are to be understood on the 'arithmetic' model of addition and subtraction. Only two potential holders are in play at a time. One of them has gained certain goods or ills from, or lost certain goods or ills to, the other. The question is whether and how the transaction is to be reversed, undone, counteracted. A norm of corrective justice is a norm that regulates (by giving a ground for) the reversal of at least some transactions."[43] As this formulation suggests, corrective justice does not demand more than a return to the status quo ante, even when the status quo ante failed to satisfy the standards of distributive justice.[44] At the moral core of corrective justice is a notion of restitution; morality demands the making good of harms suffered by individuals as a result of the actions of others.

Theories of corrective justice explain (1) which losses count as wrongful losses; (2) why those who suffer wrongful losses have a right to repair; (3) who, if anyone, is liable for those losses; (4) why the injurer has a duty to repair wrongful losses; (5) the amount of compensation owed; and (6) why fulfilling that amount counts as satisfying the demands of a distinctive kind of justice. The sixth issue is puzzling because of cases in which there

[40] I use the term *corrective justice* to include forms of compensatory justice, rectificatory justice, and reparatory justice. On this point, see Walker, "Restorative Justice." On the relationship between compensation and reparation, see Khatchadourian, Haig, "Compensation and Reparation as Forms of Compensatory Justice," *Metaphilosophy* 37, nos. 3–4 (2006): 429–48.

[41] Weinrib, *Corrective Justice*.

[42] Perry, Stephen, "The Moral Foundations of Tort Law" (1992), *Faculty Scholarship*, Paper 1153, http://scholarship.law.upenn.edu/faculty_scholarship/1153.

[43] Gardner, "What Is Tort Law For?," 11.

[44] Coleman, Jules, "Moral Theories of Torts: Their Scope and Limits: Part II," *Law and Philosophy* 2 (1983): 7.

exists a background unjust distribution of goods. Insofar as the right of repair and duty to repair take no account of the prior distribution of goods, the demands of corrective justice seem to lead to or entrench injustice, calling into question the plausibility that corrective justice's injunctions are in fact injunctions of justice. For an individual who suffers losses but suffers those losses in a context in which she did not have an entitlement to those goods as a matter of distributive justice, why does justice demand that losses be restored? In short, if things are unjust to begin with, why would justice require a return to a status quo ante that fails to satisfy the standards of distributive justice? Conversely, if justice does take into account background prior distributions, what is going on in cases of corrective justice seems to be nothing more than achieving the demands of distributive justice. In response, theorists of corrective justice recognize a moral division of labor between distributive justice and corrective justice. Distributive justice is the task for legislators to achieve through the regulations that shape legally recognized property rights and tax laws. Its concern, as we shall see in detail in Section 3, is the general distribution of the advantages and disadvantages of social cooperation. By contrast, corrective justice is interested in individual cases and individual transactions. Given their different emphases, claims of corrective justice may still arise in a distributively just state. Conversely, a distributively unjust state may nonetheless satisfy particular claims of corrective justice.

The starting assumption of theorists of corrective justice is that individuals are affected by the actions of others, and that we must take this basic fact of human life into account when thinking about justice. Justice requires that our interactions with others be predicated on respecting a certain standard of care, the following of which minimizes the risk of harming or inflicting losses on others. Grounding claims of liability is a bedrock moral intuition reflected in the idea that "if you break something, you should fix it." There is general consensus that sometimes, but not always, wrongful losses are losses that are the fault of the injurer and must be compensated or rectified. "Fault" here is not understood as necessarily entailing moral fault or the commission of a moral wrong, but rather constitutes a failure to live up to some standard of reasonable care, whether or not an individual can be morally blamed for this failure.[45] All that is

---

[45] Although this may influence the amount for which she is held liable. In cases of fault liability (as opposed to strict liability), liability can be removed if it is shown that the action was justifiable, that is, the reasonable or right thing to do. Coleman, "Moral Theories," 7; Coleman and Mendlow, "Theories of Tort Law."

necessary is that the victim's right to not be injured in a specific way is violated by the action, which constitutes an injury to the victim. Thus the losses of interest to corrective justice are not solely those that result from moral wrongdoing; responsibility or liability for harms is not only a function of the commission of wrongdoing.

Despite consensus around a range of central cases, there is disagreement among theorists of corrective justice about the precise criteria that need to be satisfied for losses or gains to count as wrongful losses or gains. According to versions of unjust enrichment theories, for example, private gains that arise as a result of the imposition of losses give rise to a duty to repair. In its simple form, as articulated in the famous case of *Vincent v. Lake Erie*, a defendant is liable whenever he or she acts deliberately in pursuing private gain and in so acting causes damages or losses to a plaintiff.[46] Transferring losses to another in the pursuit of private gain would constitute a form of unjust enrichment if one is not required to give back to the injured party that which he or she lost. In a different version of this same idea, George Fletcher argues that an individual is liable for losses when losses are incurred by another as a result of nonreciprocally risky activity taken by that individual. In such situations, an individual risks some harm befalling another but that individual is not similarly put at risk. The imposition of such losses is unjust. By contrast, in cases of reciprocally risky activity losses should lie where they fall. As Fletcher puts it, "Plaintiffs who are as likely to harm defendants as be harmed by them cannot complain when defendants' risks materialize in harm to them, for their equally risky conduct constitutes a moral waiver of their right to recover."[47] In such cases, requiring compensation from one party to another when that same party will likely be owed compensation at a different date simply creates unnecessary transaction costs.

Yet other versions of corrective justice orient the claims of corrective justice around the idea of correlativity. Here the key notion is that transactions should maintain relational equality, and when that equality is upset compensation must be given. Equality is taken to be a function of maintaining respect for legal rights. When one party violates the right of another and in the process inflicts a wrongful loss and acquires a corresponding wrongful gain, this disruption in the prior equality must be corrected. As Ernest Weinrib observes, "A remedy directed to only one of the parties does not conform to corrective justice. For the court merely

---

[46] *Vincent v. Lake Erie Transportation* 124 N.W. 221 (Minn. 1910).
[47] Hurd, "Nonreciprocal Risk Imposition," 712.

to take the away the defendant's wrongful gain does not suffice, because then the plaintiff is still left suffering a wrongful loss. Nor does it suffice for the court merely to replenish the plaintiff's loss, for then the defendant will be left holding his or her wrongful gain. The remedy consists in simultaneously removing the defendant's excess and making good the plaintiff's deficiency."[48]

Common to these different theories of corrective justice are certain orienting assumptions. Wrongful losses or gains are conceptualized as the product of deviant personal action. That is, individuals acting alone or in coordination with others fail to meet a standard of care or exercise the caution appropriately demanded. The standard of care that provides the baseline for determining whether wrongful losses or gains occurred is assumed to be characteristically followed; aberrations from the standard of due care are the exception. Thus the standard of care is not taken to be a remote ideal but generally realized in practice. Moreover, the legally defined standard of care is taken to be one that is morally justifiable.[49] As Margaret Urban Walker puts it, "Corrective justice demands 'correction' of what are presumed to be discrete lapses from that prior or standing moral baseline in particular interpersonal or institutional transactions with individuals, unacceptable impacts of the action or omission of some individuals upon others."[50] It is assumed that the state is not implicated in the wrongful losses and gains in need of correction, which is why private litigation is an appropriate form for the pursuit of justice to take. The state's role in mediating private litigation claims for compensation is thus taken to be unproblematic and appropriate. The state can act as a neutral and efficient arbitrator among private parties, thus avoiding both inefficiencies and vigilante justice.

There are three general limitations with using the framework of corrective justice in the circumstances of transitional justice. First, establishing the appropriate party to pay reparations is fraught, given the collective and political character of wrongdoing. Wrongs inflicted on individuals are a function of the actions of many different individuals, thus in many cases there may be no single individual who can appropriately be held solely

---

[48] Weinrib, *Corrective Justice*, 16. Another version of corrective justice links liability strictly to causation. If you cause certain losses, then you are required to pay. See Epstein, "Theory of Strict Liability."

[49] Thus the question of the justification for returning to a status quo ante is not a worry about the terms of interaction that were violated. It is rather a different worry concerning the failure of the distribution of goods to meet the standards of distributive justice.

[50] Walker, "Restorative Justice," 378.

liable for the damages caused. Consider individuals who were disappeared. Insofar as someone can be sued, who should be sued? The individual who ordered torture, the individual who inflicted the torture, the government that permitted and sanctioned torture? A related complication concerns attempting to individuate liability for collective wrongs in ways that will assign appropriate amounts of monetary compensation to be paid by particular individuals or individuals vis-à-vis groups.

The determination of the appropriate amount of compensation for losses is also much more complex in the case of normalized collective and political wrongdoing. What was lost is not simply a function of the impact of an action considered as an isolated incident; this misconstrues the wrong done. If an individual act of rape is considered in isolation and without reference to the connection between it and the other instances of rape that together constitute the use of rape as a tool of war, the wrong done is misdescribed. The wrongs of interest have an ineliminably collective and political character.

Consider the abduction of approximately five thousand Yazidi women and children in Iraq by the Islamic State (ISIS) in August 2014, the majority of which are still missing at the time of writing. Drawing on the experiences of the few women who managed to escape, the conditions of captivity are deprived in the following way: "Enslaved as *malak yamiin* (spoils of war), the women must endure repeated rape, forced marriage and violent abuse. Some are sold in open markets – virgins fetch the highest price – while others are given as 'gifts' to fighters in Syria and elsewhere."[51] The abduction campaign and subsequent sexual slavery are part of a broader campaign of ethnic cleaning of the ethnic minority in the northern Iraq region. Targeted on the basis of their identity, these girls and women suffer horrific physical and psychological abuse designed to devastate them individually and by extension defeat their community. Indeed, Vian Dakhil, the only female Yazidi member of the Iraqi parliament, describes the impact of rape in these words, "When something like this happens to the Yazidi people, it happens to all of us. We are family, we feel it as deeply as that." She observes that the sexual enslavement of Yazidi women is like "the public rape of our community."[52]

---

[51] Haworth, Abigail, "Vian Dakhil: Iraq's Only Female Yazidi MP on the Battle to Save Her People," *Guardian*, February 8, 2015, www.theguardian.com/world/2015/feb/08/vian-dakhil-iraq-isis-yazidi-women.
[52] Ibid.

As is the case for the abducted Yazidi women, the wrongs that are characteristic of periods prior to a transition have an expressive dimension and expressive harm.[53] Normalized political wrongdoing communicates and reinforces a widely shared sense of the diminished status of victims – and often the communities of which they are a part – within a society, and wrongdoing tangibly expresses this devaluation. Such wrongs are intended to humiliate, demoralize, and diminish the self-respect and self-esteem of victims.[54] An ISIS pamphlet states that it is permissible for fighters to "buy, sell, or give as a gift female slaves, 'for they are merely property, which can be disposed of.'"[55] Finally, the reaction by the state to such wrongs compounds the harm such wrongs entail and the losses individuals experience. Haldemann puts it thus: "When collective evils occur and mass violence or totalitarian terror tears apart whole social fabrics, those wronged suffer an additional injustice of misrecognition – they are ignored, silenced, smothered, and suppressed from the public eye. By silencing the victims, their personal and social grievances have no reality. Thus, one's suffering is reduced to a clandestine experience – overlooked and forgotten. This sort of treatment adds insult to injury, and one can describe its devastating effects as 'the wounds of silence.'"[56] For Yazidi women who manage to escape the suffering from the trauma of repeated abuse, the challenge of reintegrating into the community is enormous. Rape carries with it a powerful stigma, which undermines the willingness of women to speak about their experiences and risks the further isolation and marginalization of these women upon their return.[57]

Theories of corrective justice provide little guidance on what amount would accurately compensate individuals for losses that have a collective expressive character and are misrecognized.[58] Walker notes, "The framework of corrective justice strains, because it has never been meant to deal

---

[53] On the idea of expressive harm, see Altman, Andrew, "Speech Codes and Expressive Harm," in *Ethics in Practice*, 4th ed., ed. Hugh LaFollette, 381–88 (West Sussex: John Wiley and Sons, 2014).

[54] Haldemann, "Another Kind of Justice," 679.   [55] Haworth, "Vian Dakhil."

[56] Haldemann, "Another Kind of Justice," 693.   [57] Haworth, "Vian Dakhil."

[58] Stable democratic contexts confront not just criminal wrongdoing but often also legacies of historical injustice in which wrongdoing occurred that was collective and political in ways similar to transitional contexts. Dealing with such historical injustices in stable democratic contexts gives rise to extended theoretical discussions about how to establish who should pay for past wrongs and who should be given compensation, given the passage of time. Debates over reparations for slavery in the United States often deal with these issues. The question of what compensation is owed is also fraught; as many point out, the counterfactual to determine the appropriate amount owed is enormously complicated given the passage of time and the implications of the exercise of agency by succeeding generations. Finally, there is discussion of the possibility of superseding historical injustice. The wrongdoing with which transitional societies deal, though it has often occurred years and even decades earlier, are not properly thought of as historical injustices in the same way as the historical injustices with which stable democratic contexts deal since perpetrators as well as many

with either a massive scale of serious mayhem or a protracted and brutal subjugation and mutually ramifying indignities and atrocities that characterize oppressive and violently repressive systems."[59] As with punishment, commensurate reparations with certain kinds of horrific injury may be impossible to determine and, given competing constraints, impossible to realize. Unsurprisingly, many have expressed skepticism about the possibility of reparations for normalized collective and political wrongdoing that satisfy standards of corrective justice. Naomi Roht-Arriaza argues that reparations are impractical in such contexts and inadequate in dealing with the losses and harms of such wrongs.[60]

There are further moral reasons to doubt that attempts to overcome these obstacles are morally worthwhile. De Greiff expresses moral concerns about trying to overcome such problems of quantification. Embarking on a journey of making interpersonal comparisons among victims of normalized collective and political wrongdoing so as to accurately determine the amount of compensation owed to specific victims can be divisive and lead to troubling hierarchies of victims.[61] Such hierarchies can be counterproductive to the communication of the fundamental equality of all victims as members of a community, and can obstruct any attempt to repair victims who have been injured.

An even more fundamental concern with conceptualizing the problem of justice in circumstances of transitional justice as one of corrective justice is that it obscures a key dimension of the moral challenge in such circumstances. Redressing the wrongs of victims is at most part but not all of the problem of justice arising in transitional circumstances. Particular incidents of violence are part of a broader pattern of interaction designed to entrench and reinforce pervasive structural inequality. Such wrongdoing needs to be seen against the background of pervasive structural inequality, and as intended to reinforce and be justified by that inequality. Thus, unlike in the paradigm case of wrongdoing with which theories of corrective justice deal, the terms of interaction themselves are unjustifiable. The de facto standard of care to be realized in interaction is part of what must

---

victims are often still alive. Moreover, the concern about counterfactuals is not as acute since there is no time gap between injustice and the present.

[59] Walker, "Restorative Justice," 380.

[60] Roht-Arriaza, Naomi, "Reparations in the Aftermath of Repression and Mass Violence," in *My Neighbor, My Enemy: Justice and Community in the Aftermath of Mass Atrocity*, ed. Eric Stover and Harvey M. Weinstein (Cambridge: Cambridge University Press, 2004), 121–23.

[61] de Greiff, Pablo, "Justice and Reparations," in *The Handbook of Reparations*, ed. Pablo de Greiff, 451–77 (New York: Oxford University Press, 2006).

be corrected and changed.[62] It is for this reason that prominent accounts of the role of reparations in transitional circumstances point not just to the correction of individual injustices but the broader social function that reparations programs necessarily must have. Pervasive structural inequality signals the necessity of overhauling the basic terms on which citizens interact and the basic principles on which government operates. The background context structuring interaction, and not just individual transactions and interactions in the past, is part of the subject matter of justice.

The Problem of Distributive Justice

Theories of distributive justice highlight the importance of looking not just at the losses and gains that occur through individual transactions but also at the broader distribution of goods within a community. A theory of distributive justice addresses the following question: *What constitutes a just distribution of goods?*

Theories of distributive justice differ along a number of dimensions. There are different accounts of the relevant goods to be distributed.[63] Theorists point to primary goods, capabilities, resources, and utilities as the relevant object(s) of distribution.[64] There is disagreement about the subject matter for evaluation, in particular whether principles of distributive justice regulate institutions and/or individual actions.[65] Whether and in what way(s) principles of justice are fact sensitive,[66] and whether principles of distributive justice apply at the global level are further areas of dispute.[67] At issue in this latter dispute is the scope of principles of

---

[62] Walker, "Restorative Justice." This point is not the question of how to understand the relationship between corrective justice and distributive justice because in that debate the losses an individual suffers in a particular case are conceptualized as separate from the injustice that may be present in what an individual enjoys in the matter of distributed goods within a community. Rather, the point about the implications of normalized collective and political wrongdoing is that such wrongs impact how best to conceptualize the losses from wrongdoing themselves.

[63] On this point, see Sen, Amartya, "Equality of What?," The Tanner Lectures on Human Values, Delivered at Stanford University, 1979, http://tannerlectures.utah.edu/_documents/a-to-z/s/sen80.pdf (accessed October 16, 2015).

[64] Rawls, *Theory of Justice*; Sen, "Equality of What?"

[65] For contrasting views on this point, see Rawls, *Theory of Justice*; Liam Murphy, "Institutions and the Demands of Justice," *Philosophy & Public Affairs* 27, no. 4 (1998): 251–91.

[66] See, for example, Sangiovanni, Andrea, "Justice and the Priority of Politics to Morality," *Journal of Political Philosophy* 16, no. 2 (2008): 137–64; G. A. Cohen, *Rescuing Justice and Equality* (Cambridge, MA: Harvard University Press, 2008).

[67] See, for example, Abizadeh, "Cooperation, Pervasive Impact, and Coercion"; Blake, Michael, "Distributive Justice, State Coercion, and Autonomy," *Philosophy & Public Affairs* 30 (2002): 257–96; Nagel, Thomas, "The Problem of Global Justice," *Philosophy & Public Affairs* 33 (2005): 113–47; Julius, A. J., "Nagel's Atlas," *Philosophy & Public Affairs* 34, no. 2 (2006): 176–92. For

distributive justice, which is often taken to turn on the kind of relationship that must obtain for questions of distributive justice to arise. Answers to the question of the scope of justice are often conditional: norms of distributive justice apply internationally if international institutions that structure interaction have a given feature.[68]

Finally, theorists disagree about the substantive criteria or principles that must be satisfied for a given distribution of goods to be just. Rawls argues that the distribution of primary goods must satisfy two specific principles of justice.[69] The first requires equal distribution of rights and liberties compatible with the most extensive rights and liberties for others. The second requires social and economic goods be distributed in a manner that is based on offices and positions open to all under conditions of fair equality of opportunity. Inequality in the distribution of such goods is permissible so long as it is to the greatest benefit of the least advantaged. By contrast, Robert Nozick rejects the notion that the actual distribution of goods within a community must satisfy any particular substantive criteria; instead he argues that the process by which a distribution came about is what matters morally.[70] In particular, he argues that whatever distribution one finds within a community is just so long as the distribution of goods is a function of a just original acquisition of goods and just transfer of goods from one individual to another.

For my purposes, differences among theories of distributive justice are less important than the similarities in how the problem of distributive justice is conceptualized. I concentrate in the following on this conceptualization since it informs subsequent accounts of distributive justice. My aim is to explain why the problem as it is conceptualized, which provides the

---

different ways of interpreting why the basic structure is morally salient for questions of justice, see Abizadeh, "Cooperation, Pervasive Impact, and Coercion."

[68] For example, Rawls limits the scope of application of principles of distributive justice to single domestic communities because only when relationships are regulated by a basic structure do questions of distributive justice arise, and there is no global basic structure. See Rawls, John, *Law of Peoples* (Cambridge, MA: Harvard University Press, 1999). By contrast, Charles Beitz argues that there is a global basic structure and so principles of distributive justice are global in application; see Beitz, Charles, *Political Theory and International Relations* (Princeton, NJ: Princeton University Press, 1979). Thomas Nagel also restricts the scope of justice to domestic communities, but for different reasons. Following Hobbes, Nagel connects sovereignty and justice, arguing that justice does not apply to relationships that are not mediated by a sovereign who can enforce rules and practices, providing assurance to individuals that others will follow mutually beneficial rules if he or she does. See Nagel, "Problem of Global Justice." Drawing on Nagel's concerns about the role of coercion in shaping terms of interaction, Julius argues that some "members of different states are in the justice relation" when their interaction is sufficiently dense in "Nagel's Atlas," 178.

[69] Rawls, *Theory of Justice*.

[70] Nozick, Robert, *Anarchy, State and Utopia* (New York: Basic Books, 1974).

starting point for theoretical reflection among theorists of distributive justice, is not the salient problem of justice in the circumstances of transitional justice.

At the most general level, liberal theorists of distributive justice seek to balance two moral values: equality and liberty.[71] Equality is linked with concerns about mitigating the impact of brute luck on distributive shares. Liberal egalitarians like Rawls recognize the profound role that natural and social contingencies play in shaping the distributive shares individuals receive. Contingencies such as which natural talents we were born with, what talents the marketplace values, and the kind of support that is present or absent within families for the cultivation of our talents all profoundly impact what we are able to do in our lives. Importantly, none of these contingencies are contingencies that any particular individual can be said to deserve or merit. No child deserves to be born into an emotionally or physically abusive family; conversely, no child has done anything to be able to claim to deserve emotionally supportive parents. No individual can claim to deserve a market in which his or her particular talents are (or are not) preferred and valued. For liberal theorists, if what we can earn or what talents we develop is shaped by brute luck, the resulting distribution of goods is influenced by luck as well. Theorists then ask: What would be a fair and legitimate basis on which to distribute goods, recognizing the role that contingency and luck play in individual lives?[72] Theorists recognize that no just institutional scheme could ever eliminate the influence of luck. Natural and social contingencies will inevitably shape the distributive shares of individuals and thus how individual lives go even in the most perfectly just institutional scheme. Just institutions thus do not eliminate luck, but rather take into account luck's influence in distribution and subsequent life prospects when articulating what distributive justice requires.

---

[71] For an excellent overview of this debate, see Anderson, Elizabeth, "What Is the Point of Equality?" *Ethics* 109, no. 2 (1999): 287–337. This characterization does not fully capture theorists who appeal to desert as the basis of distributive shares, theorists such as J. R. Lucas, Wojciech Sadurski, and Michael Sandel. However, the notion that distributive shares track what individuals deserve as a function of their freely made choices will be vulnerable to the concerns I articulate in the following.

[72] On the moral salience of luck, see, for example, Arneson, Richard, "Liberalism, Distributive Subjectivism, and Equal Opportunity for Welfare," *Philosophy & Public Affairs* 19 (1990): 158–94; Barry, Brian, "Equal Opportunity and Moral Arbitrariness," in *Equal Opportunity*, ed. Norman E. Bowie, 23–44 (Boulder, CO: Westview Press, 1988); Daniels, Norman, "Equality of What: Welfare, Resources, or Capabilities?," *Philosophy and Phenomenological Research* 50 (1990): 273–96; Dworkin, Ronald, "What Is Equality? Part 1: Equality of Resources," *Philosophy & Public Affairs* 10 (1981): 185–246; Dworkin, Ronald, "What Is Equality? Part 2: Equality of Welfare," *Philosophy & Public Affairs* 10 (1981): 283–345.

Liberty as a value is linked in discussions of distributive justice with recognizing and respecting individual choices. Respect for individuals and their agency seems to mandate allowing a space for individuals to make choices and bear the consequences of those choices, and for responses to individuals to be based on choices individuals made.[73] A concern for individual liberty and individual responsibility thus seems critical. Respecting individual choice requires allowing inequality in the distributions that result from the different choices various individuals will make.

Liberal egalitarian theorists of distributive justice aim to identify a set of principles of distributive justice that can both recognize and strike the appropriate balance between (1) mitigation of the role of social and natural contingencies in shaping distributive shares and consequently life prospects and (2) respect for individual agency in holding individuals responsible for the consequences of choices they make.[74]

The circumstances of transitional justice raise important questions about the distribution of goods. However, characteristically the salient distributive question is not whether the extant distribution of goods is unjust. By whatever standard of distributive justice one might adopt (e.g., Nozickian or Rawlsian), distributions of goods in the circumstances of transitional justice fail to meet that standard. In contexts of pervasive structural inequality as well as normalized collective and political wrongdoing, life prospects and distributive shares in fact have been and continue to be grossly unequal. There is no appropriate balance between luck and choice in determining the institutionally determined distributive shares of goods individuals enjoy. Distributive shares and the life prospects they shape are instead often a function of group membership, where such membership can be a function of, for example, ethnicity, race, ideology, or religion. Some instances of normalized collective and political wrongdoing consist in the wrongful direct appropriation of goods such as land. Property acquisition stemming from appropriation by a government of

---

[73] Theorists who emphasize the role of choice include Feinberg, Joel, *Doing and Deserving* (Princeton, NJ: Princeton University Press, 1970); Lamont, Julian, "Incentive Income, Deserved Income, and Economic Rents," *Journal of Political Philosophy* 5 (1997): 26–46; Pojman, L. and O. McLeod, eds., *What Do We Deserve?* (New York: Oxford University Press, 1999); Riley, Jonathan, "Justice under Capitalism," in *Markets and Justice*, ed. John W. Chapman, 122–62 (New York: New York University Press, 1989); Lamont, Julian and Christi Favor, "Distributive Justice," *Stanford Encyclopedia of Philosophy*, ed. Edward N. Zalta (2014), http://plato.stanford.edu/archives/fall2014/entries/justice-distributive/.

[74] Theorists like Nozick focus on individual choice and liberty almost exclusively, arguing that distributive justice requires respect for individual choice and the consequences of those choices when it comes to the acquisition and transfer of goods.

land or goods left behind by those targeted in a campaign of ethnic cleansing are some examples of this phenomena.

Furthermore, with pervasive structural inequality and normalized collective and political wrongdoing some, but not all, citizens have the ability to shape the terms for interaction. This in turn shapes what goods will be produced and how goods produced as well as natural resources will be distributed.[75] As Iris Marion Young astutely notes, decision-making procedures and decision-making power have distributive impacts. In her view, in the economic arena economic domination occurs when decision-making power for wages and employment terms, for example, are held by only a few. Concentration of such power, Young argues, unsurprisingly results in inequality being reproduced as, for example, those with power increase their compensation and the wages of those without such power remain stagnant. Normalized collective and political wrongdoing further entrenches and exacerbates the unequal terms for interaction and distribution of goods by dissuading those who might resist such terms from doing so.

The main distributive issue in such transitional contexts is how should a society deal with an unjust distribution of goods? That is, the core distributive challenge is how to respond to a distributive situation that is unjust by any reasonable standard of distributive justice. There are two general dimensions to this challenge. The first concerns specifying the correction(s) to make to the existing distribution of resources that navigates tensions and dilemmas that any alteration will entail. The second is how to transform the basic structure such that the terms for interaction that shape the distribution of goods within a community are no longer pervasively unequal. Extant theories of distributive justice do not deal with these tensions because they articulate an ideal standard for distribution to be satisfied.[76]

The first issue is on what basis and to what extent should attempts be made to alter the existing distribution of goods, such as land, and reduce some of the consequences of a historically unjust distributive framework? This question is increasingly prominent in discussions of transitional justice. For example, Khanyisela Moyo discusses unjust land appropriation and distribution by the state in racially divided countries such

---

[75] On the notion of practices of domination and oppression, see Iris Marion Young, *Justice and the Politics of Difference* (Princeton, NJ: Princeton University Press, 1990).

[76] Nozick's rectification may be required for goods unjustly appropriated in violation of just principles of acquisition and transfer. However, he does not offer a principle of rectification and does not provide guidance on how to deal with questions of rectification.

as South Africa and Zimbabwe.[77] Moyo provides a critical overview of the variety of mechanisms available for and employed when dealing with a grossly unjust distribution of goods, including restitution of land taken, redistribution (where some land of large landowners is given to landless individuals), land reform (where changes are made to the character of land rights), and compensation in other forms for taken land when restitution cannot occur. She considers the South African case in depth, discussing the final constitution that permits land appropriation for public interest purposes (although only one farm has been gained through this provision), and the willing seller–willing buyer program for redistribution established by the Provision of Land and Resistance Act in 1993.[78] Moyo's discussion also highlights the tensions involved in efforts to change existing distributive patterns of goods like land. The tensions arise because restitution and redistribution on a large scale potentially undermine the stability of a regime of property rights.[79]

The second dimension of the core challenge is determining the just way to change the terms for interaction defined by the basic structure. This is not a question of how to reform existing imperfect and flawed, but legitimate, institutions such that they are closer to realizing standards of distributive justice, where ideal principles of distributive justice serve as regulative ideals guiding reform efforts.[80] Reform is necessary when limited and localized structural inequality exists, and so actual institutions fail to live up to the values at the foundation of the institutional order. Inequality in such cases does not reflect a failure or deficiency in the values underpinning that order itself.

By contrast, in the circumstances of transitional justice, transformation and not simply reform is needed. Transformation denotes a need to repudiate the basic institutional order governing a community and the values underpinning that order.[81] The institutional framework governing

---

[77] Moyo, "Mimicry," 71.

[78] Ibid., 81. Interestingly, Moyo notes that despite a target of 30 percent of transfer of land through these programs, by 2013 only 6.7 percent of land had changed hands through programs of restitution and redistribution.

[79] Ibid. This is a point emphasized by Posner and Vermeule in their discussion of U.S. efforts to give compensation to Japanese-Americans interned in World War II (see "Transitional Justice").

[80] For an overview of such discussions, see Valentini, "Ideal vs. Non-Ideal Theory"; Adam Swift, "The Value of Philosophy in Nonideal Circumstances," *Social Theory & Practice* 34, no. 3 (2008): 363–87; Gilbert, Pablo, "Comparative Assessments of Justice, Feasibility, and Ideal Theory," *Ethical Theory and Moral Practice* 15, no. 1 (2012): 39–56.

[81] On the idea that the aim of transitional justice is transformation, see Dyzenhaus, "Survey Article"; Daly, Erin, "Transformative Justice: Charting a Path to Reconciliation," *International Legal Perspectives* 12, nos. 1–2 (2002): 74–183; Duthie, Roger, "Toward a Development-Sensitive

interaction must be overhauled and the terms of interaction, including the definition of what is permissible and impermissible, fundamentally altered. Nazi Germany is an example of a society requiring such repudiation. Given the values at the core of the Nazi ideology and institutional structure, simply modifying the institutional order would not have been sufficient to make it morally justified; rather, a wholesale repudiation of the form of social order Nazism represented was needed. The institutional and social sanctioning of collective and political wrongdoing, such as genocide or apartheid, must be annulled or revoked.[82] The basic importance of human rights and their efficacy in governing conduct often needs to be established.[83]

There are also tensions in the pursuit of an overhaul of the terms of interaction. Any fundamental altering of terms of interaction threatens to inhibit the future ability of individuals to exercise their agency by forming and pursuing goals. As Lon Fuller recognized, individual agency depends on a stable institutional structure of rules that individuals can turn to in order to form reliable expectations of how other citizens and officials will respond to their actions.[84] Such expectations are needed to be able to form reliable plans for how to effectively realize individual goals and objectives. Overhauling the institutional structure governing interaction all at once would undermine the effectiveness of previous steps taken to achieve individual goals and plans, and the effectiveness of the agency of individuals previously exercised.[85] Individuals could not practically learn about the rules now shaping conduct so as to know what is permitted and prohibited.

Even if they learned part of such rules, the circumstance of serious existential uncertainty exacerbates the tensions involved in pursuing transformation while maintaining the conditions for the effective exercise of

---

Approach to Transitional Justice," *International Journal of Transitional Justice* 2, no. 3 (2008): 292–309; Gready, Paul and Simon Robins, "From Transitional to Transformative Justice: A New Agenda for Practice," *International Journal of Transitional Justice* 8, no. 3 (2014): 339–61.

[82] Theorists who refer to the importance of changing the ethos of a community include Jonathan Allen and David Dyzenhaus. See Allen, "Balancing Justice and Social Utility"; Dyzenhaus, "Survey Article"; Rama Mani, *Beyond Retribution: Seeking Justice in the Shadows of War* (Cambridge: Polity Press, 2002).

[83] On this point, see Teitel, *Transitional Justice*; de Greiff, "Theorizing Transitional Justice"; Gray, "Extraordinary Justice," 91–92.

[84] Fuller, *Morality of Law*.

[85] These debates come vividly to the fore in legal philosophy debates about how legal systems should deal with grudge informers post–World War II. On these debates, see Dyzenhaus, "Grudge Informer Case Revisited"; Fuller, "Positivism and Fidelity"; Fuller, *Morality of Law*; Hart, "Positivism"; Murphy, "Political Reconciliation."

agency. Without confidence in the future trajectory of a political community, there cannot be confidence that institutional changes will be permanent or simply be overturned. This makes it difficult for citizens to turn to newly formulated rules to form expectations that would guide their formulation and pursuit of goals and objectives. Citizens have epistemic challenges in identifying which future framework for interaction should be taken as a given for purposes of formulating effective plans for realizing one's goals.

Thus the moral question facing transitional communities is how do you pursue an overhaul of an institutional framework governing interaction in a way that will allow individuals to live their lives and effectively exercise their agency? In the midst of a process of institutional transformation, children must go to school. Marriages will take place. Businesses will try to continue to operate. All of these require a stable set of rules governing education, marriages, and commerce. Marriages depend on a stable set of rules for contracts. Businesses depend on a stable set of expectations regarding property rights and claims.[86] Yet while stability is needed, transformation is, too. Thus there must be a balance between a concern for conditions that make agency possible with a concern for altering the conditions structuring interaction.

The Problem of Transitional Justice

In Sections 1, 2, and 3, I discussed limitations with the ability of standard theories of retributive, corrective, and distributive justice to provide normative guidance in the circumstances of transitional justice. One reaction to my discussion of the limitations of retributive, corrective, and distributive theories, considered in isolation, is to conceptualize the problem of transitional justice as a conjunction of these problems. On this view, an account of transitional justice is a combination of a suitably revised theory of retributive justice with suitably revised theories of corrective and distributive justice. I have serious doubts about the value of engaging in the philosophical maneuvering needed to revise accounts to deal with the limitations discussed above.

In my view, a simpler and more promising path is to take seriously the idea that transitional justice is distinctive, and not simply reducible to the other kinds of justice with which we are familiar. Taken as distinctive, the core question of transitional justice can be put as the following: *What*

---

[86] Posner and Vermeule explore a number of these tensions in their article "Transitional Justice."

constitutes the just pursuit of societal transformation? This is the central issue
that arises in the circumstances of transitional justice. Starting with the
circumstances of transitional communities, the task for a theory of transitional justice is to flesh out an account of how the just pursuit of societal
transformation should be conceptualized.

The problem of transitional justice so defined has two parts: societal
transformation and its just pursuit. Transformation is the key overarching
moral aim of responses to wrongdoing in transitional contexts. However,
transitional justice is pursued in a very specific way: through dealing with
past wrongs that were committed by particular perpetrators against particular victims. Transformation's "just pursuit" references the need to be
attentive to the independent moral claims that wrongdoing generates for
both victims and perpetrators.

The appropriate way to conceptualize the relationship between the
fundamentally forward-looking aim of transformation and the fundamentally backward-looking claims entailed by wrongdoing is not immediately
obvious.[87] For one thing, responding to past wrongdoing is not typically
linked with broader structural or relational change either in political
theorizing or in the practice of stable democracies. Theories of criminal,
corrective, and distributive justice are developed individually rather than in
a combined or linked fashion.[88] Generally, the justice of a response to
criminal wrongdoing is not taken to depend on the success or failure of a
response to achieve broader societal transformation. Nor is societal reform
or transformation typically pursued via responding to wrongdoing.

In my view, the circumstances of justice (in both transitional and stable
democratic contexts) provide theoretical resources for understanding *why*
fundamentally forward-looking concerns with societal transformation and
backward-looking concerns with past wrongdoing get linked in the circumstances of transitional justice, but not typically in the circumstances of
stable democracies.

Consider first the circumstances of stable democracies. Deviant wrongdoing is just that, deviant, and so there is no reason to see responses to
wrongdoing as having implications for the broader institutions that structure interaction. Structural imperfections that do exist typically do not

[87] I am very grateful to Jeff Blustein for extremely valuable feedback and criticism on this part that
forced me to rethink my understanding of the relationship between the pursuit of transformation
and the moral demands bound up with dealing with past wrongs.
[88] Although some theories of retributive and corrective justice try to reduce these accounts to
principles of distributive justice, such theories are subject to the criticism that they precisely fail
to recognize the distinction between different kinds of justice.

have any relationship to or bearing on criminal wrongs done. Moreover, with limited structural inequality, there is no need to overhaul the basic institutional framework. Finally, given minor existential uncertainty, there is little doubt about what the political trajectory of a community is and so little reason to think responses to wrongdoing will have any significant implications for the trajectory of a political community.

By contrast, in the circumstance of serious existential uncertainty the future of a society is fragile. The appropriate narrative to use when interpreting current events is unclear. When the future is fragile, individuals and groups try to find tea leaves to better predict where their community is heading. Thus processes that in the context of minor existential uncertainty may not have much impact on a community can come to play a profoundly important role in determining its future trajectory. In particular, when a political trajectory is fragile, how a community responds to wrongdoing can be seen to have enormous implications and ramifications for society as a whole and prospects for transformation. In fact, precisely whether and in what way a transitional community deals with its past has a significant influence on its trajectory.

There are other reasons why societal transformation becomes linked with past wrongdoing. Pervasive structural inequality provides a setting in which normalized collective and political wrongdoing can flourish; the psychological, legal, social, and moral obstacles to the perpetration of atrocities against fellow human beings are absent or diminished. Conversely, normalized collective and political wrongdoing is often necessary to maintain a system of pervasive structural inequality, as the case of apartheid South Africa so powerfully demonstrates. Because of these linkages, failing to repudiate past wrongdoing can be read as endorsing past structural inequality, just as repudiating past wrongdoing can support repudiation of pervasive structural inequality. Given this, processes for dealing with wrongdoing have implications for fundamental uncertainty about authority since how a state deals (or fails to deal) with past wrong can signal how it plans to deal (or not deal) with pervasive structural injustice.

I have argued that the circumstances of transitional justice provide important theoretical resources for understanding why forward- and backward-looking moral aims become intertwined. Of course, understanding why an objective of transformation becomes bound up with the objective of justly dealing with past wrongs does not yet tell us *how* to combine these diverse moral claims. It matters morally that we conceptualize this relationship correctly. One way of conceptualizing the relationship is that the importance of the backward aim of dealing with past wrong-doing is derivative and secondary. Dealing with past wrongs matters only insofar as the failure to do so would inhibit relational transformation; dealing with past wrongs thus has instrumental moral significance. Past wrongs should be addressed only insofar as this is necessary to promote relational transformation. Moreover, how to deal with past wrongs should be determined by looking at what is conducive to relational transformation.

However, this way of conceptualizing the relationship between forward- and backward-looking aims is problematic because it misconstrues the importance of the moral claims related to perpetrators and victims of wrongdoing. Such claims have an independent, non-instrumental moral importance. To regard wrongdoing as valuable only instrumentally is insulting to victims and insufficiently respectful of the agency of perpetrators. It could also have morally troubling implications; what dealing with past wrongs must do to facilitate transformation need not necessarily track what seems intrinsically appropriate as ways of dealing with victims (or perpetrators) of wrongdoing. Prospects for altering the institutional framework within which the broad contours of political relationships are defined may be enhanced by paying nominal reparations and using the additional resources not given directly to victims toward programs for institutional reform. Yet such nominal payments intuitively seem prima facie inappropriate for victims of violations of human rights since they risk undermining recognition of the grave and serious nature of the wrongs with which societies in the circumstances of transitional justice are dealing. Moreover, nominal reparations risk communicating that the wrongs experienced by victims were insignificant. Any adequate conceptualization of the relationship between these claims must thus acknowledge the noninstrumental importance of the moral claims related to perpetrators and victims that normalized collective and political wrongdoing generates must be recognized and taken into account.

Yet if the importance of dealing with past wrongs is not simply derivative and instrumental, then how should we synthesize the claims associated with transformation and with past wrongdoing? I believe that the relationship between the aims of transformation and dealing justly with past wrongs can be usefully conceptualized as structurally analogous to the relationship between the *jus ad bellum* and *jus in bello* components of just war theory. There remains ongoing and robust debate about the specific criteria for the different components of just war. Philosophers have been revising just war theory on the normative level, reformulating, for example, the standard criteria of just war theory.[89] My interest is not in the particular criteria for just war but rather in the widely recognized structure of just war theory. It is this basic structure that offers a useful analogy for theorizing about transitional justice by providing a model for how two distinct sets of moral criteria interact to jointly determine the justice of a given subject.

There are many different versions of just war theory, ranging from the Christian-based theories of Augustine and Aquinas, to historical and contemporary Islamic-based just war doctrines, to the secular version defended by Grotius, and the contemporary "legalist" theory offered by Walzer.[90] Thomas Hurka articulates a standard characterization of just war theory: a just war theory determines when and why it is morally permissible to respond to political conflict via warfare and how to respond to political conflict in this way.[91] In particular, just war theory specifies the conditions under which it is permissible for actors to try to settle the question at issue in a conflict by force, and specifies the kind and amount of force that may permissibly be used in this pursuit. As Brian Orend puts it, just war theory is designed to "offer rules to guide decision-makers on the appropriateness of their conduct during the resort to war, conduct during war and the termination phase of the conflict. Its over-all aim is to try and ensure that wars are begun only for a very narrow set of truly defensible reasons, that when wars break out they are fought in a responsibly controlled and targeted manner, and that the parties to the dispute bring their war to an end in a speedy and responsible fashion that respects the requirements of justice."[92]

---

[89] See, for example, Orend, Brian, "Justice after War," *Ethics and International Affairs* 16, no. 1 (2002): 43–52; Rodin, David, "Terrorism without Intention," *Ethics* 114, no. 4 (2004): 752–71; McMahan, Jeff, "Just Cause for War," *Ethics and International Affairs* 19, no. 3 (2005): 1–21. Frances Kamm, for example, argues for the need to dramatically revise the principle of noncombatant immunity in the wake of terror killing. See Kamm, F. M., "Failures of Just War Theory: Terror, Harm, and Justice," *Ethics* 114, no. 4 (2004): 650–92. Thomas Hurka tries to rescue the proportionality condition against arguments that it fails to provide sufficient guidance in contemporary warfare. See Hurka, Thomas, "Proportionality in the Morality of War," *Philosophy and Public Affairs* 33, no. 1 (2005): 34–66. Michael Walzer continues to defend the need for a supreme emergency clause that calls for the suspension of just war criteria when circumstances present a supreme emergency to "our deepest values and our collective survival." Walzer, Michael, "Emergency Ethics," reprinted in Michael Walzer, *Arguing about War* (New Haven, CT: Yale University Press, 2004), 33.

[90] For an in-depth historical overview of such doctrines, see Johnson, James T., *The Just War Tradition and the Restraint of War* (Princeton, NJ: Princeton University Press, 1981).

[91] Hurka, "Proportionality," at 35.

[92] Orend, Brian, "War," *Stanford Encyclopedia of Philosophy*, ed. Edward N. Zalta (2008), http://plato .stanford.edu/archives/fall2008/entries/war/.

Just war theory is standardly divided into distinct sets of principles of *jus ad bellum* and *jus in bello*. As Jeffrey McMahan begins his discussion of just war theory, "The traditional theory of the just war comprises two sets of principles, one governing the resort to war (*jus ad bellum*) and the other governing the conduct of war (*jus in bello*)."[93] *Jus ad bellum* principles outline the moral considerations that must be met for war to be permissibly undertaken. Key to these principles is an account of the reasons for the sake of which war might be permissibly undertaken (e.g., in self-defense). *Jus in bello* principles, by contrast, specify the principles that must be satisfied in the conduct of war itself. For example, a central principle is the principle of discrimination, according to which only combatants may be intentionally targeted in war. Underlying *jus in bello* principles is the recognition that individuals cannot be used as mere means to the most efficient route to achieve the overarching purpose of war itself. Individuals must rather become morally liable to being killed, and *jus in bello* principles articulate who has become so liable.[94] Evaluating warfare

---

[93] McMahan, Jeffrey, "The Ethics of Killing in War," *Ethics* 114 (2004): 693. Increasingly, discussions of just war theory include a third category of analysis, *jus post bellum*, a category referenced in the Orend quote. *Jus post bellum* concerns the criteria that must be satisfied to justly end a war, and includes considerations not only of the terms that treaties may take but the way in which violations of the *jus ad bellum* and *jus in bello* criteria should be dealt. I actually prefer versions of just war theory that include *jus post bellum*; however, my point in this section is not to discuss just war theory as a substantive theory but only to draw a structural analogy that is helpful for thinking through transitional justice. For that reason I focus on *jus ad bellum* and *jus in bello* components.

One further point of clarification concerns my understanding of the substantive relationship between *jus post bellum* and transitional justice. Both deal with the general issue of cleaning up the moral mess that war leaves behind. Despite this general similarity, however, there are also a number of differences. Transitional justice is not restricted in its focus to postwar contexts, but includes in its scope postauthoritarian and postrepression contexts, as well. The scope of wrongs with which it deals is also broader, encompassing more than simply war crimes or crimes of aggression. A wide range of violations of human rights, which may or may not occur or be related to war, can be salient for transitional justice. Finally, despite the shared emphasis on the repair of relationships, the conception of relationship is different. *Jus post bellum* is concerned with the establishment of a just peace, but the notion of just peace does not conceptually entail democratic peace. Within transitional justice, by contrast, transition has been historically linked conceptually to a transition to democracy. As I noted in the Introduction, this link between transitional justice and democracy is one that has been recently contested, but, as I argue in Chapter 3, there are good theoretical reasons for maintaining this link. For a more extensive discussion of how I conceptualize the requirements of *jus post bellum*, see Murphy, Colleen and Linda Radzik, "*Jus Post Bellum* and Political Reconciliation," in *Jus Post Bellum and Transitional Justice*, ed. Elizabeth Edenberg and Larry May, 305–25 (New York: Cambridge University Press, 2014); Colleen Murphy, "Political Reconciliation, *Jus Post Bellum* and Asymmetric Conflict," *Theoria* 62, no. 4 (2015): 43–59.

[94] There is ongoing discussion in the literature about the appropriate way to conceptualize the relationship among these two sets of principles. Historically the view has been that the two sets of criteria are morally independent in the sense that the justification of the *jus in bello* criteria does not depend on the *jus ad bellum* criteria. *Jus in bello* criteria are justified by what Walzer calls the "moral equality of combatants," according to which all soldiers in combatant are liable to be killed

from the framework of just war theory requires making two distinct kinds of judgment: about the justice of the recourse to war and about the justice of conduct in war. War can fail to be just in two distinct ways, by failing to satisfy either of the sets of criteria. Thus a war may be just from the *jus ad bellum* perspective but not from a *jus in bello* point of view. Failure in either category undermines the overall justification for a war.

Just war theory provides a structural model for conceptualizing the relationship between societal transformation and its just pursuit. The overarching objective of and reason for establishing processes of transitional justice, societal transformation, is structurally analogous to the *jus ad bellum* criteria of just war theory. The ultimate end or reason for the sake of which a set of actions and responses should be undertaken is to pursue transformation of a community. However, this pursuit is conditioned on the intrinsically just nature of the means that are used. Since we are dealing with processes for responding to past wrongs, the key question is the following: What forms of accountability are perpetrators of normalized collective and political wrongdoing eligible to receive, and to what are the victims of such wrongs entitled? These criteria or conditions play the analogous role to *jus in bello* criteria, which set moral standards on the means through which war can be pursued and bar the pursuit of a just cause through cruel or inhumane means.

Using this structural analogy, we see that processes of transitional justice may be just or fail to be just along multiple dimensions. A process may be just in the sense that it promotes societal transformation and does so in a manner that treats perpetrators and victims appropriately. It may be just in the sense that it promotes societal transformation by cultivating the rule of

---

in virtue of the threat they pose, but only soldiers are so liable. However, Jeff McMahan has recently challenged this doctrine, arguing that a concern for individual moral rights, contra Walzer, does not in fact underpin *jus in bello* criteria. Taking individual rights seriously is incompatible with the moral equality of soldiers and the discrimination requirement because soldiers fighting for a just cause have done nothing to become individually liable to being killed. McMahan goes on to argue that there are epistemic and pragmatic reasons why the law does not follow morality in its prescriptions, stemming from the fact that given individuals tend to believe that the side for which they are fighting is just, even when this belief is false. If you grant permission to the just to target civilians, just war theory will end up having no constraining effect in practice. On this debate, see Walzer, Michael, *Just and Unjust Wars: A Moral Argument with Historical Illustrations*, 3rd ed. (New York: Basic Books, 2000); McMahan, Jeffrey, "The Sources and Status of Just War Principles," *Journal of Military Ethics* 6, no. 2 (2007): 91–106; McMahan, "Ethics of Killing." It is not necessary for my purposes to adjudicate this debate since my point is rather to draw on the insight that there are two conceptually distinct kinds of considerations that can inform our judgment of the justice of a particular subject. I set aside the question of the relationship or interdependency of the two distinct kinds of criteria in the case of just war theory. I consider the interrelationship of the two sets of criteria for transitional justice in Chapter 4.

law, but fails to be just in the sense that it does not treat victims appropriately by failing to properly acknowledge the wrongness of the rights abuse they experienced. Or a project may be just in the sense that it treats victims appropriately but fails to contribute to societal transformation by, for example, failing to cultivate the rule of law. In Chapter 3, I turn to the task of specifying societal transformation, the overarching aim of processes of transformation that is the structural analogue of *jus ad bellum* criteria. Chapter 4 then considers the structural analogue to *jus in bello* guidelines, namely, the criteria that must be satisfied for processes of transitional justice to treat perpetrators and victims appropriately.

Societal Transformation

In Chapter 2, I argued that the problem of transitional justice is not the same as the problems of criminal justice, corrective justice, or distributive justice as they are standardly understood. Transitional justice is concerned with *the just pursuit of societal transformation*. The core question of transitional justice is "What constitutes the just pursuit of societal transformation?" This question is morally salient in the four circumstances of transitional justice. Pervasive structural inequality and normalized collective and political wrongdoing make societal transformation necessary. The pursuit of societal transformation becomes bound up with the process of responding to past wrongs in part because of the circumstance of serious existential uncertainty.

In this chapter I develop a substantive account of societal transformation. Societal transformation is the overarching aim for the sake of which processes of transitional justice are adopted; it can be thought of as the structural analogue of *jus ad bellum* in just war theory. Civil conflict and repression leave significant damage in their wake – to people, to institutions, to infrastructure, and to relationships, all of which may be said to be need of transformation. In my view, the societal transformation at which processes of transitional justice aim is best conceptualized as relational transformation.[1] Relational transformation alters the terms of political interaction among citizens, and between citizens and officials. A relational analysis provides an account of what specifically must be changed if relationships are to be transformed and of the moral significance of such transformation. Included in an account of such change will be the

---

[1] In conceptualizing transformation in relational terms, I am drawing on a tradition of thinking in political philosophy in which a concern with relationships is at the center. Some recent examples include Radzik, Linda, *Making Amends: Atonement in Morality, Law, and Politics* (New York: Oxford University Press, 2010); Walker, Margaret Urban, *Moral Repair: Reconstructing Moral Relations after Wrongdoing* (New York: Cambridge University Press, 2006).

obstacles or impediments to the possibility of altering extant patterns of interaction which must be addressed.

Of course when individuals and/or those they care about are subject to arbitrary arrest, torture, or humiliation; denied basic political rights; or become the target of a genocidal campaign, it is difficult if not impossible to envision interacting at all with those responsible for such abuses, let alone cooperatively interacting in a morally defensible manner. However, some degree of interaction is unavoidable and necessary insofar as groups previously in conflict remain part of the same community, and if interaction is to avoid repeating the wrongs of the past it must be changed. A focus on relationships concentrates on a central core of what must be different when moving forward.

Conceptualizing transformation in relational terms connects transitional justice with reconciliation, a subject on which there is significant emphasis in the literature on transitional justice. Political reconciliation refers to the process of improving damaged relationships.[2] Below I articulate my conception of relational transformation, drawing from and building on the analysis of political reconciliation I developed in *A Moral Theory of Political Reconciliation*.

This chapter is structured as followed. Section 1 outlines the three general goals of relational transformation: cultivation of the rule of law, threshold levels of relational capabilities, and the conditions under which political trust and trust responsiveness become reasonable. Section 2 outlines the criteria we should use when evaluating the contribution of processes of transitional justice to such transformation. These criteria consider both direct and indirect contributions of processes to this goal. Section 3 discusses the relationship between transformation, human rights and democracy. Section 4 considers the objection that my conception of societal transformation is too robust.

Relational Transformation[3]

The starting point for my account of relational transformation is the circumstance of pervasive structural inequality. Relational transformation primarily targets this circumstance. As detailed in Chapter 1, pervasive

---

[2] For clarity, in what follows I use the term *relational transformation* instead of *political reconciliation*.
[3] Portions of this section were originally published in my "A Reply to Critics," *Criminal Law and Philosophy* 10 (2016): 165–77. The section as a whole draws on the analysis of political reconciliation I develop in *A Moral Theory of Political Reconciliation*.

structural inequality concerns the institutionally defined terms for inter-action among citizens, and between citizens and officials. Such terms, I noted, are defined by the various institutions that regulate and shape interaction, specifying who may or may not do what to whom. Put negatively, one rough way of defining the overarching aim of societal transformation is to transform relationships among citizens and between citizens and officials such that they are no longer pervasively structurally unequal. It is rough because relational transformation is not restricted to institutional transformation. It also requires attention to the broader attitudes and ethos that characterize relations and interactions. That is, the interpersonal dimensions of institutionally defined and structured political relationships must also be incorporated.

Relationships are in need of transformation, I argue below, because of the absence of two moral values in the interaction among citizens and between citizens and officials: reciprocity and respect for agency. By respect for agency, I mean recognition of the capacity of individuals to govern their lives and to deliberate and choose courses of action. Agents are capable of interpersonal interaction, taking into account and responding to the reasons offered by others, and capable of recognizing the second-person standing of others to make demands and claims on them. Moral agents have the capacity to respond to moral reasons and recognize the moral constraints that the agency of others imposes on how they treat them. To acknowledge agency is to treat individuals as responsible persons by structuring interaction so that individuals are in a position in choose courses of action and, in turn, appropriately be held to account for the choices they make.

Reciprocity entails that citizens and officials are willing to fulfill their responsibilities toward others when they in turn demand that fellow citizens and officials fulfill their responsibilities toward them. A commitment to reciprocity recognizes that our actions influence the legitimacy with which we can make demands and place expectations on others.

Why do the values of reciprocity and respect for agency matter? In part they matter because to be treated as an equal, individuals must be treated as agents and in a reciprocal manner. Relationships among equals are predicated on equal respect and concern.[4] Part of what equal respect

---

[4] As Stefan Gosepath notes in his "Equality" entry, "Against Plato and Aristotle, the classical formula for justice according to which an action is just when it offers each individual his or her due took on a substantively egalitarian meaning in the course of time, viz. everyone deserved the same dignity and

requires is respect for agency. A concern with equality among citizens, and between citizens and officials is a concern for justice. There is a deep connection between the ideals of justice and equality in the modern imagination.[5] There is moreover a long history in moral and political philosophy of linking reciprocity and justice.[6]

When pervasive structural inequality exists, institutions structure interaction in a manner that is differentially respectful of agency and is nonreciprocal. That is, interaction is marked by denials of the agency of some, efforts to obstruct the exercise of agency of some or all citizens, and failures to recognize or acknowledge the legitimacy of demands made by parties to a conflict or groups opposed to a political regime in power. The absence of these values in turn comes to characterize the interpersonal dimensions of interactions among citizens, and between citizens and officials.

How specifically does pervasive structural inequality undermine or deny respect for agency and reciprocity? As I discuss in detail below, three normative frameworks provide resources for answering this question: the rule of law, relational capabilities, and trust. The erosion or absence of the rule of law, the presence of deep-seated distrust, and the undermining of key relational capabilities prevent individuals from being recognized as agents and having the demands of reciprocity acknowledged. The characteristics of the structure of interaction that is pervasively unequal can be interpreted as violations of the normative requirements of the rule of law, relational capabilities, and trust.

The transformation toward which processes of transitional justice aim then is to establish conditions under which the requirements of the rule of

the same respect. This is now the widely held conception of substantive, universal, moral equality. ... This fundamental idea of equal respect for all persons and of the equal worth or equal dignity of all human beings (Vlastos 1962) is accepted as a minimal standard by all leading schools of modern Western political and moral culture"; see Gosepath, Stefan, "Equality," *Stanford Encyclopedia of Philosophy*, ed. Edward N. Zalta (2011), http://plato.stanford.edu/archives/spr2011/entries/equality/.

[5] In *Inequality Reexamined* (Cambridge, MA: Harvard University Press, 1992), 131, Amartya Sen writes that each normative theory of justice has a view of basal equality or "equality in some individual feature that is taken to be basic in that particular conception of social justice." Theorists, from libertarians to Rawlsians to utilitarians, all argue that there is something "which everyone should have and which is quite crucial to their own particular approach" (ibid., ix). Reiterating the same point, the Gosepath's *Stanford Encyclopedia of Philosophy* entry on "Equality" states, "From antiquity onward, equality has been considered a constitutive feature of justice."

[6] Buchanan, Allen, "Justice as Reciprocity versus Subject-Centered Justice," *Philosophy & Public Affairs* 19, no. 3 (1990): 227–52. However, I do not adopt the specific meaning of reciprocity used by some theorists, in which claims or entitlements to resources track or are a function of contributions by particular individuals to a community.

law, relational capabilities, and trust will be satisfied in the interaction among citizens and between citizens and officials.

In the remainder of this section, I discuss the rule of law, trust, and relational capabilities and then some of the social and moral conditions on which these depend to be realized in interaction.

Rule of Law

Lon Fuller defines law as "the enterprise of subjecting human conduct to the governance of rules."[7] The rule of law specifies a set of requirements for citizens and officials that must be satisfied if law is to govern conduct in practice. The requirements of the rule of law articulate the form that legal rules must take if such rules are to figure in the practical reasoning of citizens and officials. Thus laws must be *general*, requiring or prohibiting certain forms of conduct; *promulgated*, or publicly accessible; *prospective*, prohibiting or requiring behavior in the present and future and not now specifying what should have been done in the past; *clear*; *constant*, so that there is some stability in the demands law makes; and *noncontradictory*. Beyond figuring in practical reasoning, if law is to govern conduct the content of legal rules should *not be such that they ask the impossible*; citizens should be in a position to fulfill the demands that law makes. Finally, there must be *congruence between declared rules and their enforcement*. For example, behavior that is proscribed for officials is not behavior that officials engage in. The content of legal rules actually guides the response of officials to the actions of citizens. Fuller's criteria for the rule of law capture conditions around which there is general consensus. Some scholars include additional requirements, but few dispute the basic conditions that Fuller laid down.

According to Fuller, for law to govern conduct each of the above requirements must be satisfied to a threshold degree by a legal system. The requirements of the rule of law provide a basis for distinguishing between lawful and unlawful conduct on the part of citizens, and for identifying legal, illegal, and extralegal behavior on the part of officials. Failure to satisfy the threshold for any requirement undermines the ability of a system of rules to govern conduct. For example, systematic incongruence between declared rules and their enforcement means that legal rules do not as a general matter govern conduct; legal rules do not influence the actions of citizens and/or inform the way officials respond

---

[7] Fuller, *Morality of Law*, 106.

to conduct by citizens or fulfill their legally proscribed role-related responsibilities. Similarly, a system of rules that is largely unpromulgated cannot figure into the practical reasoning of citizens because such citizens do not know what the rules actually demand when they deliberate about how to act.

According to Fuller, adhering to the requirements of the rule of law is morally significant for both instrumental and noninstrumental reasons. In this section I focus on the noninstrumental moral value of the rule of law. In Section 4 I discuss law's instrumental moral value. First, the rule of law facilitates and respects the exercise of agency among legal subjects. Implicit in the rule of law is a conception of the legal subject as an agent, capable of deciding how he or she will act and properly held responsible for his or her actions. Law facilitates agency by creating a predictable environment for action. When the requirements of the rule of law are respected, legal rules shape the general contour of political relationships. One can turn to legal rules for information about conduct that is permitted, prohibited, or required on the part of citizens and officials. In looking at what behavior is officially proscribed or required, one can form reliable expectations regarding how other citizens and officials will act. Citizens know what forms of behavior or treatment from other citizens are prohibited, and can reliably expect that permitted treatment will in fact be the norm. When declared legal rules actually govern conduct, citizens can also form reliable expectations, based on legal rules, of how other citizens and officials will respond to their actions. This allows citizens to determine what course of action will be most effective in realizing their goals and objectives.

More fundamentally, governance by law shapes relationships predicated on respect for agency in virtue of the way in which political power is exercised. As Jeremy Waldron puts it, "The principles of legality aim to correct abuses of power by insisting on a particular mode of the exercise of political power–namely, governance through law–which is thought more apt to protect us against abuse than (say) managerial governance or rule by decree."[8] One of the orienting purposes of the rule of law is to constrain those in power from abusing their power by placing limits on what they are permitted to do. The rule of law entails a set of restrictions on the way government officials exercise their authority by requiring that legal rules governing the conduct of legal subjects and officials have a certain form

---

[8] Waldron, Jeremy, "Hart and the Principles of Legality," in *The Legacy of H. L. A. Hart*, ed. Matthew H. Cramer, Claire Grant, Ben Colburn, and Antony Hatzistavrou (Oxford: Oxford University Press, 2008), 78.

and that such rules actually guide the response of officials to the actions of legal subjects. The rule of law demands restraint on the part of those governing, even when this is not the most efficient means for achieving policy objectives.

When a society governs by law, the exercise of power by officials is put in the service of creating a framework that facilitates self-directed actions and interaction.[9] Citizens are put in a position in which their choices, and not the whim of officials, determine the official response to their conduct. Implicit in the rule of law, Fuller states, is the view that an individual subject to law "is or can become a responsible agent capable of understanding and following rules and answerable for his defaults."[10] Citizens know what they need to do to avoid arrest, and can form reliable expectations of the treatment and process to which they will be subject if arrested. When they willingly choose to violate legal rules, citizens choose the consequences that follow according to other declared rules that exist.

The rule of law is also noninstrumentally valuable because of the way it structures reciprocal relationships among citizens and officials. The rule of law structures relationships among citizens and officials based on reciprocity in a number of respects. First, for Fuller, the stringency of the obligation on the part of citizens to obey legal rules is conditional on the extent to which officials abide by the requirements of the rule of law. Insofar as officials demand obedience to the law on the part of citizens, they do so legitimately only if declared legal rules can figure in the practical reasoning of citizens and declared legal rules provide the actual standard against which the conduct of citizens is assessed.[11] In Fuller's words, "Certainly there can be no rational ground for asserting that a man can have a moral obligation to obey a legal rule that does not exist, or is kept secret from him, or that came into existence only after he had acted."[12]

Furthermore, for Fuller, governing conduct on the basis of rules is possible only if there is ongoing cooperative interaction among citizens

---

[9] Fuller famously distinguishes between managerial governance and governance by law. In managerial governance, relationships between superior and subordinate are structured as a one-way projection of authority; a superior issues orders to a subordinate that are designed to help the superior fulfill his or her objectives. From the perspective of managerial governance, there is no necessity of congruence between declared rules and their enforcement. The importance of congruence and other requirements only makes sense if you assume the purpose of the exercise of power is to facilitate self-directed action and interaction. On this point, see Winston, Kenneth, ed., *The Principles of Social Order: Selected Essays of Lon F. Fuller*, rev. ed. (Oxford: Hart Publishing, 2001).

[10] Fuller, *Morality of Law*, 162.

[11] There may be additional conditions that need to be satisfied for government officials to act legitimately. Satisfaction of the requirements of the rule of law is one condition.

[12] Fuller, *Morality of Law*, 39.

and officials. Reciprocal cooperation is thus not just morally desirable, but also has consequences for the possibility of the rule of law itself. One aspect of cooperative interaction is systematic adherence to the requirements of the rule of law on the part of officials and systematic efforts to obey the demands of law on the part of citizens. The absence of systematic effort on the part of either group renders futile effort on the part of the other. Officials may maintain scrupulous adherence to the requirements of the rule of law, but unless citizens are willing to obey the law declared rules will not govern conduct. Citizens may be willing to obey declared rules, but unless they know what the rules are ahead of time and the standards for behavior are clear and relatively stable, citizens will not be able to govern their conduct by such rules in practice.

The reciprocal cooperative interaction required for the rule of law to exist goes beyond this basic willingness to fulfill duties of obedience and duties for officials prescribed by the eight criteria. Legal rules offer general prescriptions, and interpretation is needed to understand how such general prescriptions apply to conduct in a particular case. Only if citizens and officials by and large apply general prescriptions in a similar manner to particular cases will shared rules govern conduct.[13] Fuller argues that citizens formulate judgments about how general rules apply by drawing on their knowledge of social practices and meanings; officials must do the same in order for shared understanding of how general rules apply to particular cases to develop.[14] Without cooperative effort to develop shared understanding of how rules will be applied to particular cases, citizens will become dependent on "what officials and formal institutions do" rather than exercising their agency in determining the meaning of rules.[15] Moreover, from the citizen's perspective the interpretation of rules will seem arbitrary and unreasonable.

How does the framework of the rule of law help us understand how relationships need to be transformed in the circumstances of pervasive structural inequality and collective and political wrongdoing? The rule of

---

[13] For an extended discussion of this dimension of the rule of law, see Murphy, Colleen, "Political Reconciliation and International Criminal Trials," in *International Criminal Law and Philosophy*, ed. Larry May and Zach Hoskins, 224–44 (Cambridge: Cambridge University Press, 2010); Murphy, *Moral Theory*, chap. 7.

[14] Fuller illustrates this point with a rule that states, "No vehicles are allowed in a park." A baby carriage and truck are both plausibly vehicles in the sense of modes of transportation. However, from the social context and knowledge of the function of parks in communities, it is clear that this rule does not allow a truck but would allow a baby carriage in a park. See Fuller, Lon, *Anatomy of the Law* (Santa Barbara, CA: Prager Press, 1977), 58.

[15] Ibid.

law articulates the moral significance of an important orienting objective of processes of transformation, namely, the cultivation of the rule of law. The importance of establishing and rebuilding the rule of law is widely recognized in the literature on transitional justice. What Fuller's framework provides are resources for explaining the content and the moral significance for relational transformation of this objective.

The Fullerian framework also provides conceptual resources for interpreting patterns of action and interaction in societies characterized by pervasive structural inequality and normalized collective and political wrongdoing as corrosive to the rule of law and, consequently, corrosive to relationships predicated on respect for agency and reciprocity. To illustrate this latter theoretical contribution, it is not uncommon in contexts of pervasive structural inequality and normalized collective and political wrongdoing for there to be a gap or disconnect between the framework for conduct laid out by declared legal rules (including, importantly, the rights protections that are guaranteed) and the actual conduct of citizens and officials "on the ground." Gaps are indicative of lack of congruence between declared rules and their enforcement. The framework of the rule of law provides resources for both identifying and explaining the moral consequences of any such gap.

For example, lack of congruence arises when security forces engage in extralegal or illegal rights violations. The systematic disappearing of citizens by security forces in Argentina during its Dirty War discussed in Chapter 1 is one such instance. Other examples of such violations are easy to find. La Comision de la Verdad, created as part of a peace accord in the conclusion of a decade-plus-long civil war in El Salvador between the government and the Frente Farabundo Marti para la Liberacion Nacional (FMLN), found in its 1993 report that 85 percent of the violations it investigated were linked to paramilitary groups with ties to the state, death squads, and armed and security forces. The violations involved torture, disappearances, and extrajudicial executions.[16] In its report the Sierra Leone Truth Commission found that prior to the onset of civil war, "the rule of law was well and truly dead. Those in power became a law unto themselves."[17] In writing specifically about security forces prior to and during the war it states, "The Commission has found that the security

---

[16] Kaye, Mike, "The Role of Truth Commissions in the Search for Justice, Reconciliation, and Democratisation: The Salvadorean and Honduran Cases," *Journal of Latin American Studies* 29, no. 3 (1997): 700.
[17] Sierra Leone Truth Commission, *Report of the Sierra Leone Truth & Reconciliation Commission* (Accra, Ghana: Graphic Packaging Ltd, 2004), 2:31.

forces, the army and police, failed the people of Sierra Leone during their time of greatest crisis. Significant elements within these forces desecrated the Constitution and acted against the wishes of the people. Successive political regimes abused their authority over the security forces and unleashed them against their political opponents in the name of national security."[18]

Lack of congruence is not only a function of explicit violations of proscribed conduct on the part of government officials; it also includes failures by government officials to properly investigate and deal with claims as their roles require. In its report the Sierra Leone Truth Commission harshly criticized members of the legal profession and judiciary:

> Lawyers and jurists in Sierra Leone have failed to stand up to the systematic violation of the rights of the people. Lawyers should be the first line of defense whenever the human rights of the people are transgressed. This has not happened in Sierra Leone. Indeed lawyers – through their collective inaction – have contributed substantially to the massive abuse of human rights before, during and after the war. The conspicuous failure, on the part of lawyers and judges, to speak up on behalf of Sierra Leoneans held in illegal detention for more than four years in Pademba Road Prison is a terrible indictment.[19]

Turning to a different example, concern and skepticism about legal proceedings was characteristic during the "Troubles" in Northern Ireland. Brendan O'Leary and John McGarry discuss how "departures from traditional English legal procedures have become normal as a result of the conflict in Northern Ireland," including fabrication of evidence in politically charged investigations.[20] Fionnuala Ní Aoláin and Colm Campbell further emphasize this point, stating, "The damage to the rule of law in democratic societies that have experienced conflict can be particularly acute. This is because, as has been thoroughly documented in the Northern Ireland context, law operates to both manage and ameliorate the experience of conflict for the state."[21]

There is variation in the form that the erosion of the rule of law takes in particular contexts. Lack of congruence is not the only way in which the rule of law erodes or is absent. Rules can be so vague as to render unclear what is included or excluded. Secret rules are another recurring issue. Such

---

[18] Ibid., 150–52.   [19] Ibid., 90–91.
[20] O'Leary, Brendan and John McGarry, *The Politics of Antagonism: Understanding Northern Ireland*, 2nd ed. (London: Althone Press, 1996), 48.
[21] Ní Aoláin and Campbell, "Paradox of Transition," 188.

variations are important for understanding what must be cultivated or addressed for the rule of law to be (re)established or strengthened. The source of the gap between declared rules and their enforcement can be a function of limited resources that undermine the ability of government officials to protect rights, or a function of a concerted effort on the part of officials to pursue a campaign of abuses designed to terrorize a population into submission. Failures of congruence can be across the board and general, or partial and targeted. Partial legality refers to segmentation in how the law operates. The requirements of the rule of law are respected by officials toward one group but not another. Thus there is not a general corrosion of the rule of law but a specific erosion. As Cindy Holder notes, "In partial legality breakdown in the rule of law is differentially distributed, so that its failure to obtain is systematic but not necessarily system-wide."[22]

The unpredictable environment created by uncertain, undeclared, and retrospective legal rules undermines the ability of legal subjects to exercise their agency in the sense of being in a position to choose courses of action that they can be reasonably confident will further their goals and objectives. The ability of some or all citizens to exercise agency is compromised. Without being able to determine the standards of behavior to which they are being or will be held, either because such standards are unclear or because such standards are not the standards enforced by officials, it is difficult for citizens to form reliable expectations about other citizens or officials. In flouting the requirements of the rule of law, officials erode the ability of legal subjects to determine what official treatment they will receive. Determining safe courses of action to avoid confrontation with security forces becomes more difficult, as does determining the actions to take to realize other important goals. The result is a context in which the whims and objectives of government officials, rather than the choices of legal subjects and whether such choices conform to legally defined expectations for actions that legal subjects are in a position to know and follow, determine whether and in what way government officials respond to the actions of such subjects. Reciprocity is also compromised insofar as citizens are expected to continue to adhere to legal standards, despite such standards being unclear or unenforced. Nonreciprocal demands are one dimension of the unequal status citizens enjoy and are seen to hold vis-à-vis officials when the rule of law is undermined or absent.

[22] Holder, Cindy, "Transition, Trust and Partial Legality: On Colleen Murphy's *A Moral Theory of Political* Reconciliation," *Criminal Law and Philosophy* 10 (2016): 159.

This dimension of relational transformation captures a key emphasis on the rule of law and its cultivation as a central objective in transitional justice.[23] Focusing on the case of South Africa and drawing on the work of legal scholar Lon Fuller, David Dyzenhaus argues that the production of order is fundamentally a legal, not just political, problem. That is, it is not just about changing the content of laws (a political task), but is also about altering how law is conceptualized within a transitional community. Law, Dyzenhaus argues, is often thought of as simply a set of social facts, and judicial obligation amounts to being deferential to facts such as legislative intention. By contrast, following Fuller, Dyzenhaus claims that law should be conceptualized as an order characterized by certain constraints on officials. The purpose of these constraints outlined above is to make law intelligible to subjects, which requires demonstrating that it makes sense for a subject to follow a law given her interests.

Relational Capabilities

Pervasive structural inequality is not simply a function of erosions in or absence of the rule of law, and promoting the rule of law is insufficient for restoring or establishing political relationships among equals. The framework of capabilities provides resources for conceptualizing many of the additional dimensions along which relationships need to be transformed in order for respect for agency and reciprocity to guide and structure political interaction.[24]

Capability refers to the genuine opportunity or freedom open to an individual to do or become something of value.[25] Genuine opportunities are a function of two broad factors: what an individual has, and what an individual can do with what she has.[26] "What an individual has" includes

---

[23] See Dyzenhaus, "Judicial Independence"; Dyzenhaus, David, "*Leviathan* as a Theory of Transitional Justice," in *NOMOS LI: Transitional Justice*, ed. Melissa S. Williams, Rosemary Nagy, and Jon Elster, 180–217 (New York: New York University Press, 2012). Other theorists emphasize the rule of law but build into it substantive commitments that go beyond the eight requirements for the rule of law outlined above. See, for example, de Greiff's "Theorizing Transitional Justice." I think these substantive requirements are best conceptualized as implications of a commitment to threshold levels of capabilities. Blending the formal criteria of the rule of law with substantive commitments to particular rights risks obscuring the key contribution of the rule of law as articulating the kind of governing order that law represents.

[24] In the course of explaining these four capabilities, I highlight the relationship between capabilities and human rights since that relationship was not sufficiently clear in *A Moral Theory of Political Reconciliation*. I am grateful to Darrel Moellendorf for pressing me on this point in his review of my book in *Ethics* 122, no. 1 (2011): 198–203.

[25] Nussbaum, *Women and Human Development*; Sen, *Development as Freedom*.

[26] On this way of putting the factors that influence opportunities, see Wolff and de-Shalit, *Disadvantage*.

internal resources, such as talents and skills, as well as external resources such as income, wealth, and family support. "What an individual can do with what she has" captures the role of legal, political, and economic institutions, social norms, and the built infrastructure in shaping what an individual is able to do or become, given what she has. On this view, a genuine opportunity for education is not just a function of internal talents and skills possessed by individuals; it is also a function of other things that an individual may have or lack in any particular case, such as familial support for that individual's education and financial resources. These conditions are not sufficient for a genuine opportunity for education, however. An individual who has the talents and skills needed to learn, family support for education, and the resources to pursue it will still lack a genuine opportunity to be educated if there are no schools at a reasonable distance from home; or if there are schools but few qualified teachers; or schools and teachers but strong social norms, often gendered in orientation, against educating that individual that create risks of harm if the individual attempts to go to school.

Capabilities are possibilities for agents, those who have the capacity to determine how their lives go and the ways in which they will interact with others. Expanding capabilities is a way of expanding opportunities for the exercise of reciprocal agency. As Nussbaum puts it, "The core idea [of capabilities] is that of the human being as a dignified free being who shapes his or her life in cooperation and reciprocity with others."[27] Applied to relationships, the idea of capabilities draws attention to the scope of freedom of individuals within their relationships to shape the terms of interaction and the character of interaction itself.[28] Of particular salience in contexts of pervasive structural inequality are the following capabilities: being respected, being recognized as a member of a political community, participating in the political, social, and economic institutions of their community, and avoiding poverty.[29] These four capabilities are constitutive of relationships among equals in a community. To be an equal member of a political community, individuals must enjoy each of these capabilities to a certain threshold level.[30]

Being respected is a necessary condition for recognizing one's equal moral status simply as a human being. The presence or absence of respect

[27] Nussbaum, *Women and Human Development*, 72.
[28] In saying this I am using capabilities to capture both the opportunity and process aspects of freedom discussed in Chapter 2.
[29] The framework of capabilities is the subject of Murphy, *Moral Theory*, chap. 3.
[30] On the notion of thresholds, see Nussbaum, *Women and Human Development*.

in our interactions with others matters deeply to human beings. Indeed, one of the core dimensions of individual well-being that Nussbaum identifies is the capability for affiliation, and this capability is linked in turn with respect. Nussbaum writes of the moral necessity for individuals to have "the social bases of self-respect and non-humiliation; being able to be treated as a dignified being whose worth is equal to that of others."[31] Unsurprisingly, anger over humiliating treatment of individuals or particular group(s) within a given community fuels conflict, and indicates the absence of relationships structured among equals. One important source of the moral wrongness of the basic structure of apartheid, with its differential restrictions and constraints on all activities and opportunities for black South Africans, was that it failed to treat all citizens equally and was fundamentally disrespectful to black South Africans. One important source of the ban on torture in international law is recognition of the incompatibility of torture with basic respect for the humanity of other human beings.

Being recognized and respected as a human being is not sufficient for relationships among equals in a political community; basic recognition of an individual as a member of a political community also matters. Being treated or regarded as fundamentally and permanently an outsider, by law or according to social norms, is incompatible with this capability. The conception of the identity of a political community and who counts as a genuine member are reflected in, for example, how a political community is conceptualized in citizenship laws and the requirements that must be satisfied for citizenship; languages used in schools and government offices and recognized as official languages of a community; and the symbols a state adopts and the official holidays it recognizes.

The third capability is a genuine opportunity for participation at a threshold level in economic, political, and social institutions. Such opportunities for participation depend on what one has and what one can do with what one has. Minimum conditions for political participation include legal rights to have a say in political processes through voting, freedom of speech, and freedom of association. All of these rights ensure that an individual has the opportunity to shape the political agenda of their community and the candidates who will be eligible for election to the roles that shape the political agenda.[32] Beyond such rights, social norms

---

[31] Ibid., 79.
[32] This mirrors Nussbaum's discussion of what she labels the capability of having control over one's environment in *Women and Human Development*, 80.

matter. Norms rendering members of certain ethnic groups ineligible for certain positions in government diminish the genuine opportunities of members of a particular group to participate in political institutions. In the economic realm, freedom from forms of formal or informal discrimination in employment is necessary, as is a genuine opportunity for education so that an individual can cultivate the skills needed to participate. Participation in market transactions depends on what individuals have (including monetary resources and financial literacy), as well as what they can do with what they have, given, for example, the existing surplus, the legal rules structuring who is eligible to buy certain goods, and the extent to which legal title to goods like land are respected in practice.

The three capabilities discussed so far – being respected, being recognized as a member of one's community, and participating in economic and political processes – are fundamentally relational in the sense that they concern our interactions with others. The fourth capability is not relational in this sense; rather, it specifies a capability whose absence in practice results from diminishment in the first three capabilities: poverty. I conceptualize poverty from a capability perspective. From this perspective:

> at its most general level, poverty is the absence of acceptable choices across a broad range of important life decisions—a severe lack of freedom to be or to do what one wants. The inevitable outcome of poverty is insufficiency and deprivation across many of the facets of a fulfilling life:
>
> • Inadequate resources to buy the basic necessities of life;
> • Frequent bouts of illness and an early death . . .;
> • Living conditions that imperil physical and mental health.[33]

Poverty thus refers to the lack of opportunity to achieve basic functioning essential for survival, such as being adequately nourished or having sufficient income to pay for resources such as food or the medical care necessary to avoid death.

Having a genuine opportunity at a threshold level to avoid poverty is necessary in practice for the first three capabilities to be realized. Being unable to avoid poverty is also a consequence of the absence of the first three. Vulnerability to disrespect and isolation or marginalization from institutions and processes can be consequences of living an impoverished life. The relative impoverishment of a segment or majority of a population

---

[33] Foster, James, Suman Seth, Michael Lokshin, and Zurab Sajaia, *A Unified Approach to Measuring Poverty and Inequality* (Washington DC: World Bank, 2013). This study explicitly draws on Sen's general understanding of poverty.

while a small minority flourishes renders it more difficult to participate meaningfully in processes, and renders one vulnerable to a range of human rights abuses. Poverty, however, is not only a consequence of these capabilities. Disrespect and isolation or marginalization from institutions and processes can both reduce avenues for avoiding poverty. The description in Chapter 1 of the economic oppression in apartheid South Africa demonstrates that poverty can be a consequence of limited capabilities of participation, respect, and recognition as members of a community since discrimination and segregation led to lower income and wealth as well as reduced health outcomes. Government appropriation of land and goods is another source of impoverishment.[34]

The erosion or undermining of central relational capabilities and the opportunity to avoid poverty constitutes a failure to respect agency insofar as capabilities themselves capture genuine opportunities to exercise one's agency by, for example, participating in social or political institutions or have one's agency acknowledged (in the case of the capability of being respected). The range of ways that these capabilities are undermined varies. The range of individuals suffering from diminished capabilities differs, and when diminished capabilities are a function of group membership the salient group identity is not always the same. The scope of capabilities diminished and the depth of their diminishment can vary as well. In some contexts, there is severe diminishment of all four capabilities discussed, with the overwhelming majority of citizens suffering from significantly reduced opportunities for participation, bases for respect, diminished recognition as full members of a political community, and opportunities to avoid poverty. In other contexts, the reduction of capabilities is less severe and/or more targeted.

Trust

Relationships are characterized and defined not just by actions but also by reactive attitudes.[35] Reactive attitudes like trust, hope, resentment, and anger contain moral judgments and assessments about the subject(s) of our attitude, and inform and shape how we interpret and respond to the actions of others.[36] The final dimension of transformed relationships is

---

[34] This is described by the Sierra Leone Truth Commission in its *Report*, 3:185.

[35] Strawson, *Freedom and Resentment*; Shoemaker, "Moral Address."

[36] For conceptions of trust as a reactive attitude, see Jones, Karen, "Trust as an Affective Attitude," *Ethics* 107, no. 1 (1996): 4–25; Govier, Trudy, "Self-Trust, Autonomy, and Self-Esteem," *Hypatia* 8 (1993): 99–120; Becker, Lawrence C., "Trust as Noncognitive Security about Motives," *Ethics* 107, no. 1 (1996): 43–61; Lagerspetz, Olli, *Trust: The Tacit Demand* (Dordrecht, The Netherlands: Kluwer Academic Publishers, 1998), 34.

reasonable default political trust and trust responsiveness. I focus specifically on trust because deep distrust is characteristically a basic feature of relationships among former combatants, groups in contexts of ethnonational conflict, and toward government and officials in authoritarian regimes. Trust is often linked to reconciliation, and the instrumental value of trust in terms of its role in facilitating cooperative interaction is often lauded.[37] My analysis does not question the instrumental significance of the cultivation of trust; rather, it adds to the moral importance of cultivating trust by articulating why trust matters noninstrumentally in virtue of the ways in which default trust, when reasonable, can express respect for agency and reciprocity. Articulating noninstrumental reasons for why trust has moral significance increases concern about the presence of deep and widespread distrust.[38]

In defining political trust, I draw on the general definition of *trust* developed by Karen Jones.[39] For Jones, *trust* refers to an attitude of optimism about the competence and goodwill of the trusted as well as the expectation that the trusted will prove trust responsive if relied on. The content of trust is relationship specific in the sense that competence and goodwill are defined in terms salient for a given role (e.g., parent, friend, technician, politician). The attitude of optimism reflects confidence in the ability of the trusted in a specified domain (e.g., moral, social, or technical). To trust is not to have a particular belief, but rather to have a certain outlook or perspective on the object of our trust. Trust is also defined by a specific expectation of trust responsiveness; that is, the trusted individual will be motivated to prove reliable if trusted and will be motivated because of the fact she is being relied on, as opposed to, say, fear of retaliation. A trusted

---

[37] Examples of views that link relational repair and trust include Walker, *Moral Repair*; de Greiff, "Theorizing Transitional Justice." On the instrumental value of trust, see, for example, Gambetta, Diego, ed., *Trust: Making and Breaking Cooperative Relations* (Oxford: Basil Blackwell, 1988); Hardin, Russell, *Trust and Trustworthiness* (New York: Russell Sage Foundation, 2002); Luhmann, Nicklas, *Trust and Power* (Toronto: Wiley Press, 1979); Hardwig, John, "The Role of Trust in Knowledge," *Journal of Philosophy* 88, no. 12 (1991): 693–708; Jones, Karen, "Second-Hand Moral Knowledge," *Journal of Philosophy* 96, no. 2 (1999): 55–78; Baker, John, "Trust and Rationality," *Pacific Philosophical Quarterly* 68 (1996): 1–13; Baier, Annette, "Demoralization, Trust, and the Virtues," in *Setting the Moral Compass: Essays by Women Philosophers*, ed. Cheshire Calhoun, 176–90 (New York: Oxford University Press, 2004); Pettit, Phillip, "The Cunning of Trust," *Philosophy and Public Affairs* 24, no. 3 (1995): 202–25; Weinstock, Daniel, "Building Trust in Divided Societies," *Journal of Political Philosophy* 7, no. 3 (1999): 287–307. For views that challenge the instrumental value of trust, see Cook, Karen S., Russell Hardin, and Margaret Levi, *Cooperation without Trust?* (New York: Russell Sage Foundation, 2007); Hardin, Russell, ed., *Distrust* (New York: Russell Sage Foundation, 2009).

[38] This discussion draws on Murphy, *Moral Theory*, chap. 4.   [39] Jones, "Trust."

individual is anticipated to be willing and able to fulfill the responsibilities or expectations the truster makes on him or her. In Jones's view, both the truster and trustee have some degree of discretion in determining what would count as proving reliable.

The degree of confidence in the competence and goodwill of another can vary, but must be beyond some minimal threshold to qualify as trust. Similarly, there can be differences in the domain(s) of interaction over which our trust for a particular individual extends. Although Jones does not discuss this in her analysis, I take trusting as a default to consist in presuming the competence, goodwill, and trust responsiveness of the trusted. Evidence of incompetence and ill will need to be shown for distrust or lack of trust to be warranted, rather than competence needing to be proven in order for an individual to be worthy of trust.

Political trust I define specifically as referring to an attitude of optimism taken with respect to the competence and lack of ill will of fellow citizens and officials qua citizens and officials. Competence indicates knowledge of and ability to fulfill the role-related responsibilities associated with citizenship or occupying an official role (e.g., president, member of the military, or legislative member). For citizens this entails competence in the ability to follow the rules and norms structuring interaction and to exercise rights. Lack of ill will captures the absence of a desire to intentionally harm others. It involves a willingness to abide by the institutional order that structures interaction; in other words, there is a commitment to fair play.[40] Lack of ill will is not the same as complacency; indeed, part of lacking ill will can consist in a commitment to drawing attention to issues or problems in need of being addressed.

For officials, competence consists in knowledge of the scope of duties and responsibilities and powers associated with their office, and the limits on the power they are permitted to exercise. Competence also consists in an ability to act on and fulfill responsibilities related to the particular official role assumed for the purposes for which those responsibilities are given. As part of competence officials must recognize the fact that they act on behalf of a community and, as such, are supposed to act and decide with the interests of that community in mind. For officials lack of ill will consists in the absence of an interest in harming the community or portion of a community over which power is exercised, as well as more minimally indifference to the welfare of the community or portion of a community over which power is exercised.

---

[40] On the duty of fair play, see Rawls, *Theory of Justice*.

Officials also have a commitment to fair play, abiding by the rules that govern their office. Political trust requires trust responsiveness, the disposition to take seriously the fact that trust has been placed in oneself when deliberating about what to do.

When trust is the default, citizens presume a minimal threshold level of competence and lack of ill will of fellow citizens and officials in their domain of interaction and anticipate trust responsiveness; fellow citizens and officials are not presumed to be incompetent and possessing ill will until proven otherwise. Officials similarly presume a minimum threshold level of competence on the part of citizens to responsibly exercise freedoms given and act within the boundaries set by law, as well as a willingness to do so. This default can in particular cases be present to different degrees, ranging from a minimum threshold assumption of confidence in the lack of ill will, to a robust confidence in competence. The default can exist toward all or some citizens, or to all or some officials.

When reasonable, in my view, default political trust and trust responsiveness manifest respect for agency and reciprocity in our interactions with others. The default manifests reciprocity insofar as individuals take a view of others (e.g., competent, lacking ill will, and trust responsive) that individuals normally desire others to take of them. Proving trust responsive as a default constitutes a reaction to the fact of being relied on that individuals desire from others they trust. It manifests respect for agency by presuming the capacity of citizens and officials to govern their lives according to shared rules and responsibly exercise the freedoms given in rights. Moreover, it is respectful in the assumption it makes regarding the motivation of others: individuals are assumed be basically decent and so not wanting to harm others, and committed to fair play.

In the circumstances of pervasive structural inequality and normalized collective and political wrongdoing, default trust is not the norm. Deep, at times absolute, distrust of the competence and decency of others as well as skepticism about the willingness or capacity of others to fair play characterize interaction. There is variation in the character of distrust across societies in the circumstances of transitional justice. Distrust may be targeted toward certain groups of citizens or be general. It may be toward all officials, officials in certain roles, or officials from certain groups. Distrust can be minor, barely failing to meet the threshold-level expectations of confidence and lack of ill will and anticipation of trust responsiveness, or it can reflect profound absence of such expectations and anticipation.

The manner in which distrust is expressed will vary. It may be reflected in anticipations of harm should interaction with government officials take place, or an anticipation that officials and (groups of) citizens are planning to or are in the midst of a campaign to inflict serious harm. Officials may be viewed as incompetent, unable to full their responsibilities out of ignorance or powerlessness. Or they may be viewed as lacking the appropriate concern for the well-being and interests of members of the general population, instead using the political system and rules to enrich themselves and their close associates. Officials may express distrust for (groups of) citizens by denying them the civil and political rights extended to other groups, thus reflecting a refusal to see such distrusted groups as competent, or as lacking ill will toward other members of a political community. This kind of distrust reflects suspicion about the willingness of some to exercise their agency appropriately.

Default distrust in the circumstances of pervasive structural inequality and normalized collective and political wrongdoing is often reasonable.[41] Default political trust and trust responsiveness is neither present nor reasonable in the circumstances of transitional justice. That is, ordinary citizens cannot reasonably assume that government officials and/or (all or some groups of) fellow citizens lack ill will and are competent in the sense of being knowledgeable of and capable of adhering to basic standards for conduct reflected in, for example, fundamental human rights norms protecting bodily integrity as well as more demanding role-related responsibilities such as those entailed by the rule of law. Pervasive structural inequality can reflect an unreasonable refusal by some groups within a community to acknowledge the competence and lack of ill will of members of certain marginalized groups, a refusal that is reflected in justifications for differential rights or differential application of rules as well as such rights and differential application themselves. Anticipating trust responsiveness sets an individual up for disappointment when the fact of being relied on is disregarded and ignored; one cannot reasonably assume that others will take seriously the fact that trust is being placed in them when others deliberate how to act. Normalized collective and political wrongdoing can further ground this reasonableness. Adopting a default stance of trust in such contexts very often renders oneself vulnerable to serious harm or exploitation.

---

[41] I say "often" and not "always" because there will be contexts of pervasive structural inequality in which the underlying justification for such inequality is based on racist or stereotyped views of members of the subordinated group. In such cases distrust of the competence of such individuals or groups is unwarranted.

What the framework of trust highlights is an additional moral cost of normalized collective and political wrongdoing and pervasive structural inequality to individuals and their interactions with others. In such circumstances the possibilities for expressions of respect for the agency of others and commitment to reciprocity not only in action, but also in the reactive attitudes adopted in interaction are foreclosed as reasonable options. The absence of grounds that make trust reasonable reflects a failure to acknowledge the second-person authority of others to make demands on us, as is the case when trust is placed in another.

Relationship among the Frameworks

I have analytically separated out three normative components of relational transformation. In practice, the relationship among the frameworks is dynamic and mutually reinforcing. The promotion of the rule of law can provide some conditions for the reasonableness of default trust of citizens and officials, just as the erosion of the rule of law generates distrust and resentment.[42] Distrust arises and is reasonable because citizens cannot turn to declared rules to have any meaningful understanding of the standard of conduct to which they will be held, and the response of officials to conduct that contravenes that standard. Denying opportunities for individuals to be recognized as members of their community can erode the rule of law insofar as it generates alienation from institutions and reduced willingness to abide by the rules structuring political interaction. In their discussion of disadvantage, Jonathan Wolff and Avner de-Shalit reference empirical evidence regarding the relationship between a sense of membership and the rule of law: "Once there is a loss of a sense of community, respect for these rules drains away, and they become increasingly difficult to enforce."[43] In this way the erosion of recognition of the membership status of individuals or groups can negatively impact the rule of law.

Evaluating Processes of Transitional Justice

An account of transitional justice must provide resources for morally evaluating the various ways societies might pursue societal transformation. In Section 1, I articulated the broad features of the relational

---

[42] On distrust as a product of violations of the rule of law, see Fuller, *Morality of Law*.
[43] Wolff and de-Shalit, *Disadvantage*, 140.

transformation toward which, I claimed, processes of transitional justice ought to aim. In this section I outline the general set of criteria to use to evaluate the contribution of any process to such transformation. The criteria are divided into two categories. The first set articulate how processes may directly contribute to the main characteristics of transformed relationships by, for example, directly enhancing mutual respect for the rule of law, reasonable default trust and trust responsiveness, and relational capabilities. The second reflects indirect contributions to transformation. Through such contributions, processes help to cultivate the basic conditions on which the rule of law, trust, and relational capabilities depend. In addition to articulating the aims in terms of which a process would be effective, I identify moral side constraints on the permissible pursuit of such transformation derived from the ideal of transformation itself. Directly or indirectly promoting societal transformation would demonstrate that a process of transitional justice is just in the *jus ad bellum* analogue sense of contributing to the overarching moral objective of such processes.

Direct Effectiveness

A process of transitional justice directly contributes to transformation by strengthening the rule of law, increasing trust among citizens and officials and among citizens, and/or enhancing the relational capabilities and capability to avoid poverty of citizens. Here the important work being done by social scientists to assess contributions of particular processes will be critical in understanding what sort of response will achieve such direct contributions and under what conditions.[44]

To assess such contributions, a variety of indicators can be used. For example, evaluations of the strength of the rule of law may look for reduced gaps between declared rules and the activities and policies of government officials, especially in areas where there was discrepancy before. Increases in the legal enforcement of violations of legal rules that were previously unenforced could be another such indicator. Yet other areas where the rule of law may be enhanced include reforming particular legal rules to enhance clarity or to remove inconsistency. The overarching aim of such contributions is to increase the openness and transparency of the legal standards for conduct that citizens and officials are expected to fulfill, and to ensure such standards are enforced in practice. Which specific indicator(s) is/are appropriate in a particular case will

---

[44] See, for example, Olsen et al., *Transitional Justice in Balance.*

depend in part on what the source(s) of the erosion of the rule of law was (were) in the past.

In terms of trust, the aim of direct contributions is to foster tangible changes in the general perceptions of citizens and officials of one another.[45] Surveys can provide some information regarding such attitudes and through them we can track changes.[46] Of particular interest will be attitudes regarding the competence of citizens and officials, as well as the presence of absence of ill will. Here context is important. Depending on the history of conflict or repression, the fault lines of distrust will vary, and so the reductions in distrust or increases in trust that are important to examine will vary as well.

For capabilities, the enhancement of capabilities is a function of increasing what individuals have and what they can do with what they have that are salient for each relational capability. For example, processes may attempt to alter social norms that play a role in precluding certain groups from participation in economic, political, or social processes. Symbolic representations of the identity of the political community can be addressed so as to broaden the groups reflected in such symbols. Processes may address the social and material conditions that impact individuals' opportunity to avoid poverty, including how land is distributed and the structure and quality of educational institutions. Sabina Alkire and James Foster have developed a multidimensional poverty index precisely for the purpose of measuring poverty from a capability perspective. It provides policy makers with guidance on specific indicators to consider when assessing the level of poverty within communities.[47]

Indirect Contributions

Turning now to what I am calling indirect contributions, there are some general conditions that influence prospects for relational transformation.[48] I concentrate on four such conditions in particular: hope, acknowledgment of the need for transformation, recognition of respect for agency, and a commitment to reciprocity.

---

[45] I discuss the importance of cultivating the conditions that make such changes in perception reasonable in the next section.

[46] An example of such surveys is Gibson, James, *Overcoming Apartheid: Can Truth Reconcile a Divided Nation?* (New York: Russell Sage Foundation, 2006).

[47] Alkire, Sabine and James Foster, "Counting and Multidimensional Poverty Measurement," *Journal of Public Economics* 95, no. 7 (2011): 476–87.

[48] I discuss these as well as some additional conditions in depth in Murphy, *Moral Theory*, chap. 5.

Hope

Hope is an attitude of optimism toward the prospect of realizing a sought-after state of affairs or objective, the achievement of which is uncertain.[49] The attitude of optimism is not in place when one only wishes for, and in that sense seeks, a state of affairs. It also requires active effort to realize the sought-after state of affairs or objective by looking for ways to promote that state of affairs or communicating the desire for the objective to others.[50] Hope is always conditioned on the recognition of the deep uncertainty of actually achieving the sought-after goal of our actions.[51] Hopeful actions are an exercise of agency in the face of serious limitations that reduce confidence in the ultimate success of one's actions.

Hope is an especially important attitude in the circumstances of transitional justice, specifically the circumstance of serious existential uncertainty. To motivate the exercise of individual and communal action needed to transform relationships, individuals must share the sense that such transformation is in some remote sense possible. Hope provides that motivational impetus to engage in actions and attempt the institutional reform needed for the transformation of political relationships, but does so in a way that is conditioned on acknowledgment of the serious existential uncertainty present in transitional communities. Hope can thus lead members of transitional societies to engage in efforts to transform relationships, actively seeking ways to make this happen in the face of serious challenges to this possibility.[52] Equally important, hope can act as a constraining force, leading members of transitional societies to exercise restraint so as not to undermine the already fragile prospect of relational change.[53] Critical for the pursuit of transitional justice, then, is an understanding of the conditions that contribute to or undermine hope among members of a transitional community. One plausible condition that could contribute to hope is a cessation of violence, especially if in the form of a truce. As Nir Eiskovits convincingly argues in his defense of what he calls "truce thinking," pauses in violence can create a space in which citizens can come to enjoy the benefits gained from a reduction in hostilities, and

---

[49] I take this general idea from Walker, *Moral Repair*, 44–49; Walker also mentions beliefs and desires as constitutive of hope.

[50] Ibid., 53.

[51] McGeer, Victoria, "Trust, Hope, and Empowerment," *Australasian Journal of Philosophy* 86, no. 2 (2008): 237–54. See also Walker, *Moral Repair*, 27.

[52] Walker, *Moral Repair*, 50, 246.   [53] On the constraining character of hope, see McGeer, "Trust."

thereby hesitate to return to hostilities as well as a space in which circumstances can change politically in ways that are conducive to longer-term peace.[54]

Not only can hope serve as a general condition for the possibility of relational transformation, it also serves as a specific condition for the possibility of trust. As Victoria McGeer notes, "Substantial trust in others is critically dependent upon our capacity to feel hopeful about them, about their capacities and dispositions as agents, as well as hopeful about how these capacities and dispositions can be positively affected by our actively and explicitly putting trust in them."[55] Hope can in turn ground a willingness to engage in the reciprocal effort needed to maintain the rule of law by encouraging citizens and officials to restrain themselves in the way that the rule of law demands.

Acknowledgment of the Need for Societal Transformation

Actions that are a product of hope will only be directed toward relational transformation if there is a prior acknowledgment that such transformation is necessary. Absent such recognition of the need to transform the terms of political relationships, there will be no recognition of the reason to engage in transformation-oriented actions. One prominent obstacle to such acknowledgment in the circumstances of transitional justice is denial.[56] Denial is the refusal to acknowledge difficult information. The range of individuals who deny the need to transform relationships will vary across transitional societies, from small groups to officials to the majority of citizens. The scope of what is being denied will vary as well, ranging in the context of relational transformation from a general refusal to acknowledge problems with the basic terms structuring political relationships to more specific denial of particular areas where change is needed.[57]

Sociologist Stanley Cohen defines three forms of denial. One form of denial is an explicit rejection of factual statements regarding, for example, the existence of structural inequality, what Cohen labels "literal denial." Denials that differential capabilities for political participation exist would be one such form. Even when the fact that something occurred is recognized, its moral significance can fail to be acknowledged. In Cohen's words, "By

[54] Eisikovits, Nir, *A Theory of Truces* (New York: Palgrave Macmillan, 2015); Eisikovits, Nir, "Truces: What They Mean, How They Work," *Theoria* 62, no. 145 (December 2015): 60–81.

[55] McGeer, "Trust," 243. On this point, wee also Walker, *Moral Repair*, 44.

[56] On denial, see Cohen, Stanley, *States of Denial: Knowing about Atrocities and Suffering* (Cambridge: Polity Press, 2001).

[57] For a comprehensive discussion of political denial, see ibid.

euphemism, by technical jargon, the observer disputes the cognitive meaning given to an event and re-allocates it to another class of event."[58] In cases
of such interpretive denial, actions like torture become "regrettable
excesses," isolated instances of actions done by rogue state agents, and/or
necessary responses to absolute evil. The egregiousness of the torture and
the fact that torture is impermissible as a form of treatment toward any
human being is being denied in such cases. Interpretive denial is likely to be
prevalent in contexts where wrongdoing has been normalized. Finally, in
implicatory denial, individuals or groups fail to acknowledge their responsibility for wrongs that took place. Ordinary citizens may refuse to acknowledge their role in maintaining and supporting a system of pervasive
structural inequality predicated on selective application of legal rules.

The source of denial can be either citizens or officials, and denial is
strongest when mutually reinforced by (parts of) both groups. Denial on
the part of officials, Cohen argues, is often "initiated, structured and
sustained by the massive resources of the modern state."[59] Official denial
influences how citizens and often international observers interpret events
and a society, yet the interpretation of events is not solely a product of
official action or inaction. Social norms influence what is acceptable to say
or ideas it is acceptable to express, and the success of official campaigns of
denial is influenced by the receptivity of a public to such denial. Cohen
notes that "denials draw on shared cultural vocabularies to be credible.
They may also be shared in another powerful sense: the commitment
between people – whether partners or an entire organization – back up
and collude in each other's denials."[60]

Respect for Moral Agency and Reciprocity

Beyond hope and acknowledgment, two further general conditions are
important for the possibility of transformation of political relationships:
recognition of the moral importance of respect for agency, and a commitment to reciprocity. Such recognition and commitment are needed
because it is these two values that underpin the normative requirements
of the rule of law, trust, and relational capabilities. By recognizing and
committing to these values, citizens and officials are in a position to both
understand the rationale for the requirements each normative framework
imposes and also be motivated to satisfy such requirements.

Acknowledgment of respect for agency is in one sense tied to the
previous general condition of acknowledgment of the need for

---

[58] Ibid., 8.   [59] Ibid., 10.   [60] Ibid., 64.

transformation. Proper acknowledgment of the need for transformation includes recognition of the ways in which the erosion of the rule of law, the reasonableness of default trust, and relational capabilities all constitute failures to respect the agency of others because eroding this value is one important source of the morally problematic character of pervasive structural inequality and the subsequent need for transformation. However, respect for agency goes beyond this previous condition in other respects. In addition to recognizing the source of the failure of respect for agency in the current structure of interaction, certain capacities must be cultivated for individuals to be motivated to respect the agency of others when moving forward. Drawing on philosopher David Shoemaker's analysis, we can see why systematic failures of respect for agency become possible when there is an absence of the capacities to care about, empathize with, and acknowledge the second-person reasons of others. It is these three capacities, Shoemaker argues, that are exercised in interpersonal interactions among moral agents who see and treat one another as moral agents.[61] These capacities are especially important to cultivate toward members of marginalized individuals and groups within a given transitional community, those toward whom relationships were structured to be unequal.

Shoemaker argues that reactive attitudes are a key component of interpersonal relationships. Reactive attitudes are a form of communication and address through which we express moral judgments and sentiments that convey such judgments, and invite the subject of our attitude to respond. Through resentment we express our judgment that we have been wronged by the action of another, and our anger at having been so wronged.

Engaging with others interpersonally depends on the presence of certain capacities, Shoemaker argues. One must be able to "recognize and apply second-personal moral reasons."[62] That is, the subject of a reactive attitude must recognize the standing and authority of the individual expressing such an attitude to give the subject reasons for action. The fact that an individual is communicating her anger toward the subject of resentment and judgment that the subject wronged her is sufficient for the subject of resentment to have reason to respond to this attitude. The subject of a reactive attitude is being held responsible for her failing by the individual expressing resentment, and the wronged has the standing and authority to so hold an individual to account. Once recognized, the subject of resentment reacts appropriately, either by feeling remorse at his or her failing, or feeling compelled to offer a justification for his or her action if judging that

---

[61] Shoemaker, "Moral Address," 71–75.   [62] Ibid., 86–89.

the resentment is misplaced. Part of being motivated to respond to the reactive attitudes of others as well as more generally engage in interpersonal interactions depends not only on recognizing the authority of others to hold us to account for our actions but also to feel moved to respond to the emotional address constitutive of such attitudes.[63]

Interacting with and responding appropriately to others interpersonally requires an ability to be moved by the emotional address of another. Being so moved depends on being able to empathize with and understand the anger, indignation, or other emotion being expressed; in the case of wrongdoing this entails in part seeing what our actions have done. Engaging interpersonally with others requires an individual to be "emotionally vulnerable with respect to the fortunes of the items the person with whom one empathizes cares about, and vulnerable in a roughly similar way to the person with whom one empathizes."[64] Such comprehension better enables individuals to understand how to respond appropriately.

A willingness to be vulnerable to the emotional address of others and recognize and be motivated to act on the second-personal reasons of others depends on an individual caring for that other in the sense of having a "disposition to experience mature, complex emotions corresponding to the up-and-down fortunes of X."[65] Shoemaker argues that we implicitly assume a connection between care and motivation when interacting with others. The absence of care is indifference, and one complaint by those subject to injustice is the failure of others to care about what is taking place. Implicit, in other words, is the assumption that if someone can promote a certain good through her actions and is not motivated to do so, this is because she does not care about the good in question.[66] Unsurprisingly, a recurring complaint among members of marginalized groups as well as victims of human rights violations regards indifference to their suffering, either on the part of perpetrators responsible for inflicting suffering or on the part of the broader domestic community and/or international community when the suffering is made known. Writing about Peru in the aftermath of its TRC (Comisión de la Verdad y Reconciliación), the ICTJ notes, "The TRC findings and recommendations have been strongly opposed by traditional political sectors and some local elites. The trials of people accused of grave crimes are proceeding at a slow pace, the needs of victims do not receive adequate

---

[63] Ibid., 91.   [64] Ibid., 98.   [65] Ibid., 83.   [66] Ibid., 91.

attention, and the demands of the families of thousands of disappeared people are met with inaction and indifference."[67]

In the circumstances of transitional justice where there is an absence of care for certain individuals and groups, the failure to recognize the authority of certain individuals and groups to make demands on others and the inability to empathize all diminish the conditions required for respect for the moral agency of others. Moral agents have the standing to give others second-personal reasons for action, including demands regarding how they should be treated. Moral agents have the standing to hold others accountable for their failure or success in meeting these demands, as the reactive attitudes individuals form and express in response to treatment by others do. Respect for moral agency will succeed only when individuals are motivated to treat others with such respect, which the absence of care and subsequent indifference toward others erodes. Indifference in the face of injustice and the suffering of others is a core complaint expressed among those who are targeted by pervasive structural inequality.

As noted earlier, reciprocity captures the idea that the legitimacy of (at least some of) the demands and expectations I make on others is conditional in part on my willingness to recognize and fulfill the expectations that others make of me. Erosions of the rule of law, the reasonableness of trust, and relational capabilities all constitute erosions of reciprocity in the relationships among citizens, and between citizens and officials. Legal rules govern conduct only if there is mutual willingness on the part of citizens and officials to restrict their conduct as the requirements of the rule of law demand. Yet characteristically mutual fidelity to the rule of law breaks down, leaving a context in which officials disregard or fail to fulfill the demands that legal rules for conduct be publicly knowable in advance by citizens, and yet continue to claim the authority to punish citizens for infractions of such rules despite undermining the basis on which a duty of obedience to law by citizens could be made. Similarly, the absence of the conditions where default trust and trust responsiveness would be reasonable signals an asymmetry in what individuals would like or demand that others presume of them (e.g., decency, competence, and reliability in the sense of being trust responsive) and what they can presume of others.

Finally, processes should themselves reflect and respect the central moral values realized in political relationships predicated on equality: respect for agency and reciprocity. Objection to the absence of these values underpins

[67] ICTJ, "Ten Years after Peru's Commission," www.ictj.org/news/ten-years-after-peru-truth-commission (accessed January 6, 2017).

certain kinds of criticisms of the pursuit of transitional justice in particular cases. For example, concern about the lack or insufficiency of local participation in decision-making processes of transitional justice is becoming increasingly pronounced. Such concern is implicit – and in some cases explicit – in calls for greater local participation by members of transitional communities in response to concerns about the external, top-down imposition of transitional justice choices.[68] The decision-making process through which a transitional society determines which particular response(s) to which wrongs will be adopted should be inclusive, incorporating representatives of all members of a community. This is especially the case in circumstances of pervasive structural inequality where members of particular groups may have been marginalized from participation in social or political processes on the basis of a particular ethnic identity, ideological commitments, or gender. Achieving broad participatory objectives of fair and equal deliberation requires explicit and targeted attention to the circumstance of pervasive structural inequality. The United Nation Security Council's Resolution 1325 in 2000, which called for greater inclusion of and participation by women in negotiations leading to peace agreements and in peacemaking, is a response to one important source of deliberative democratic deficit.[69]

Conditions for the Rule of Law

Beyond the general conditions to cultivate, there are conditions more specific to each of the normative frameworks discussed. I turn first to consider the conditions for mutual respect of the rule of law. From the Fullerian perspective described earlier, the rule of law is at its core governance of conduct of officials and citizens on the basis of legal rules.[70] Certain conditions must obtain for such conduct to be governed by rules in fact. According to Fuller, there must be faith in the law on the

---

[68] See, for example, McEvoy, "Beyond Legalism"; United Nations General Assembly, Sixty-Second Session, Agenda Items 34 and 86: Comprehensive Review of the Whole Peacekeeping Operations in All Their Aspects, UN Doc. A/62/885, June 19, 2008, www.icc-cpi.int/iccdocs/asp_docs/RC2010/Stocktaking/Nuremberg%20Declaration%20UNGA.pdf; McEvoy, Kieran and Lorna McGregor, "Transitional Justice From Below: An Agenda for Research, Policy and Praxis," in *Transitional Justice from Below: Grassroots Activism and the Struggle for Change*, ed. Kieran McEvoy and Lorna McGregor, 1–13 (Portland, OR: Hart Publishing, 2008); Pouligny, Béatrice, Simon Chesterman, and Albrecht Schnabel, "Introduction: Picking up the Pieces," in *After Mass Crime: Rebuilding States and Communities*, ed. Béatrice Pouligny, Simon Chesterman, and Albrecht Schnabel, 1–16 (Tokyo: United Nations University Press, 2008); Viaene and Brems, "Transitional Justice."

[69] United Nations Security Council, Resolution 1325 (2000), http://daccess-dds-ny.un.org/doc/UNDOC/GEN/N00/720/18/PDF/N0072018.pdf?OpenElement.

[70] Fuller, *Morality of Law*, 106.

part of citizens, legal decency on the part of officials, cooperative action and interaction between citizens and officials that is ongoing, and congruence between the law and informal social practices.[71] I discuss these conditions in turn.

Faith in Law

As Fuller notes, in order for citizens to be willing to engage in the cooperative interaction necessary to maintain a system of rules that govern conduct in practice and to correspondingly restrain themselves in the way that legal rules stipulate, they must have faith in law. This faith captures a confidence and trust that officials are, in Fuller's words, "playing the game of law fairly" and so formulating public and general rules that are actually respected and enforced in practice.[72] Moreover, the inclination of citizens to restrain their conduct according to legal prescriptions is impacted by their faith in law and legal processes. Only when such faith is widespread will citizens in general be willing to constrain their conduct in the way declared rules demand. Governing by law requires citizens to be willing to restrict their conduct to what legal rules require, permit, or prohibit. The willingness of citizens to do this is influenced by their view of the consequences of so doing. Insofar as citizens have little faith in the law as regulating the conduct of either fellow citizens or officials, their willingness declines. Following rules that require them to forbear benefits that may come, for example, from tax evasion while most citizens ignore such rules becomes less compelling. Similarly, forbearance is futile when citizens can have little confidence that officials will actually take such obedience into account when determining how they will act toward or interact with citizens. When there is a widespread sense that obedience is futile because officials do not respond to individuals on the basis of whether they have violated the law or because it is impossible to determine how legal rules will be interpreted, such faith breaks down and disobedience is more likely to become widespread. Faith is also necessary if law is to facilitate agency. Chronic suspicion can motivate a continual scrutiny of government actions that impedes and interferes with interaction.

There is often little faith in the law on the part of (some or all) citizens in the circumstances of transitional justice. Studies of transitional societies

---

[71] Fuller refers to these conditions in *Morality of Law*; see also Fuller, *Anatomy of the Law*; Lon Fuller, "Human Interaction and the Law," in *The Principles of Social Order: Selected Essays of Lon F. Fuller*, rev. ed., ed. Kenneth Winston, 231–66 (Portland, OR: Hart Publishing, 2001).

[72] Fuller, "Human Interaction," 255.

articulate a loss of faith in law in many contexts. In his study of courts in contemporary sub-Saharan Africa, H. Kwasi Prempeh argues that during the transitions from authoritarian rule in the 1990s a central concern became establishing the formal conditions for judicial independence found in stable democracies, including powers of judicial review and safeguards from political interference. However, the postauthoritarian judiciary continues to fail to be seen as legitimate among the general population. He writes that many groups of citizens share a "longstanding public perception of the judicial system as corrupt and biased in favor of the powerful, and the result is an African public that is both distrustful of judicial power and doubtful of the relevance of courts to the lives of the ordinary citizen."[73] As a result, citizens do not turn to the law or legal processes to resolve disputes or enforce rights. Their faith in the outcome of legal resolutions of disputes is absent. In Prempeh's words, "As far as the majority of Africans were concerned, the courts existed only to enforce the criminal law against the poor and socially disadvantaged."[74] Making a similar point, the Sierra Leone Truth Commission concluded, "Much has to be done to restore the faith and confidence of the people of Sierra Leone in the Army."[75]

There will be variation in the scope and depth of the loss of faith in any given society. In cases of partial legality, for example, groups targeted by violence or injustice frequently lack faith in law, a faith that may be present in the group whose experience of law is that of congruence between declared rules and their enforcement. In cases of a general absence or breakdown of the rule of law, lack of faith can become more widespread.

Legal Decency

Prospects for generating faith in the law increase when officials themselves demonstrate fidelity to the law. Fuller argues that such fidelity requires decency on the part of officials, who must be willing to restrain themselves as legal rules specify and require.[76] Structural factors can influence the demandingness required for such decency to be exercised. As Prempeh emphasizes, formal conditions for judicial independence, including powers of judicial review and safeguards from political interference, are not sufficient to ensure that the judiciary will have independence and the authority based on this independence. If the legislative and executive branches control the resources required for courts to function and the judiciary

---

[73] Prempeh, "*Marbury* in Africa," 62.   [74] Ibid., 31.
[75] Sierra Leone Truth Commission, *Report*, 3:151.   [76] Fuller, *Anatomy of Law*, 65.

remains chronically underfunded, this creates an incentive for judges to do whatever is necessary to secure the requisite funding and makes judges more vulnerable to political interference.[77] Similarly, rulers dismissing judges who become too active in challenging executive authority make decency that much more difficult.[78]

Ongoing Action and Interaction

Decency among officials and faith in the law can undergird the third condition, which is ongoing cooperative activity among citizens and officials. Cooperative interaction depends on both faith in the law and decency. Neither citizens nor officials can maintain the rule of law on their own. A system of clear, prospective, and promulgated rules will be mere words on paper if citizens are not willing to take legal rules into account when deliberating about how to act. Conversely, a population of citizens willing to take such rules into account will not be able to do so if officials fail to promulgate rules or articulate rules in a clear manner. Absent ongoing cooperative action and interaction among citizens, law cannot govern conduct.

Successful cooperative action and interaction depends as well on congruence between law and informal social practices.[79] Legal rules are general rules that must be interpreted and applied to the particular situations in which individuals are acting. Drawing on social practices when determining how such rules apply to particular cases is a way of ensuring that the interpretations of officials and citizens will be similar. As a result, citizens will be held to a standard of conduct they have a genuine opportunity to meet.[80]

The conditions for the rule of law are mutually reinforcing and interactive. To illustrate, the lack of faith in courts among a population can in turn undermine the capacity of courts to strengthen the constitution and rights that are constitutionally guaranteed.

Conditions for Political Trust

In the case of trust, the possibility of restoring trust may depend on altering the way in which certain social groups are viewed within a given

---

[77] Prempeh, "*Marbury* in Africa," 66.   [78] Ibid., 25–32.

[79] This was part of Fuller's point in his illustration of the example of a legal rule prohibiting vehicles from entering the park discussed in footnote 14. See Fuller, *Anatomy of the Law*, 58.

[80] Postema, Gerald J., "Implicit Law," *Law and Philosophy* 13 (1994): 365.

community. Political trust characteristically has a group dimension; that is, trust is a phenomenon mediated by group identities and affiliations. Who individuals view in a given context as competent and lacking ill will often depends on to which groups the individual in question belongs; prejudice can impede recognition of the competence of members of certain groups. Stereotypes and prejudice may need to be countered before the competence of groups that have been historically discriminated against is acknowledged. Moreover, stereotypes underpin justifications of structurally unequal institutions by, for example, appealing to the incompetence of certain groups, and justifications of wrongdoing targeting particular groups may appeal to the intrinsic ill will possessed by the targeted group's members.

Trust's reasonableness is a function of the reasonableness of assuming as a default the lack of ill will and competence of the subject of trust, and the reasonableness of assuming that another will prove trust responsive. Conditions like ongoing violence or systematic corruption render such presumptions unreasonable.

Conditions for Relational and Basic Capabilities

Capabilities exist as a function of what individuals have and what they can do with what they have given the institutional and infrastructure context in which they act and interact. These are the conditions that must be examined when identifying how to enhance relational and basic capabilities. Promoting genuine opportunities for participation in economic processes requires recognizing the source of pervasively differential opportunities among members of certain groups. This could be a function of discriminatory laws and/or discriminatory practices. It could be a function of variation in the quality of education available to members of certain groups, or differences in the rates of attendance in school that are of similar quality that reflect social norms on who should be educated. When underpinning pervasively structurally unequal institutions, stereotyping can lead to employment discrimination and reduced opportunities for participation in a society. Stereotypes can be humiliating for the targeted group, thereby diminishing the capability for respect.[81] Stereotypes can become internalized, and belief in the inherent laziness or inferiority of groups of which one is a member can further diminish the personal resources on which all capabilities depend.[82] Increasing relational capabilities requires attending to the conditions that diminish opportunities.

---

[81] Cudd, *Analyzing Oppression*, 163.
[82] This point is also emphasized by Benson, Paul, "Free Agency and Self-Worth," *Journal of Philosophy* 91, no. 12 (1994): 650–68; and Cudd, *Analyzing Oppression*.

Transformation, Human Rights, and Democracy

How should we understand the relationship between societal transformation, defined above, human rights, and democracy? A prominent
theme in the literature on transitional justice is human rights, which
need to be respected in both formal law and in practice. Promotion of
such respect is characterized by some as the core overarching aim of
transitional justice. In the words of de Greiff, processes of transitional
justice have "as a point reestablishing the force of the human rights
norms whose systematic violation characterized the predecessor
regime."[83] Processes of transitional justice, he writes, must aim to "draw
a line between a past in which rights meant nothing or very little and a
future in which rights do matter."[84] That is, transitional justice contributes to the process of having those norms that call for respect for
human rights regulate and govern behavior in practice. Thus "legal
remedies are ... instruments for the constitution or reconstitution of
a legally medicated system of justice as such."[85]

It is important to recognize that the conception of relational transformation articulated above has human rights requirements. Respect for
human rights is a necessary condition for any threshold level of the
relational capabilities discussed above to be realized. For example,
respect for human rights is an important component of respect for
individuals. The idea that all human beings have a basic dignity often
underpins and justifies human rights claims and entitlements. The basis
of dignity is the subject of debate, but one powerful view is that the
dignity of individuals stems from their agency.[86] In virtue of this
dignity, certain forms of treatment or deprivations are morally out of
bounds. Fulfilling such claims is a form of demonstrating respect for
other human beings and recognizing the worth they have that forecloses

---

[83] De Greiff, "Theorizing Transitional Justice," 70. Daniel Philpott also articulates the standards
for what he calls "right relationship" in terms of respect for human rights norms and restrictions
on the use of force in individual actions, laws, and constitutions; see Philpott, *Just and Unjust
Peace*.

[84] De Greiff, "Theorizing Transitional Justice," 62.

[85] Ibid., 64. Paige Arthur also notes that the transitional justice movement has taken up human rights
norm "entrepreneurship" following the human rights movement. See Arthur, "How 'Transitions'
Reshaped Human Rights." The theme of norm affirmation is an important dimension of Walker,
Moral Repair; Gray, "Extraordinary Justice."

[86] For contemporary views that make this connection, see Gewirth, Alan, *Human Rights: Essays on
Justification and Applications* (Chicago: University of Chicago Press, 1982); James Griffin, *On
Human Rights* (Oxford: Oxford University Press, 2008).

certain forms of treatment. The relationship between respect for human rights and respect for individuals is reflected in the experience of humiliation, degradation, and shame that accompanies violations of basic human rights, especially violations of rights to bodily integrity. One function of violations of basic rights in the form of rape, torture, and mutilation is precisely to humiliate and degrade the individual whose rights are violated, and by extension the groups or communities of which these individuals are a part.

Furthermore, genuine opportunities to participate in political processes depend on legal rights, both to speech so as to voice one's opinions on political matters and to vote to express the candidate of one's choosing and affiliation. Opportunities for participation depend on the economic rights to property being recognized and respected. The rule of law's commitment to congruence entails that any rights recognized in law must be protected and enforced in practice. Respect for human rights or its absence plays an important role in shaping whether or not trust of officials or citizens is reasonable.

In addition to explicitly requiring respect for human rights, my normative conception of transformation articulates conditions that must be in place for the force of human rights norms to be realized and respected in practice. The formal conception of the rule of law outlined above is particularly important in this respect. It highlights the necessity of basic knowledge of what policies and practices are de facto governing interaction so that the justice of such practices can in turn be evaluated. Absent threshold levels of satisfaction of the basic requirements of the rule of law, the epistemic knowledge needed to assess whether or not rights are being respected becomes much more difficult to acquire.

More generally, I have argued at length in previous work that there is an intimate connection between the formal criteria of the rule of law and substantive injustice; one form of substantive injustice is violations of human rights. As Fuller famously (and controversially) claimed, the rule of law is morally significant for instrumental moral reasons, because of the ways in which the rule of law curtails the pursuit of injustice.[87]

---

[87] The idea that there are limits to the kind of policies, objectives, and action that can be pursued compatibly with the rule of law is the subject of ongoing debate. For many scholars a purely formal conception of the rule of law of the kind Fuller articulates and that is laid out in this chapter is compatible with the pursuit of policies of discrimination, slavery, and violations of rights. An eloquent articulation of this view is in Raz, Joseph, *Authority of Law* (Oxford: Clarendon Press,

The rule of law is incompatible with certain objectives of repressive regimes or groups in combat; the predictability created by the rule of law is ill suited to a campaign of terror. Thus, as Waldron observes, "The outward appearance of the rule of law may be important for the external reputation of a regime. But those who reflect seriously on humanity's experience with tyranny know that, in the real world, this problem of the scrupulously legalistic Nazi is at best a question about the efficacy of cosmetics."[88] Waldron's quote is important for drawing attention to the fact that what matters in an assessment of the rule of law within a community is not just what is claimed but what is actually done in practice. The facade of legality is not the same as actually achieving legality where a system of declared legal rules actually has purchase on governing interaction in practice.

In defending Fuller's claim that scrupulous adherence to the rule of law constrains the pursuit of injustice, I also discuss historical and contemporary cases in which human rights abuses occur as officials violate requirements of the rule of law.[89] I offer an argument for why officials violate the rule of law when committing such abuses. Systematic adherence to the requirements of the rule of law entails openness and transparency. This makes abuse publicly knowable at the time it is occurring. Such transparency renders individuals and communities vulnerable to criticism. Citizens domestically as well as the international community can both identify and challenge the policies a government is pursuing and the practices it is endorsing in terms of how citizens are treated. Governments and communities have to own and take responsibility for what they are doing, and provide justifications for actions in the face of critique. Such transparency

---

1979). I offer an extended argument against Raz's view in "Lon Fuller." I further develop this argument in chapter 2 of *Moral Theory* and in Murphy, Colleen, "Political Reconciliation, the Rule of Law, and Post-Traumatic Stress Disorder," in *Trauma, Truth, and Reconciliation: Healing Damaged Relationships*, ed. Nancy Nyquist Potter, 83–110 (Oxford: Oxford University Press, 2006).

[88] Waldron, Jeremy "Why Law–Efficacy, Freedom or Fidelity?," *Law and Philosophy* 13 (1994): 264. For a detailed examination of legality during the Nazi period, see Rundle, Kristin, "The Impossibility of an Exterminatory Legality: Law and the Holocaust," *University of Toronto Law Journal* 59, no. 1 (2009): 65–125.

[89] Fuller's claim about the constraining effect of the requirements of the rule of law is made at the system level; thus there may be particular rules that are morally fraught that legal systems introduce. Indeed, limited structural inequality may be compatible with general respect for the rule of law. What is precluded is pervasive structural inequality and robust adherence to the requirements of the rule of law. There may also be variation in the strength of the criticism to which a community is subject by the international community, reflecting differences in power or interest among nations. In contexts of partial legality we see an erosion of legality precisely where injustice is being pursued. The absence of the restraint demanded by the rule of law occurs with groups whose experience of law is of fundamental incongruence between declared rules and their enforcement.

can create tension with an orienting psychological assumption of individuals, which can be extended by analogy to communities, that they are good.[90] Criticism challenges the ability of individuals, and by extension communities, to maintain this belief in the face of their actions. This is why there is strong incentive to maintain the façade of legality. Were the rule of law scrupulously adhered to during periods of conflict and repression in which rights abuses occurred, there would be no need for truth commissions because who did what to whom would already be known and the scale of rights abuses would be part of the public record.

Turning now to democracy, as I noted in the Introduction, democracy as a necessary component of transitional justice is increasingly being contested as both a descriptive and normative matter. Descriptively, theorists include societies not in fact moving in a democratic direction in discussions of transitional justice. Normatively, scholars question the significance of democracy, instead for example invoking notions of peace as a broader aim to ascribe to the pursuit of transitional justice.[91]

There is significant debate and disagreement over how best to define democracy and the criteria by which the presence or absence of democracy in a particular context should be assessed. We speak of democracy, constitutional democracy, liberal democracy, and/or deliberative democracy. Liberal and constitutional versions of democracy emphasize the rights democratic governments must recognize and respect and that constrain democratic decision making. Deliberative democratic theory articulates the processes and conditions required for inclusive and public deliberation that is premised on a fair resolution of policy questions among free and equal individuals, and so provides theoretical resources for considerations to be attentive to when communal deliberation takes place.[92]

Just as there are different definitions of democracy, there are different ways of measuring democracy. Minimally, democracy may be evaluated

---

[90] See my "Political Reconciliation." I discuss in detail the psychological work done on these assumptions and their bearing for the rule of law. Especially salient psychological studies include Janoff-Bulman, R., "Assumptive Worlds and the Stress of Traumatic Events: Applications of the Schema Construct," *Social Cognition* 7 (1989): 113–36; Janoff-Bulman, R., *Shattered Assumptions: Towards a New Psychology of Trauma* (New York: Free Press, 1992); Joseph, S., R. Williams, and W. Yule, *Understanding Post-Traumatic Stress: A Psychosocial Perspective on PTSD and Treatment* (Chichester, UK: John Wiley and Sons, 1997).

[91] Sriram, Chandra Lekha, "Justice as Peace? Liberal Peacebuilding and Strategies of Transitional Justice," *Global Society* 21, no. 4 (2007): 579–91; Lambourne, Wendy, "Transitional Justice and Peacebuilding after Mass Violence," *International Journal of Transitional Justice* 3, no. 1 (2009): 28–48; Sharp, "Emancipating Transitional Justice."

[92] Crocker, David, *Ethics of Global Development: Agency, Capability, and Deliberative Democracy* (New York: Cambridge University Press, 2009) (accessed January 8, 2017).

on the basis of whether elections take place. Elections are often viewed as a necessary but not sufficient indication of democracy. As Kofi Annan puts it, "Democracy is not just about one day every four or five years when elections are held, but a system of government that respects the separation of powers, fundamental freedoms like the freedom of thought, religion, expression, association and assembly and the rule of law. Any regime that rides roughshod on these principles loses its democratic legitimacy, regardless of whether it initially won an election."[93] Many theorists advocate procedural and institutional criteria that reflect Annan's basic ideas, such as the holding of elections, introduction of constraints on the executive branch, establishment of the rule of law, and respect for human rights. Others concentrate on the attitudes of citizens and officials toward the new order, marked by acceptance of the rule of law and liberal democracy, and recognition of the legitimacy of the new regime.[94] Still others advocate a mix of criteria, such as the presence of executive constraints, the openness of the media, and the formation of associations "championing civic causes."[95]

Thomas Christiano distills the core notion of democracy shared by competing conceptions in this way: democracy is a "method of group decision making characterized by a kind of equality among the participants at an essential stage of the collective decision making."[96] To explain why democracy is a necessary component of transitional justice, I begin with Christiano's definition of a minimally egalitarian democracy.[97] Using a thin, minimal notion avoids including in my discussion of democracy features that may be more controversial. In a minimally egalitarian democracy three conditions hold. First, all persons have formally equal voting rights that are effective aggregately in determining who holds power. Second, all persons have equal opportunities to run for office, influence political deliberation and influence what gets on the agenda for such deliberation. This requires freedom to organize political parties, freedom to enter and leave such parties, freedom of speech (at least concerning political matters), and competition among political parties. Third,

---

[93] Annan, Kofi, "Are Elections Giving Democracy a Bad Name?," www.linkedin.com/pulse/elections-giving-democracy-bad-name-kofi-annan?trk=mp-author-card.

[94] Teitel, "Transitional Jurisprudence."

[95] Epstein et al., "Democratic Transitions," 555; Herbst, J., "Political Liberalization in Africa after Ten Years," *Comparative Politics* 33, no. 3 (2001): 357–75.

[96] Christiano, Tom, "Democracy," in *The Stanford Encyclopedia of Philosophy*, ed. Edward N. Zalta (2015), http://plato.stanford.edu/archives/spr2015/entries/democracy/.

[97] Christiano, Thomas, "An Instrumental Argument for a Human Right to Democracy," *Philosophy & Public Affairs* 39, no. 2 (2011): 142–76.

minorities have protection afforded by the rule of law and freedoms guaranteed in law such that they have a presence in the legislature.

Democracy, so defined, is necessary (though not sufficient) for societal transformation aimed at establishing relationships among equals based on the values of reciprocal agency for two reasons. First, the normative core of democracy is that all individuals have a right to have a say in how they are governed and by whom they are governed.[98] Democracy is a form of governance predicated on the equality of all citizens in the sense that no one group is excluded from the opportunity to reciprocally rule and be ruled.[99] A democratic form of government, broadly understood in Christiano's terms, is constitutively required for relationships among equals, for it is a form of government in which no individual or group has the right to unilaterally rule over others. As the United Nations Declaration on Human Rights states, "Everyone has the right to take part in the government of his [or her] country."[100] It is also instrumentally significant. As Christiano argues in detail, minimally egalitarian democracy has been shown empirically to be essential to the protection of fundamental moral rights, including rights to personal integrity guarding against torture, arbitrary imprisonment, or being disappeared. That is, minimally egalitarian democracy is normally necessary for protecting basic rights to personal integrity and reliably protects these rights; non-democracies and partial democracies are normally not reliable in protecting these rights.[101] Given that rights to personal integrity are a constitutive component of the capability to be respected, we thus have instrumental reasons as well to include democracy as a component of transformation.

An Objection

I have argued that transforming relationships in the circumstances of transitional justice requires promoting the rule of law, the conditions that make default political trust reasonable, and four specific capabilities. As defined, relational transformation is robust and comprehensive, and may

---

[98] Christiano, Thomas, "The Authority of Democracy," *Journal of Political Philosophy* 12, no. 3 (2004): 266–90.

[99] Griffin, Christopher, "Democracy as a Non-Instrumentally Just Procedure," *Journal of Political Philosophy* 11, no. 1 (2003): 111–21; Gould, Carol, *Rethinking Democracy: Freedom and Social Cooperation in Politics, Economics and Society* (New York: Cambridge University Press, 1999).

[100] Popovich, Neil A. F., "In Pursuit of Environmental Human Rights: Commentary on the Draft Declaration of Principles on Human Rights and the Environment," *Columbia Human Rights Law Review* 27 (1995–96): 554–56.

[101] Christiano, "An Instrumental Argument."

for that reason seem to be irrelevant precisely in the context of pervasive structural inequality, normalized collective and political wrongdoing, and serious existential uncertainty, where the possibility of avoiding another massacre or violent campaign seems unclear and the possibility of trust ever being reasonable seems extremely remote.

In response, I want to note first a robust characterization is appropriate given the distinction drawn in Chapter 2 between reform and transformation. If indeed transformation, and not simply reform, is the general challenge in the circumstances of transitional justice, then the kind of interaction toward which processes aim must indeed be substantively different from current interaction.

Second, an account must provide resources for recognizing and identifying variation and difference across transitional contexts, including differences in transitions from conflict versus from repression or from a society in which the state has broken down versus a society where state institutions, though corrupt, are largely intact. The three normative frameworks provide theoretical tools for identifying and describing variation and difference across specific transitional contexts.

Finally, my analysis of transformation is scalar in the way that an adequate account of justice demands. Justice is not, as argued in Introduction, an all-or-nothing matter. Justice comes in degrees and processes may promote more or less justice in relational transformation in their operations. To be sufficiently nuanced, the scalar character of the demands of justice should also be recognized so that it is possible to judge that a given response to wrongdoing is more or less just, or more or less unjust. The complexity of my analysis provides resources for making such judgments. Processes of transitional justice may begin to cultivate some of the characteristics outlined above, strengthening or contributing to the establishment of the rule of law, or expanding opportunities for citizens to avoid poverty or be recognized as members of their community.[102] In its robustness, my analysis draws attention to the myriad ways in which societal transformation can be promoted by processes of transitional justice, and it keeps in mind the ways a given process leaves aspects of relationships unchanged. As part of the scalar character of justice, processes may contribute to relational transformation not only by directly cultivating the rule of law, trust, or relational capabilities but also by fostering the social and moral conditions on which these depend.

---

[102] For a discussion of the general scalar character of reconciliation, which provides the foundation for the view of societal transformation I develop here, see Radzik and Murphy, "Reconciliation."

CHAPTER 4

The Just Pursuit of Transformation

I have argued that *transitional justice* refers to a particular type of justice. This type of justice becomes salient when a specific moral problem arises in a particular set of circumstances of justice. The circumstances of transitional justice I laid out in Chapter 1 are pervasive structural inequality, normalized collective and political wrongdoing, serious existential uncertainty, and fundamental uncertainty about authority.

The central problem of justice in the circumstances of transitional justice is not, I claimed, the problems dealt with by theories of retributive, corrective, and distributive justice. Nor do the corresponding principles of justice designed to address these problems articulate the standard against which transitional justice processes should be evaluated. That is, victim-oriented claims of justice are not fundamentally aimed at making victims whole by restoring them to a status quo ante position, as corrective justice asserts. Nor are perpetrator-oriented claims directed toward the intentional infliction of suffering proportionate with the gravity of the wrong and the culpability of the perpetrator, as retributive justice asserts.

The core problem of transitional justice is how to justly pursue societal transformation. In Chapter 3, I argued that transformation is best defined relationally, that is, as overhauling the terms of interaction structuring political relationships among citizens and between citizens and officials; processes of transitional justice aim to promote these. At its core, relational transformation is concerned with establishing relationships predicated on mutual respect for agency and reciprocity. Fostering the rule of law, establishing grounds that would make default political trust reasonable, and promoting relational capabilities are all part of this structure.

Transitional justice processes pursue relational transformation by dealing with past wrongdoing. The wrongs addressed were committed by specific perpetrators with the support and aid of complicit individuals, and were committed against specific victims who suffered in particular ways. The "just pursuit" of transformation signals the importance of respecting the core moral claims to which wrongdoing independently gives rise. The fact of having committed a wrong and the fact of having been wronged are morally significant in their own right. Ignoring the intrinsic moral claims associated with being a perpetrator of wrongdoing and a victim of wrongdoing would result in a theory that failed to ensure that transformation was justly pursued.

In Chapter 2, I suggested that we should conceptualize the relationship between the aim of transformation and the intrinsic claims associated with wrongdoing as structurally analogous to the relationship between the *jus ad bello* and *jus in bello* components of just war theory. Transitional justice is undertaken with the overarching aim of societal transformation. However, the justice of that pursuit is conditioned on respect for the moral claims that the moral status of being a perpetrator or victim of wrongdoing generates. Just as we can recognize that a war may fail to be just in two distinct ways – by failing to satisfy the *jus ad bellum* and *jus in bello* criteria – so too may a process of transitional justice fail to be just in two ways. A process may fail to satisfy the *jus ad bellum* analogue criteria by not contributing to societal transformation, or it may fail to satisfy the *jus in bello* analogue criteria by not satisfying the criteria for morally permissible responses to perpetrators and victims.

This chapter concentrates on the *jus in bello* analogue of transitional justice, and specifically the justice-based claims associated with wrongdoing itself that must be satisfied if transformation is to be pursued in a just manner.[1] There is a set of general moral objectives of responses to victims and perpetrators of wrongdoing widely recognized in the literature on transitional justice as well as in moral and political philosophy. My central thesis in this chapter is that to satisfy these objectives, the design, implementation, and evaluation of responses to victims and/or perpetrators must be holistic.

Responses must be holistic in two respects. First, as the just war theory metaphor suggests, responses to wrongdoing must be holistic in the sense of satisfying two distinct sets of requirements.[2] Responses to wrongdoing

---

[1] In this chapter I broadly understand "perpetrators" to include individuals complicit in wrongdoing.

[2] Discussions of what I call holism are found in Olsen et al., *Transitional Justice*; de Greiff, "Theorizing Transitional Justice." De Greiff concentrates on holism as needed for both what I call the *jus ad bellum* analogue requirements and the *jus in bello* analogue requirements. Olsen et al. discuss what they call the justice balance as well as a holistic approach, which advocates the adoption of "combinations of methods" for dealing with wrongdoing. They argue that holism seems to work empirically in fostering the *jus ad bellum* aim of transitional justice, transformation, while isolated responses to wrongdoing do not. Olsen et al. identify from their empirical analysis two especially useful combinations of responses: (1) trials, truth commissions, and amnesties and (2) trials and

must be just in the sense that they contribute to societal transformation defined as the transformation of political relationships. They must also be just in the sense of responding in an intrinsically fitting and appropriate manner to victims and perpetrators, thereby satisfying the *jus in bello* analogue requirements. Responses must be designed and evaluated in a way that keeps in mind both sets of requirements that processes must meet. In practice, as I discuss in detail in this chapter, the satisfaction of both of these requirements will often be interdependent. In such cases, failure to keep in mind both sets of requirements will result in a process satisfying neither set.

Responses must be holistic in a second sense. No single kind of response to wrongdoing should be designed, implemented, or evaluated in isolation, but must take into account what other response(s) to wrongdoing are being pursued. Responses to wrongdoing designed, implemented, and evaluated in isolation will not fulfill the general *jus in bello* analogue moral aims of responses to victims and perpetrators. There are two general reasons for the failure of isolated responses to wrongdoing. First, in the circumstances of transitional justice, the expressive meaning of responses to wrongdoing is not fixed but is shaped by other responses to wrongdoing. Second, in the circumstances of transitional justice, no single response to victims or perpetrators has the ability to fulfill the broad moral objectives of such responses. Individual trials, for example, are insufficient for holding accountable perpetrators of normalized collective and political wrongdoing. A program of reparations is insufficient to repair the multiple forms of damage experienced by victims of wrongdoing.

In Section 1 of this chapter, I outline the *jus in bello* analogue requirements of transitional justice. To meet these *jus in bello* demands, a response must be intrinsically fitting or appropriate as a response to victims or perpetrators of wrongdoing. Section 1 outlines the four general factors that influence evaluations of the fittingness or appropriateness of a response. In Sections 2, 3, and 4, I discuss in detail three case studies of moral failure in which a particular response to wrongdoing failed to satisfy the *jus in bello* analogue requirements of transitional justice. I trace the limitations of a response – to victims in the first case, to perpetrators in the

---

amnesties (154). With (2), they argue that "balance involves the legal imperative for justice with protecting public safety by granting amnesty to perpetrators." (ibid., 154). Truth commissions can compensate for lack of prosecution of everyone, while still achieving some kind of acknowledgment. They write, "Two important goals for transitional justice policy are to strengthen democracy and to reduce human rights violations. The empirical study suggests that the best method for achieving those two goals is via multiple mechanisms" (ibid., 159).

second, and to complex victims in the third – to the absence of both senses of holism in the design and implementation of responses to wrongdoing.

Background

Although they do not capture the core moral problem of transitional justice, retributive justice and corrective justice do share a key insight: there are noninstrumental moral reasons to respond to the victims and perpetrators of wrongdoing. Part of the grounds for such reasons is that we treat victims and perpetrators as agents when we respond to their actions or experiences for their own sake. More specifically, we acknowledge the agency of perpetrators by having their actions and choices be the basis for our response to them. Thus, for example, insofar as they fail to fulfill the duties that the human rights of others place on them, perpetrators of human rights violations become eligible for censure and sanction. In terms of victims, Hampton aptly notes that human rights abuses not only harm victims but also communicate the message that victims are not entitled to better treatment. Wrongdoing constitutes a failure to acknowledge the dignity of moral agents, and the intrinsic constraints and demands on the behavior of others that recognizing and respecting the dignity of agents place on others. By responding to victims, we recognize that it was agents who were wronged, and that agency generates a moral duty to respond.

Theories of retributive and corrective justice also correctly recognize that not only must there be a response to victims or perpetrators of wrongdoing but also any such response must be in some sense fitting or apt. One dimension of fittingness is whether a response to wrongdoing facilitates the widely recognized victim- and perpetrator-oriented moral objectives of such responses. The literature in moral and political philosophy on responding to wrongdoing and the literature on transitional justice empha-size a similar, broad set of such moral aims. With responses to perpetrators, the overarching moral aims of responses are repudiation of the wrong and accountability for those responsible for such wrongs.[3] With responses to

---

[3] Walker, "Restorative Justice," 383; Bennett, Christopher, *The Apology Ritual: A Philosophical Theory of Punishment* (Cambridge: Cambridge University Press, 2008). On repudiation as important, see Duff, Antony, *Punishment, Communication and Community* (Oxford: Oxford University Press, 2001); Duff, Antony, *Answering for Crime: Responsibility and Liability in the Criminal Law* (Oxford: Hart Publishing, 2007); Minow, Martha, *Between Vengeance and Forgiveness: Facing History after Genocide and Mass Violence* (Boston, MA: Beacon Press, 1998); Radzik, *Making Amends*; Nick Smith, *I Was Wrong* (New York: Cambridge University Press, 2008); Smith, Nick, *Justice through Apologies: Remorse, Reform, and Punishment* (Cambridge: Cambridge University Press, 2014); Walker, *Moral Repair*; International Center for Transitional Justice, "From Rejection

victims, the overarching aims are acknowledgment of the past wrong, recognition of the status of victims as moral agents who are rights bearers,[4] as well as members of a political community, and reparation.[5] A shared moral objective of responses to both perpetrators and victims is nonrecurrence.[6] In Sections 2, 3, and 4, I fill out the meaning of each of these objectives in the context of responses to victims and perpetrators of normalized collective and political wrongdoing.

Responses to wrongdoing involve interpersonal interactions among agents. A second dimension of fittingness is relational. Specifically, judgments of whether a response is or is not appropriate are influenced by the relationship between the responder (e.g., victim, perpetrator, or third party) and the subject of the response (e.g., victim, perpetrator, or third party).[7] This is because only individuals in certain relationships have the standing or authority to issue certain forms of responses to wrongdoing. The form of response and the standing to respond at all and/or in particular ways are interwoven.

Christopher Kutz provides a very simple but useful example to illustrate the influence of relationships on judgments of the appropriateness or fitness of a response to wrongdoing. Consider a case in which I break my neighbor's vase through carelessness. We generally recognize that my neighbor is entitled to feel resentment toward me and to make a certain range of moral demands, including seeking an apology or compensation from me. By contrast, it is inappropriate for onlookers who witness or hear about my action to feel resentment, though they may be indignant. Like most theorists, Kutz recognizes that resentment is a reactive attitude appropriate for victims to express toward perpetrators; indignation is the reactive attitude that is appropriate for third parties to wrongdoing to express

---

to Redress: Overcoming Legacies of Conflict-Related Sexual Violence in Northern Uganda," October 2015, www.ictj.org/publication/rejection-redress-overcoming-legacies-conflict-sexualviolence-northern-uganda.

[4] Roht-Arriaza, Naomi and Katharine Orlovsky, "A Complementary Relationship: Reparations and Development," in *Transitional Justice and Development: Making Connections*, ed. Pablo de Greiff and Roger Duthie, 170–213 (New York: Social Science Research Council, 2009).

[5] Walker, "Restorative Justice," 383; Blustein, Jeffrey, *Moral Demands of Memory* (New York: Oxford University Press, 2008); Blustein, Jeffrey, "Human Rights and the Internationalization of Memory," *Journal of Social Philosophy* 43, no. 1 (2012): 19–32; Hampton, "Correcting Harms"; Haldemann, "Another Kind of Justice"; Gray, "Extraordinary Justice"; Smith, *I Was Wrong*; ICTJ, "From Rejection to Redress."

[6] Radzik, *Making Amends*; Smith, *I Was Wrong*; Walker, *Moral Repair*; de Greiff, "Theorizing Transitional Justice."

[7] On the relational dimension of different actors' appropriate and inappropriate responses, see Kutz, *Complicity*; Maibom, Heidi, "The Descent of Shame," *Philosophy and Phenomenological Research* 80, no. 3 (May 2010): 566–94.

toward perpetrators. As Kutz's distinction between those who do and do not have the standing to feel resentment indicates, appropriate reactive attitudes are influenced by roles and relationships.[8] Tasioulas makes similar distinctions in his discussion of appropriate responses to an individual who has violated the human rights of another without justification or excuse. Third-party bystanders may blame the perpetrator, while the victim of the human rights violation may react with resentment. The perpetrator may respond in turn to his own failure with guilt or self-blame.[9] Guilt would be an inappropriate reactive attitude for the victim to have toward herself, and blame would be inappropriate for third parties to express to the victim. The category of third parties may not be uniform, but may in some cases be a category within which we can make further distinctions. Kutz, for example, argues that those who bore direct witness to the event "are probably warranted" in different sorts of responses than those who hear about it secondhand.[10]

The overall character of the particular relationship will also influence judgments of fittingness. What counts as a fitting or appropriate response is informed not just by the relationship that wrongdoing creates (e.g., between victim and perpetrator, or between witness and perpetrator) but also by the relationship that existed prior to the harm or wrong. As Kutz puts it, "The moral relations that make up the everyday troubles of life are, essentially, relations between well-defined roles and characters: colleagues, buyers and sellers, supervisors and subordinates, parents and children. Moral disturbances in these relations – disagreements, betrayals, self-dealing – can only be thought through, and responded to, by reference to the grainy texture of those very relations."[11] The implications of this point are significant in transitional contexts. It suggests that we cannot define the appropriate backward-looking way to hold those implicated in past wrongdoing accountable without taking into account the existing structure of relationships within which this wrongdoing occurred, which is a structure of pervasive inequality in the relationships among citizens and between citizens and officials. Similarly, the demands that victims make must be shaped by the broader relational context within which wrongdoing happened.

In the context of pervasive structural inequality, the structure of relationships is generally morally unjustifiable precisely because of the absence, erosion, or diminished character of the respect for agency and reciprocity

[8] Kutz, *Complicity*, 59.   [9] Tasioulas, "On the Nature of Human Rights," 28.
[10] Kutz, *Complicity*, 21–22.   [11] Ibid., 25.

governing interaction. This background context of injustice alters what constitutes a reasonable response to specific wrongs. For example, and as noted in the Introduction, the fittingness of forgiveness as a response to wrongdoing is most plausible in the context of normal personal relationships. In such relationships wrongdoing is the exception or aberration, not the rule. This makes the claim that an individual who was wronged should overcome his or her resentment through forgiveness reasonable and appropriate. Through forgiveness a valuable relationship can be restored. However, in transitional contexts the conception of a prior normal acceptable political relationship that has been ruptured by wrongdoing does not pertain.[12] Rather than being reasonable and appropriate, urging forgiveness and the overcoming of resentment in contexts where wrongdoing is systematic and ongoing seems at best naive and at worst a form of complicity in the maintenance of oppression and injustice.

In addition to examining whether a response to wrongdoing facilitates the general moral functions of such responses and is appropriate given the relationship between responder and the subject of a response, the nature of the wrong itself is a third factor that influences judgments of the fittingness or aptness of a response to wrongdoing. Responses must be apt in the sense of accurately identifying and appropriately dealing with the actual harms caused by wrongdoing. The harm and damage to acknowledge will vary depending on the nature of the wrong at issue. Harms can differ in both type and magnitude. It is intuitively clear that the harm caused by burglary is not identical to the harm caused by rape. The former wrong entails loss of goods and violation of property claims, while the latter involves a form of physical assault that violates rights to physical integrity, is frequently traumatizing and has other important psychological ramifications, and can lead to social ostracism. Appropriate reparations for harms stemming from rape will be different than for land dispossession, and reparations need not take the form of monetary payment in either case.

The specific kind of wrongfulness being responded to is an additional salient dimension of the nature of the wrong. Wrongdoing violates different rights, and through such violations communicates different messages about what treatment for the victim is taken to be permissible. The reasons

---

[12] Murphy, *Moral Theory*. There may also be personal relationships in which the idea of a prior normal acceptable relationship does not hold as well. Abusive relationships seem a paradigm case. However, such relationships seem the exception and are not typically treated as constituting the cases that should serve as the starting point for theoretical reflection on how to appropriately respond in the aftermath of wrongdoing. Instead, we are inclined to judge that forgiveness, while normally appropriate, is not appropriate in such cases.

for which wrong was done will also shape its wrongfulness. Responding in a fitting manner to the acts of terrorism carried out by ISIS for political reasons in Paris on November 14, 2015, which left 129 dead, will require engagement with the political dimension of the wrong. This engagement will be different from the engagement needed when responding to the act of the serial murderer Gary Ridgway, nicknamed the Green River Killer, who was responsible for the murder of at least seventy women during the 1980s and 1990s and committed these crimes for individual and personal reasons. The importance of this distinction is reflected in protests among prisoners classified as ordinary criminals when the acts for which they are being punished were political in nature. In Northern Ireland prisoners, including most famously Bobby Sands, conducted a hunger strike to protest the removal of their Special Category Status as prisoners. Special Category Status was granted to prisoners convicted for "Troubles"-related offenses. With this status, prisoners were recognized as de facto prisoners of war, provided with protections outlined in the Geneva Conventions, and not required to wear prison uniforms. The British Labour secretary eventually phased out this status in 1976. After this phasing out, a number of prisoners whose convictions were Troubles related refused to wear the new prison uniform, arguing that they were political prisoners and not ordinary criminals. By 1978 approximately three hundred Irish Republican prisoners were participating in the blanket protest, which was followed by a hunger strike. The strike was aimed at forcing the British government to re-recognize these prisoners as political prisoners and not ordinary criminals.[13] Implicit in the message of the hunger strike was that the British government's response was inappropriate because it was based on a misrepresentation of the nature of the wrong for which they were being punished.

In taking account the nature of the wrong, responses must be sensitive to whether a perpetrator was acting individually or as part of a group, and whether the harm stemming from wrongdoing was limited to individuals or was experienced by groups of which the individual is a part. Indeed, developing a legal doctrine that appropriately captures the collective dimension of many of the crimes with which international criminal law deals is the subject of extensive discussion and debate in that field.[14]

---

[13] Mulraney, Frances, "Leader of 1981 IRA hunger strike, Bobby Sands, Died 34 Years Ago Today," *Irish Central*, May 5, 2015, www.irishcentral.com/roots/history/Leader-of-1981-IRA-hunger-strike-Bobby-Sands-died-34-years-ago-today.html. The status was eventually reintroduced.

[14] In identifying potential candidates for responsibility, Kutz distinguishes between what he calls the *basis of accountability* and the *object of accountability*. The basis of accountability specifies the

Informing such debates is the recognition that any process for dealing with responses to wrongdoing must be such that there is a process for determining the guilt of perpetrators. Such processes are designed to establish to a sufficient degree of confidence that those to whom we are responding do in fact fall into the category under consideration. It ensures to a sufficiently satisfactory degree that we are in fact responding to the actions committed by or harms suffered by particular individuals. The burden of proof for guilt and procedural safeguards are especially demanding, and rightly so, in the case of criminal trials because of the consequences that follow a guilty verdict. The loss of liberty that is typically constitutive of criminal punishment is serious, and should only be visited on someone for whom a rigorous standard of proof has been met. Similarly, in civil law there are standards of proof to be met to demonstrate that the defendant ought to be held legally liable for the damages suffered by the plaintiff. The background idea at work is that respect for the dignity and moral worth of individuals that stems from being a moral agent is shown in part through respect for due process.

Debates about the appropriate standard of proof to use to establish the status of an individual as a perpetrator and/or as a victim attempt to deal with two challenges that come from somewhat opposite directions in the literature on transitional justice. From one direction is the concern about how to balance the risk of impunity against the risk of guilt by association. Especially in contexts of criminal trials, there is a worry that the law lacks an adequate standard of proof to fairly secure conviction of perpetrators of normalized collective and political wrongdoing. In discussing the doctrine of joint criminal enterprise (JCE), legal scholar Jens David Ohlin worries that it is insufficiently nuanced in its understanding of liability. According to JCE, when an organized group with a common plan commits a crime each individual member can be held responsible for the crimes the group commits. Ohlin writes, "The collective moral guilt suggested by these crimes cannot be used as a justification to blindly impose criminal liability to all members of a conspiracy, regardless of their level of participation."[15] Similarly, Allison Marston Danner and Jenny Martinez are concerned that

---

conditions that need to be satisfied for an individual to be eligible to be held accountable for a given harm; the basis is individualistic. Specifically, according to the complicity principle Kutz defends, individuals become eligible to be held accountable by virtue of what they do, in particular when they "intentionally participate in the wrong." Here intentional participation is understood broadly to include cases of unstructured collective harms. See Kutz, *Complicity*, 115–22.

[15] Ohlin, Jens David, "Three Conceptual Problems with the Doctrine of Joint Criminal Enterprise," *Journal of International Criminal Justice* 5 (2007): 74.

JCE, as well as the doctrine of command responsibility (whereby supervisors can be held liable for the conduct of their subordinates), "if not limited appropriately, have the potential to lapse into forms of guilt by association, thereby undermining the legitimacy and the ultimate effectiveness of international criminal law."[16] A related worry is sometimes expressed about truth commissions and reparations programs. For named perpetrators in the reports of truth commissions, there are worries that individuals will be named unjustly in the absence of adequate corroboration of claims about their responsibility for wrongdoing. For reparations programs, a worry is that reparations will be granted to individuals who were not victims.

At the same time, there are concerns that impunity will not be countered if there is an overly rigorous standard of proof.[17] Setting a demanding standard may guard against guilt by association, but at the risk of presenting an insuperable bar to actually reaching a guilty verdict, especially for those most responsible in an intuitive sense for normalized collective and political wrongdoing. The difficulty stems not only from the paucity of evidence that may be available, especially in contexts in which evidence has been systematically destroyed, nor does it only stem from the difficulty of getting witnesses to testify in particular cases. More fundamentally, it stems from limits in the ability of existing legal doctrines of responsibility to adequately cover collective wrongdoing. In debates about the proper legal doctrine to utilize in dealing with wrongs with a collective dimension, the discussion centers on the relevance of causation. The necessity of causation for liability is controversial because in many cases of wrongdoing causation is overdetermined.[18]

---

[16] Danner and Martinez, "Guilty Associations," 79.

[17] Nancy Combs is an important critic in this context. See her *Guilty Pleas in International Criminal Law* (Stanford, CA: Stanford University Press, 2007); Combs, Nancy, *Fact-Finding without Facts: The Uncertain Evidentiary Foundations of International Criminal Convictions* (New York: Cambridge University Press, 2010).

[18] See Stewart, James, "Overdetermined Atrocities," *Journal of International Criminal Justice* 10 (2012): 1189–1218. It is beyond the scope of this book to resolve the ongoing debates in international criminal law about the appropriate standard for criminal responsibility. What I want to note, however, is that the standard of proof need not be identical across all range of responses. What standard of proof is appropriate for a given process may be plausibly seen as a function in part of what is at stake for determining a judgment of guilt or a judgment of being a victim of a harm eligible for redress. The more serious the consequences, the more robust the standard of proof may be plausibly taken to be. A concern for agency justifies tying the consequences of a judgment that an individual was a perpetrator or victim to the standard of proof required. The more demanding the terms of holding an individual responsible for a wrong, the heavier the burden to demonstrate we are not erring in our process.

The fourth factor that influences our evaluation of appropriate and fitting responses to victims and perpetrators is culture. The cultural context in which a particular response takes place matters in evaluations of its appropriateness. In the case of the moral objectives of responses to wrongdoing, cultural variation will exist because many of the moral aims of responses to victims and perpetrators are expressive in nature; they involve communicating a particular moral message about what happened in the past. Successful expressions of moral censure or acknowledgement of wrongfulness, as well as successful recognition of an individual as an equal member of a political community will be influenced by cultural norms for communicating censure, acknowledgment, and recognition. Evaluations of whether morally appropriate acknowledgment of the past occurred should be informed by whether a response could plausibly be seen to have such a particular moral meaning, given the cultural context in which it took place. Cultural variation can be an important source of conflict and potential misunderstanding. Conflict can arise because within any particular community there will be contestation over culture itself. Misunderstanding is likely in cases of wrongdoing that occurred across cultures.

Not only will considerations of culture affect whether particular responses achieve their overarching moral aims; cultural variation will also impact the nature of the harm victims experienced or suffered as a consequence of a particular violation of human rights. For example, the physical consequences of rape for two individuals may be similar, but the social consequences of being a victim of rape may vary quite significantly. Rape may have the consequence of serious coercion being brought to bear on the victim to marry her rapist in one culture, while that coercion does not exist in another. The degree and kind of social ostracism experienced as a rape victim may vary as well.

The *jus in bello* analogue moral requirements of transitional justice specify the criteria that a response to wrongdoing must satisfy for it to be intrinsically fitting or appropriate. These requirements are predicated on a recognition that the justice of responses to wrongdoing is not only a function of whether a given response is instrumentally effective in contributing to the *jus ad bellum* aim of relational transformation, though the justice of a response is also necessarily a function of this consideration. As the discussion in this section suggests, there will be a range of appropriate or fitting responses to victims and/or perpetrators of wrongdoing in the circumstances of transitional justice; that is, there is no single uniquely warranted or required response to victims and perpetrators of wrongdoing.[19] We may, for example, hold a perpetrator accountable through the judgments we make, our reactive attitudes, through social punishment, legal punishment, and/or by holding them liable for compensation or reparation. There may be permissible cultural variation in the form of appropriate or fitting responses to victims and perpetrators as well.

At the same time it is important to recognize that there will be a limit to this range. The four general factors that inform judgments of the inherent appropriateness of a response as a response to victims or perpetrators of wrongdoing provide theoretical resources for specifying this limit. The first factor is whether a response facilitates the widely recognized moral purposes of responding to victims and perpetrators, including, for example, acknowledgment and recognition. The second factor is the relationship between the subject of a response (e.g., perpetrator or victim) and the respondent (e.g., perpetrator, victim, or third party). What matters is who the respondent is and to whom the response is directed since only some respondents have the standing to react in certain ways, such as through specific reactive attitudes, to particular subjects. Furthermore, as my discussion of forgiveness emphasized, the existing terms of interaction between subject and respondent influence evaluations of the fittingness of a particular response. The third factor informing the *jus in bello* analogue justice of a response is the nature of the wrong itself. Here both the harm and wrongfulness of the violation of human rights under consideration as well as the political or personal character and the collective or individual nature of the wrong done are salient. Finally, the cultural context in which the wrong occurred and in which a response is offered matters. When a mismatch occurs between a response and the factors listed in the preceding, then the moral aim that a response was designed to facilitate will not be achieved and the justice of the response will be compromised.

The just pursuit of transitional justice, the *jus in bello* analogue, requires responses to wrongdoing to be fitting or appropriate responses to perpetrators and victims. This section outlined the four factors influencing the appropriateness or fittingness of responses.[20] In Sections 2, 3, and 4, I argue that in the circumstances of transitional justice holism in the process of designing and implementing responses to perpetrators and

---

[19] Kutz argues for this assumption drawing on the relational dimension of responses in *Complicity*, 19.

[20] These factors are also salient when evaluating the inherent justice of responses to wrongdoing in the circumstances of stable democracies. For example, in stable democracies the paradigm wrongdoing of interest is individual and personal, and appropriate responses need to take into account such differences in the nature of the wrongs to which a response is aimed.

victims is necessary. That is, the ability of any single response to victims or perpetrators of wrongdoing to satisfy the *jus in bello* analogue of transitional justice will be affected by which other responses to wrongdoing are pursued. I argue for the *jus in bello* analogue aspect of holism through a discussion of cases in which a nonholistic approach to wrongdoing in the circumstances of transitional justice failed to achieve the generally recognized moral aims of responses to perpetrators and victims of wrongdoing.

Victims

My first case study looks at the absence of the *jus in bello* analogue dimension of holism in Uganda and draws on a recent report by the ICTJ on abducted girls and women and their children who were born from sexual violence. The report focuses on northern Uganda, specifically the Acholi, Lango, Teso, and West Nile subregions, and evaluates the extent to which redress has or has not been provided to this particular group of victims.[21] In April 2015 the authors of the report consulted with 249 individuals, including children born from sexual violence and their fathers and mothers, as well as relatives, local leaders, and government officials. A range of groups were responsible for sexual violence, including the UNLA/UNRFII, Lord's Resistance Army (LRA), Uganda People's Defense Force (UPDF) and National Resistance Army (NRA), UPA, and the Arrow Boys militia. In some cases a woman suffered violations at the hands of more than one group. The UDPF and NRA, responsible for protecting communities from the LRA, were instead accused of raping women. Women in displacement camps in particular underwent sexual exploitation for food.

It is estimated that since 1986 fifty-four thousand to seventy-five thousand individuals, including twenty-five thousand to thirty-five thousand children, have been abducted by the LRA.[22] Secure Livelihoods Research Consortium (SLRC) estimated that three thousand to eight thousand households in the Acholi and Lango areas include a child born from rape.[23] Many of those kidnapped were subject to repeated sexual violence, in some cases being used as sex slaves and in others as "wives" of a particular rebel. According to the ICTJ, the "systematic abduction of females [was]

---

[21] ICTJ, "From Rejection to Redress," 3. The report noted that because of barriers to speaking with women whose children were born from violations by government forces, the majority of women interviewed had children through violations from rebel forces.
[22] Ibid., 5, citing Berkeley study.   [23] Ibid., 6.

followed by forced marriage, rape, and forced pregnancy leading to forced child bearing."[24] Girls and young women between ten and eighteen years old were particularly targeted by the LRA. Following their abduction experiences, these women in many cases returned to their home villages with children born from violence.

The Ugandan government passed the Amnesty Act of 2000 as a means to ending the ongoing conflict in northern Uganda. As part of its terms, all combatants engaged in armed conflict were eligible for immunity from prosecution if they agreed to give up their weapons. An Amnesty Commission was established and charged with demobilization, granting amnesty, and the reintegration of "reporters" (the label used for those who came to the commission and repudiated the rebellion).[25] Reporters were given an amnesty certificate and reinsertion kit, which consisted of a cash payment, information about available reintegration services, and household items.[26] In practice, the greatest emphasis of the Amnesty Commission was on granting legal immunity from prosecution. Indeed, partly as a function of its limited funding and capacity, many received their reintegration kit only after they had returned home. Those eligible to participate in the program included abducted women.

The Amnesty Commission constituted a third-party response by the Ugandan government to the abducted women and the children born from their abduction. As noted in Section 1, there are three widely recognized general moral functions of responses by third parties to victims: acknowledgment, recognition, and reparation. In the following sections, I first discuss acknowledgment of the past, followed by reparation, and finally recognition. My discussion concentrates on the ways in which its failure in satisfying these victim-oriented moral claims can be traced to an absence of holism.

Acknowledgment of the Past

Acknowledgment of the past entails admitting (a) what happened, (b) that what happened to victims was wrong and unjustified, (c) that what happened damaged victims in particular ways, and (d) one's role in the wrongdoing.[27]

---

[24] Ibid., 4. [25] Ibid., 9. [26] Ibid.

[27] Walker, "Restorative Justice," 383; Blustein, *Moral Demands*. Issue (a) is often enormously significant in the circumstances of transitional justice. Very often victims and their family members do not know exactly what happened to victims or who was responsible for the wrong suffered. Queries to government officials may be met with denials either that wrong has been done

The basic premise of the Amnesty Commission failed to satisfy (b). To apply for amnesty necessarily implied that these women were guilty of a criminal wrong for which they would otherwise be liable. The commission defined the women who had been abducted as complicit in their own abuse. They were responsible for allowing or permitting the abduction that took place. The commission thus failed to acknowledge that these women were victims, not complicit perpetrators in wrongdoing. Interestingly, many women who were victims of sexual violence and bore children rejected the basic frame of the commission itself. The ICTJ report found that a large percentage of women did not report to the Amnesty Commission. One reason many women did not report was that they viewed themselves as victims of sexual violence, and neither perpetrators nor collaborators of wrongdoing.[28] In addition, many women did not participate in the proceedings because they worried about the stigma that would follow them if they were identified as a reporter, and consequently perceived as "perpetrators or rebel collaborators."[29] The fear of stigma turned out to be well founded and unavoidable even for those women who did not report. Members of the broader community targeted their resentment about the ways in which the conflict had impacted them and resentment about their own poverty on these women and children.[30] By failing to acknowledge these women as victims, the commission also thereby failed to acknowledge that the women had been treated in morally egregious ways by those responsible for their abduction and subsequent sexual violations. Proper acknowledgment of the past includes expressing that what happened to victims was morally wrong because it was incompatible with the treatment fitting or appropriate to moral agents.

To achieve (b) in Uganda it would not have been sufficient to revise the structure of the Amnesty Commission. The failure to acknowledge that the women who were abducted were victims and had been wronged in ways for which they were not responsible went beyond the structure of the Amnesty Commission. Other kinds of stigmatization of the women occurred, kinds that the Amnesty Commission could not have forestalled merely by changing the categorization of the women from reporters to victims.

---

or that the state was responsible for the wrongdoing that took place. Reflecting the basic importance of knowing what took place, the "right to truth" is an emerging rule in international law. Viaene and Brems's "Transitional Justice and Cultural Contexts," 201, discusses this, citing Inter-American Court of Human Rights, *Trujillo-Oroza v. Bolivia*, February 27, 2002, IACHR database, www .corteidh.or.cr.

[28] ICTJ, "From Rejection to Redress," 8.   [29] Ibid., 9–10.   [30] Ibid., 22.

The report notes the general stigmatization of women in Uganda who have children outside marriage.[31] Compounding this stigmatization was the fact that many within the communities to which the mothers returned held the women responsible for the condition they were forced into involuntarily. The abducted women were labeled prostitutes; in this way these women – and their female children who were often given the same label – were penalized for being victims of kidnapping and sexual violence.[32] Although no woman (or man) merits being raped or abducted, blaming women for being raped is a widespread phenomenon, and a gendered aspect of existing circumstances of pervasive structural inequality. Such inequality compounded and entrenched the consequences of being a victim.

Implicitly or explicitly blaming women for the abuse to which they were subject is also a way of denying the wrongness of the treatment to which they were subject. By blaming women for the treatment they experienced, the wrongness and impermissibility of that treatment can be diminished. Insofar as wrongdoing buttresses a false conception of the victim's value, failing to counter this false conception in turn leaves women vulnerable to being subject to similar treatment by others.[33] Acknowledgment of the wrongfulness of the sexual violence experienced by the abducted women thus required tending to the social norms and beliefs that lead members of a community to blame or otherwise stigmatize victims for the treatment to which they were subject. In contexts of normalized collective and political wrongdoing and pervasive structural inequality, the failure to acknowledge the wrongness of the behavior to which victims were subject characteristically requires going beyond the actions of a single perpetrator to address the basic norms and institutional rules governing interaction.

Recognition of the Status of Victims as Moral Agents and Members of the Political Community

The third moral objective of responses to victims by third parties is recognition of the status of victims as moral agents and members of the political community. The Amnesty Commission was not well situated to

---

[31] Ibid., 16.
[32] Women being blamed for being raped is a widespread and long-standing phenomenon, with women being seen as polluted and ruined rather than as "wrongdoers."
[33] Hampton, "Correcting Harms," 1670.

foster this recognition.[34] Recognition of victims not just as moral agents and rights bearers but also as equal citizens within a political community is characteristically critical in the circumstances of transitional justice. As Frank Haldemann argues, political wrongs are public acts communicating to victims that their views will not be heard and that they are not full members of a community.[35] Very often part of what normalized collective and political wrongdoing aims to accomplish is the removal or marginalization of a certain group or groups of citizens from the political arena. Reiterating the standing of victims as citizens of a political community – and *equal* citizens – is critical to repudiate the wrongdoing that occurred and its impact.

Broad social stigmatization crucially undermined the recognition of such women and their children as equal members of the political community.[36] More formal forms of recognition of citizenship were negatively impacted as well, especially for the children born from conflict. Mothers whose children are children of rebels face increased problems in proving the nationality of their children. The ICTJ report notes that a "significant number" of children whose fathers were LRA members did not have a birth registration, which precluded them from receiving a national identity card and claiming rights to free education, voting, and health care.[37]

Reparation

The Amnesty Commission failed to satisfy the condition (c), acknowledgment, which concerns recognizing the ways in which wrongdoing damaged victims. Failing to accurately understand the damage victims experienced in turn led to a flawed program of repair. Reparation is a moral objective of responses because to acknowledge that what was done was wrong does not remedy many of the sources of damage created by wrongdoing and harm suffered by wrongdoing's victims. In the following I discuss how the restitution measures offered reflect the limitations of the acknowledgment of the ways in which wrongdoing damaged victims and the Amnesty Commission's attempts at repair.

One general limitation with the reparations offered was conceptual. The restitution kit provided by the commission was not defined as a form of reparations; thus the restitution kit itself did not acknowledge that the

---

[34] ICTJ, "From Rejection to Redress," 2; Walker, "Restorative Justice," 383.
[35] Haldemann, "Another Kind of Justice."   [36] ICTJ, "From Rejection to Redress," 2.
[37] Ibid., 17.

women receiving the kit were damaged in any way by having been wronged. Another structural flaw in the program, according to the ICTJ report, was that it did not include the children themselves who were born from conflict.[38] Such children suffered significant harms by being born from sexual violence, as I document here, but were not considered in the transitional justice scheme established.

Especially important for my purposes, the ICJT report documents in extensive detail the reasons why a restitution program – even if it was conceptualized properly as offering reparations to victims of sexual violence, even if it included children, and even if it properly factored in variations among victims (such as whether they bore children as a result of their violations) – would have been inadequate to fully repair and acknowledge the damage stemming from wrongdoing. This is because of the ways in which the existing circumstances of pervasive structural inequality compounded and entrenched the consequences of being a victim of collective and political wrongdoing. The social isolation and social punishment these women and their children experienced upon their return, coupled with existing pervasive structural inequality, left many women and their children in a position where they continue to struggle to have access to the basic necessities of life.[39] The cumulative impact of the collective and political wrongdoing perpetrated against northern Ugandan women committed in a context of pervasive structural inequality is summarized by the ICTJ report thus: "While the majority of families in northern Uganda struggle to meet their basic needs following two decades of conflict, recent studies have found that women and girls who experienced sexual violence and/or who returned from the LRA with children were among the most vulnerable categories of war-affected people across northern Uganda in relation to most measures of well-being, including wealth; food security; physical, mental and emotional health; access to health care; and experience of crime in the last three years."[40] The victims remained the poorest individuals within their communities.

During the period of their abduction these women missed out on opportunities for education and skill acquisition that could have enabled them to secure employment. Other pathways to securing increased resources, including, importantly, marriage, were often foreclosed owing to their abduction and sexual abuse. Women faced a stigma associated with having been abducted and abused, and reduced marriageability because of the children they now had. Stigma stemming from abduction,

[38] Ibid., 8–9.   [39] Ibid., 1.   [40] Ibid., 15.

rape, and/or from being born to a rebel parent created multiple additional burdens for women and their children; indeed, it was characterized by Ugandans interviewed for the ICTJ report as "one of the greatest problems facing the children and their mothers today."[41] Those marriages that did occur posed an increased risk of abuse and neglect of women and their children.[42]

Access to land is a critical pathway to some sort of financial support in Uganda. Remarriage is one main way women can gain greater access to land and resources since, as the ICTJ report notes, men disproportionately own land in Uganda. However, as just stated, social norms and stigma pose a significant obstacle to the realization of this option. Moreover, for those women who were single heads of households with land, the legal system offers limited remedy for women whose land or property rights are violated or contested.[43] Consequently, real access to land directly by women who were heads of households is limited.[44]

The consequences for mothers facing stigma, lack of access to land, and subsequent poverty were then passed down to their children. As the ICTJ report notes, "For many children, not knowing their father leads to a situation where they cannot access land and thus are not able to earn an income. As a result, they cannot pay their school fees or courses in skills training, leaving them with very limited opportunities for the future."[45] Even for those who can afford schooling, success in school is more difficult because of the ostracism they face as a result of being children of rebels.[46]

No program of reparations could have repaired the layered damage that the wrongdoing to which abducted women were subject faced. Any such program that focused narrowly on the physical and psychological harms suffered through repeated sexual abuse would fail to capture the social consequences of returning to a community in which being a victim of such crimes entails loss of the basic recognition of oneself as a member of one's community. Ignoring the normalized character of wrongdoing that is collective and political can lead to inadequate attempts to reassert and recognize the equal standing of victims as members of the moral community and citizens. Only broader initiatives that deal with the reform of land rights and their recognition, an accurate characterization of the abduction and experiences surrounding a victim of sexual violence, and countering obstacles to the recognition of women and their children as victims of wrongdoing and as equal members of the political community could have

---

[41] Ibid., 21.   [42] Ibid., 18–19.   [43] Ibid., 2.   [44] Ibid., 15.   [45] Ibid., 17.   [46] Ibid., 20.

mitigated the damage from wrongdoing.[47] Absent such measures, "the mothers and their children are re-victimized," as the ICTJ report puts it.[48]

The Ugandan experience illustrates the importance of holism in responses to victims of wrongdoing. When it comes to reparations programs, as Peter Dixon notes, "there will always be forms of harm, types of violence and immediate needs that fall outside the boundaries of any given reparations program" in the circumstances of transitional justice.[49] Dixon's quote points to the multiple kinds of wrongs that must be dealt with in the circumstances of transitional justice that no single response can feasibly take up. Truth commissions have a circumscribed mandate, circumscribed in terms of type of violation and time period within which such violations took place. Reparations programs are circumscribed in similar ways. However, even for those victims included within the scope of a single program and those wrongs addressed, no single reparations program, for example, can fully repair harms experienced by victims of normalized collective and political wrongdoing in part because the circumstance of pervasive structural inequality. Pervasive structural inequality, as demonstrated in the preceding, compounds the direct harms stemming from particular violations of human rights. Pervasive structural inequality can also result in wrongdoing having broader social consequences that prevent or impede recognition of victims as equal members of a political community. Reparations programs are limited in their ability to deal with the social norms and social consequences of being a victim that are bound up with pervasive structural inequality. To adequately achieve the reparatory and recognition aims of a *jus in bello* analogue of transitional justice requires forms of response that address this larger context.

Perpetrators[50]

Section 2 considered limitations in transitional justice from the perspective of the moral aims associated with responding to victims of wrongdoing. My example in this section traces the consequences of the absence of holism in responses to perpetrators. I consider the use of international criminal trials as a third-party response to perpetrators of wrongdoing in

---

[47] Walker, "Restorative Justice," 378. Walker cites de Greiff, "Justice and Reparations."

[48] ICTJ, "From Rejection to Redress," 7.

[49] Dixon, Peter, "Reparations, Assistance, and the Experience of Justice: Lessons from Colombia and the Democratic Republic of the Congo," *International Journal of Transitional Justice* 10 (2016): 88–107.

[50] I am grateful to Jelena Subotic for her comments on this section.

the former Yugoslavia. My discussion highlights why without multiple, coordinated responses to wrongdoing, the wrongdoing being acknowledged is at risk of being distorted. Trials individualize guilt, and without additional responses the complicity of ordinary citizens and government officials gets obscured. Furthermore, individual trials cannot counter or reverse the normalization of wrongdoing, which is necessary for nonrecurrence to be achieved; this requires relational transformation which individual trials are insufficient to promote.

The International Criminal Tribunal for the Former Yugoslavia (ICTY) was established in 1993 in The Hague by the United Nations Security Council to deal with war crimes committed during the wars in the Balkans following the breakup of Yugoslavia in the 1990s. The ICTY was the first international war crimes tribunal to take place since the Nuremburg and Tokyo tribunals following World War II. It was also the first tribunal established by the United Nations. The mandate of the ICTY covered war crimes committed in "1991–2001 against members of various ethnic groups in Croatia, Bosnia and Herzegovina, Serbia, Kosovo and the Former Yugoslav Republic of Macedonia."[51] A range of actors composed the more than 160 charged, from midlevel leaders in the military and police to heads of state and state ministers.

One especially prominent trial was that of Radovan Karadžić, who both helped establish and served as president of the Serbian Democratic Party (SDS).[52] Karadžić also served as president of what was called the Serbian Republic of Bosnia and Herzegovina (later Republika Srpska [RS]), first as part of a three-person presidency and then as exclusive president and head of the armed forces. Following the warrant issued for his arrest, Karadžić evaded arrest for eleven years before finally being caught and arrested in 2008. Karadžić was charged on eleven counts, consisting of genocide (two counts), crimes against humanity (five counts), and violations of the laws or customs of war (four counts).[53] These charges covered crimes committed in Bosnian municipalities, the siege of Sarajevo, hostage taking of UN peacekeepers, and the Srebrenica massacre.[54] Opening statements for the trial began in October 2009, and closing arguments were heard in September and October 2014.[55] In March 2016, eight years after his arrest, Karadžić was acquitted on one count of genocide in seven Bosnian municipalities other than Srebrenica,

[51] See www.icty.org/en/about.   [52] See www.icty.org/x/cases/karadzic/cis/en/cis_karadzic_en.pdf.
[53] See www.icty.org/x/cases/karadzic/tjug/en/160324_judgement_summary.pdf.
[54] Milanovic, "ICTY Convicts Radovan Karadzic."   [55] Ibid.

but convicted on all remaining charges including genocide in Srebrenica. He was sentenced to forty years in prison.

As detailed in Section 1, there are three overarching objectives of responses by third parties such as the ICTY to perpetrators of wrongdoing: repudiation, accountability, and nonrecurrence.[56] Repudiation entails rejecting the permissibility of the treatment the victim experienced.[57] Repudiation presupposes acknowledgment that wrongdoing occurred; thus denial of the fact that certain events took place is incompatible with repudiation. Acknowledging that *wrongdoing* occurred requires condemning as morally impermissible what is being acknowledged. In repudiation, acknowledgment of the fact that the victim experienced certain treatment at the hands of the perpetrator(s) is coupled with condemnation of what took place.

Beyond repudiation, responses aim at holding perpetrators to account for what they did.[58] What does it mean to hold someone to account for what they did? At a minimum, it is to judge that the perpetrator is responsible for the wrong to which the response is directed. Through processes of accountability we recognize that what was done was done *by the perpetrator* we are holding accountable, either acting alone or in conjunction with others. To hold to account is to demand that perpetrators assume responsibility for the wrong they committed. At a minimum, assumption of responsibility can entail that a perpetrator acknowledge his or her responsibility for wrongdoing. It was *his* or *her* actions that wronged and harmed a victim or victims. Beyond this, to hold a perpetrator to account may entail encouraging or requiring a perpetrator to repair the consequences of the damage and harm stemming from the wrong done. Through repudiation and accountability, responses aim to provide perpetrators with reasons to avoid participation in wrongdoing in the future.[59]

There is a range of forms that third-party responses to perpetrators may take. In the case of reactive attitudes such as indignation, repudiation and accountability come together. Through indignation third parties to wrongdoing express their moral outrage over what occurred, thereby repudiating its permissibility. As with other reactive attitudes, indignation is fundamentally interpersonally oriented. The moral judgment expressed in indignation is coupled with an invitation for the target of this reactive attitude

---

[56] Walker, "Restorative Justice," 383.
[57] On the importance of repudiation, see Hampton, "Correcting Wrongs"; Duff, *Punishment*; Duff, *Answering for Crime*.
[58] Minow, *Between Vengeance and Forgiveness*; Walker, "Restorative Justice."
[59] Kutz, *Complicity*, 123.

to respond, ideally by responding to the emotional appeal with remorse and regret. Beyond reactive attitudes, other forms that responses might take include criminal punishment, social punishment, and requiring private reparations.

Individual criminal trials are lauded as an especially promising way of achieving the objectives of third-party responses to perpetrators of wrong-doing. According to justifications of legal punishment, trials are predicated on recognition of the agency of perpetrators. They focus on specific wrongs in which individual perpetrators are implicated, determine the responsibility of the perpetrator for such wrongs, and hold the perpetrator accountable through the verdict and subsequent punishment. Trials and punishment are taken to express condemnation and repudiation of the crimes for which perpetrators are held liable, the condemnation that the suffering constitutive of punishment following a guilty verdict reinforces.[60] In the following sections, I argue that these potential benefits of trials are unlikely to be realized in the circumstances of transitional justice if trials are pursued as the single form that a response to perpetrators takes.

Accountability

A fitting way of holding perpetrators accountable must be appropriate to the nature of the wrong done. One central concern with pursuing trials in isolation from other mechanisms is that the focus on individual perpetrators obscures the collective character of the wrongs done.

Individual trials are limited in their ability to recognize and take into account the collective nature of wrongdoing. Single trials hold individual perpetrators accountable for their roles in a wrong. Some trials deal with crimes that are collective in nature. However, even when examining the relationship of that perpetrator's actions to the actions of others who were part of a JCE, for example, individual trials, and the narrative of the actions of a single perpetrator on which trials focus, separate perpetrators from the context in which they acted. The trial narrative necessary for conviction thus cannot easily capture the full picture of the conditions that made possible and facilitated the wrongs in which a particular perpetrator was involved.

Unsurprisingly, as a consequence, trials can also strengthen, rather than counter, denial on the part of ordinary citizens and other officials regarding their complicity in wrongdoing. Jelena Subotic notes that both the Serbian

---

[60] This is at the core of expressive accounts of punishment, including Hampton, "Correcting Wrongs"; Duff, *Punishment*.

and Croatian governments framed the war crimes trials that took place after the wars in the former Yugoslavia as responses to "individual, isolated crimes that are removed from Serbian and Croatian state wartime efforts."[61] Through this conceptualization, the role of the state in the wrongs that took place was displaced. This is why in some cases "domestic elites can be enthusiastic supporters of individual human rights trials – not because they want to bring about justice, but because they want to shield the state and society from complicity in past crimes."[62] Similarly, responses to wrongdoing that consist only of trials directed at specific individuals obfuscate the complicity of ordinary citizens in such atrocities, obscuring the larger societal context in which atrocities were planned, supported, and executed. In this way, trials have little prospect of countering denial among citizens about their complicity.[63] Most people who live in regimes of horror are neither leaders nor dissidents; instead, they passively tolerate abuses done to others, or they join in because they themselves are coerced into it or because going along is easier than standing up to the powerful. Against this background, doing the right thing in an abusive regime requires far more courage than doing the right thing in a nonabusive regime. Properly acknowledging wrongdoing entails trying to capture this complex reality.

Isolated trials that address specific wrongs also confront two different kinds of risks that, when realized, undermine the accountability that trials aim to achieve. First, trials deal with a specific scope of wrongs. However, the consequences of other kinds of wrongs with which trials do not characteristically deal, in particular economic wrongdoing, influence the efficacy of trials as a response to wrongdoing. For example, Rueben Carranza examines the relationship between economic wrongdoing in the form of embezzlement and criminal trials, discussing ways that such funds can be used to undermine criminal trials. He cites Liberian Charles Taylor's use of money to fund efforts to threaten witnesses and secure impunity.[64]

---

[61] Subotic, Jelena, "Expanding the Scope of Post-Conflict Justice: Individual, State and Societal Responsibility for Mass Atrocity," *Journal of Peace Research* 48, no. 2 (2011): 157–169, 159. See also Subotic, Jelena, "Legitimacy, Scope and Conflicting Claims on the ICTY: In the Aftermath of *Gotovina, Haradinai and Perisic*," *Journal of Human Rights* 13 (2014): 170–85.

[62] Subotic, "Expanding the Scope," 157.

[63] On the importance of countering such denial, see Leebaw, "Irreconcilable Goals." On the risks of processes such as trials designed to individualize guilt contributing to denial of complicity, see Fletcher and Weinstein, "Violence and Social Repair"; Drumbl, *Atrocity*; Subotic, "Expanding the Scope."

[64] Carranza, Ruben, "Plunder and Pain: Should Transitional Justice Engage with Corruption and Economic Crimes?," *International Journal of Transitional Justice* 2 (2008): 314.

Second, the strong interest among members of transitional societies and the international community in countering impunity can lead to serious pressure being brought to bear to relax procedural restrictions and due-process guarantees in ways that secure conviction.[65] Ending or countering historical impunity for collective and political wrongdoing is generally taken to require holding perpetrators of such wrongdoing accountable. In the case of trials, successfully holding a perpetrator accountable is often equated with securing that perpetrator's conviction. By contrast, with multiple processes in place, the frustration that guilty individuals will not be held accountable can be mitigated, even if not all put on trial are convicted.

Repudiation

A key moral aim of third-party responses to wrongdoing is repudiating the permissibility of the wrongs that occurred. However, for the message of repudiation to be heard by both victims and the broad group of perpetrators and individuals complicit in wrongdoing, the legitimacy of the messenger must be recognized. Calling the credibility of such a response to perpetrators into question can distract attention from or strengthen denial about the wrongs that occurred. Undermining the sense of the legitimacy of the proceedings is also a way of discounting its findings and the justice of holding perpetrators to account.

Legitimacy concerns by a local population about individual trials conducted by a third-party actor that is international, regional, or otherwise an "outsider" can be especially pronounced. Questions of the legitimacy of such proceedings can stem from conditions such as a perception of bias in the way cases are selected and the remoteness of such trials to a local population. According to Subotic, 86 percent of Serbians surveyed during the course of the Karadžić trial believed the ICTY "was biased against the Serbs."[66] Such Serbians repudiated the ICTY and not wrongdoing. The reactions to the guilty verdict for Karadžić reflected this skepticism. Marko Milanovic notes that "while many Bosniaks welcomed the conviction they also decried the acquittal for genocide outside Srebrenica, whereas the current Bosnian Serb president has decried the judgment as yet another example of the ICTY's anti-Serb bias."[67]

---

[65] On this point, see Combs, *Fact-Finding.*   [66] Subotic, "Expanding the Scope," 158.
[67] Milanovic, Marko, "ICTY Convicts Radovan Karadzic," Blog of the European Journal of International Law, www.ejiltalk.org/icty-convicts-radovan-karadzic/ (accessed January 6, 2017).

Even when not perceived as biased against a particular group, the remoteness of certain respondents from the communities in which wrong-doing took place can itself be a source of questions about the legitimacy of a respondent, and consequently the legitimacy of that respondent's response. The international criminal court's isolation from local transitional societies in terms of its operations and processes has had an impact on citizens' perceptions of its legitimacy and effectiveness. Framed as justice meted out by unaccountable foreign experts with little knowledge of or connection to a particular society within which atrocities occurred, the legitimacy of such proceedings can be challenged.[68] Reactions to the Karadžić verdict bear out these concerns in his particular case. In an article deeply skeptical about the impact of the Karadžić trial, Nidzara Ahmetasevic writes:

> the judgment is spelled out over 2,500 pages, and only a limited number of people will actually read it and understand it. Additionally, the judgment is available only in English. In this case, as in other ICTY cases, it will take probably years for it to be translated into local languages ... The ICTY was, and is, an institution distant from the region – not only geographically, but in every possible way. The official language used by the institution is not one of the regional languages; personnel by large do not come from the region; the law they operate under has nothing to do with regional laws; when and if judges or prosecutors are coming to the region, they often act as aliens towards locals, being distant and reserved in their contacts.[69]

She concludes, "After 23 years of work, the international tribunal in The Hague did not succeed in having a real impact on the people of the region."[70]

Finally, trials cannot deal with the normalized character of wrongdoing. They cannot counter the broader social narratives and ideologies that justified wrongdoing and reinforce denial. Subotic notes, "It is particularly necessary, indeed imperative, for the perpetrator society to come to an understanding that what was done was wrong, that it was not how a 'normal' and decent society operates, and that politics has to change. In the absence of this type of responsibility, political ideologies will remain intact and a renewed cycle of violence can begin."[71] The sources of the

---

[68] Mihai, Mihaela, *Negative Emotions and Transitional Justice* (New York: Columbia University Press, 2016). See also Drumbl, *Atrocity*; Eric Stover, *The Witnesses: War Crimes and the Promise of Justice in The Hague* (Philadelphia: University of Pennsylvania Press, 2007); Henham, Ralph, "Some Reflections on the Legitimacy of International Trial Justice," *International Journal of the Sociology of Law* 35 (2007): 75–95.

[69] Ahmetasevic, Nidzara "The Radovan Karadzic Verdict Will Change Nothing," *Al Jazeera*, March 27, 2016, www.aljazeera.com/indepth/opinion/2016/03/radovan-karadzic-verdict-change-bosnia-serbia-160327093504907.html.

[70] Ibid.   [71] Subotic, "Expanding the Scope," 161.

normalization of wrongdoing must be countered, yet single trials are ill equipped to fulfill this task. Each trial concentrates on a discrete set of acts and the actions that were criminal, not on the conditions that make such criminal conduct feasible in the first place. Moreover, trials cannot alter pervasive structural inequality, which often underpins justifications for violence targeting particular groups.

The Karadžić trial bears out the consequences of failing to address the normalization of violence and pervasive structural inequality. A product of such narratives and reflecting such denial, thirty-three percent of respondents viewed Karadžić as a national hero, while only 17 percent saw him as a war criminal.[72] In lauding him as a hero rather than a criminal, respondents displayed denial of the possibility that atrocities were done, and done in their name. When discussing the impact of the single count on which Karadžić was acquitted, for genocide in Bosnian municipalities, Milanovic argues that "the acquittal will now inevitably be used in the nationalist politics of the Balkans, with Serbs saying, for example, that it confirms that the Republika Srpska was not a 'genocidal creation' and that its continued existence is therefore legitimate."[73]

The overarching *jus in bello* analogue moral aims of third-party responses to perpetrators are accountability and repudiation. In this section I have outlined the limits of single responses like trials as appropriate and fitting third-party responses to perpetrators. Trials are ill equipped to deal with individuals complicit in wrongdoing. Recognizing the collective character of wrongdoing requires responding to the broad group of individuals who are often complicit in collective wrongs. Absent coordinated efforts to establish the legitimacy of institutions dealing with wrongdoing and to respond to multiple perpetrators, including complicit individuals who were responsible for wrongdoing that took place, criminal trials stand little chance of holding particular perpetrators accountable for their role in collective and political wrongdoing and little chance of expressing an effective message of repudiation of the wrongdoing that took place.

Complex Victims

In Sections 2 and 3, I explained why a single form of response to victims in the first case, and perpetrators in the second is limited in its ability to fulfill the moral claims of victims and respond to the moral demands associated with perpetrators. I traced the source of these failures to insufficient

---

[72] Ibid.   [73] Milanovic, "ICTY Convicts Radovan Karadzic."

attention to the collective and political character of the wrongs done and the existence of pervasive structural inequality. No single response can fully deal with the collective character of wrongdoing, leading to inadequate recognition of the range of individuals implicated in the wrongdoing that took place, nor can a single response deal with the range of harms victims of collective and political wrongdoing experience, especially when such harms are bound up with pervasive structural inequality. Holism, in the form of coordinated responses to perpetrators and victims that target relational transformation as well, is needed.

My discussion implicitly assumed victims and perpetrators as separate groups of individuals. However, in the circumstances of transitional justice the categories of victim and perpetrator frequently overlap. As Luke Moffett writes, "Individual identities in protracted armed conflicts and political violence can be more complex than the binary identities of victim and perpetrator – individuals can be both victimized and victimizer over time."[74] This overlap points to an additional source of the need for holism, and specifically to coordination of the responses to victims and to perpetrators.

Victims are often what Moffett terms "complex victims" who are "not just vulnerable objects victimized by others, but are responsible for victimizing others."[75] In many cases perpetrators become perpetrators as a consequence of previous victimization. Abducted child soldiers may in turn abduct and brutalize others. Indeed, as the ICTJ report notes of LRA rebels in Uganda, "While in many cases those who were abducted into the LRA may have committed violations, their status is complicated by the fact that they were forced into that context in violation of their own rights. Therefore, individual responsibility for violations does not fit into a simplified victim-perpetrator binary, but needs to be contextualized and nuanced."[76]

Previous victimization can compromise the ability of perpetrators to fulfill their responsibilities to victims. There are three primary *jus in bello*

---

[74] Moffett, Luke, "Reparations for 'Guilty' Victims: Navigating Complex Identities of Victim–Perpetrators in Reparation Mechanisms," *International Journal of Transitional Justice* 10 (2016): 146–167, 147–8. See also Borer, Tristan Anne, "A Taxonomy of Victims and Perpetrators: Human Rights and Reconciliation in South Africa," *Human Rights Quarterly* 25, no. 4 (2003): 1088–1116.

[75] Moffett, "Reparations," 5.

[76] ICTJ, "From Rejection to Redress," 12–13. The ongoing trial of Ugandan Dominic Ongwen at the International Criminal Court precisely illustrates this complexity. Ongwen was abducted by the LRA when he was nine years old and was forced to become a child soldier. He then went on over three decades to become one of its top commanders and stands accused at the time of writing of the unlawful recruitment of child soldiers and enslavement. In Mark Drumbl's words, "Ongwen shatters the binaries in that he is a child, abducted and brutalized, who then became a zealous adult abuser"; see Drumbl, Mark, "Atrocity, Crime, and Justice: Thick and Thin Accounts," *InterGentes Op-Ed*, January 21, 2016, http://intergentes.com/atrocity-crime-and-justice/?platform=hootsuite.

analogue moral objectives in the responses of perpetrators of wrongdoing to those who were their victims, all of which are designed to enable the perpetrator to make amends to the victim.[77] The first is *repudiation of the action done*. As with third parties, the wrongdoer must repudiate the moral permissibility of their action against the victim.[78] This entails that the perpetrator must assume responsibility for the action committed. In assuming responsibility, the perpetrator is assuming responsibility for something that was wrongful; that is, the manner in which the perpetrator treated the victim was incompatible with recognition of the victim's equal moral status as an agent and as a member of the political community.

The second moral aim is *reparation*.[79] Here the perpetrator seeks to repair the harm and damage experienced by the victim as a result of the wrong committed. The form that reparation may take will vary according to the nature of the harm experienced by the victim.

The third general aim is *a commitment to nonrecurrence*;[80] that is, the wrongdoer demonstrates a resolve not to permit or commit similar wrongs in the future. This is necessary for providing a reasonable basis for the possibility of a new moral relationship with the victim. In committing to nonrecurrence, the perpetrator aims to demonstrate that he or she is morally trustworthy and can be relied on to adhere to normative standards that regulate morally defensible relationships.[81] With such (re-)commitment, it may become possible to imagine or develop relationships not structured simply in terms of the wrongdoer-victim roles once assumed.[82]

The ICTJ report highlights the limited ability of individual rebels, who were responsible for sexual violations of abducted women and subsequently became fathers of the children born from such violations, to make good on their obligations to victims. This inability is linked to the previous victimization of rebels in many cases. The context into which former rebels returned did not facilitate their ability to assume responsibility for the wrongs done and demonstrate a commitment to nonrecurrence. Many rebels were themselves abducted as children and forced as part of the campaign to take on wives and have children. Like the women who were abducted, male rebels returned to a community without the education or skills needed to be able to provide for themselves, or a wife and child. Moreover, in a number of cases they returned unable to claim land that

---

[77] Radzik, *Making Amends*.

[78] On this point, see Radzik, *Making Amends*; Smith, *I Was Wrong*; Nick Smith, *Justice through Apologies*.

[79] Radzik, *Making Amends*; Smith, *I Was Wrong*; Walker, *Moral Repair*.   [80] Ibid.   [81] Ibid.

[82] Radzik, *Making Amends*.

would have been a gateway for income and resources. When families believed an abducted son was killed or dead, they gave their land to another claimant or sold it. The restitution kit provided by the Amnesty Commission did not adequately address the resource deficit facing rebels to be able to claim and support the children they had during conflict and take responsibility for wrongs done.[83]

Through recognition of the complexity of victims and coordination of responses to wrongdoing, transitional societies can address the consequences of prior victimization for perpetrators, consequences that in turn impact their ability to fulfill their obligations to their own victims. Moreover, this can mitigate the risk that complex victims will fail to be considered victims or addressed by the responses to victims that take place.

Summary

This chapter discussed the *jus in bello* analogue requirements that must be satisfied for societal transformation to be justly pursued. It is these requirements that distinguish the just from the unjust pursuit of societal transformation. I have argued that just responses to wrongdoing are intrinsically appropriate or fitting responses to perpetrators and victims. Four general factors influence the fittingness of a response to perpetrators or victims. First, a response must facilitate the widely recognized general moral claims of victims or claims on perpetrators. The second factor is the relationship between subject and respondent, and the third factor is the nature of the wrong itself. Finally, the cultural context within which wrongdoing occurred and in which a response is offered influences whether it is fitting or not.

After articulating these requirements, I went on to argue that holism in the design and implementation of responses to wrongdoing is needed if these *jus in bello* analogue requirements are to be satisfied in the circumstances of transitional justice. My discussion focused on the importance of coordination in the design and implementation of multiple responses to victims and perpetrators. Given collective and political wrongdoing as well as pervasive structural inequality, a single response to perpetrators or victims is limited in its ability to achieve the moral aims of such response. The absence of holism risks undermining the limited contribution of any single response to the moral functions of such responses. The extent to which transitional justice is pursued holistically influences the moral meaning and impact of each of the responses considered individually.

---

[83] ICTJ, "From Rejection to Redress," 18–19.

Ignoring the limits of what any single response can do can be both self-defeating and contribute to needless further suffering.

Holism is important not just when designing and implementing responses to victims and perpetrators, but is also necessary when evaluating whether the *jus in bello* requirements of transitional justice have been satisfied. The *jus in bello* justice of punishment in the circumstances of transitional justice is conditional or dependent on what actions or reforms the transitional government is or is not taking. For example, given the collective character of wrongdoing, the appropriateness or fittingness of the punishment of a single perpetrator will be influenced by how other individuals complicit in the wrongs done are treated.

My analysis explains why it is necessary for a moral division of labor to take place among different institutional mechanisms, necessary because no single mechanism can adequately deal with all the moral objectives that wrongdoing leaves in its wake. While it is necessary and permissible for a given response to deal with only part of the problem that wrongdoing creates, it is also necessary for those selecting and establishing a single response to wrongdoing to have some plausible grounds for claiming that what is being established will in fact contribute to a holistic balance. Such grounds will not likely exist through an unguided working of the invisible hand. An established group of processes that together adequately respond to wrongs done must be the product of intentional action and active coordination by the actors already involved in the pursuit of transitional justice.[84] Such active coordination should include third-party international actors who increasingly play a prominent role in the pursuit of transitional justice in many societies, as well as domestic actors. How best to structure this coordination may be somewhat context specific and a function of the actors involved in the process.

Perceptions of victims also shape what is done.[85] Victims of human rights abuses have a special standing and consultative role to play in determining the form that a response to wrongs done to them should take. One reason for such a role is epistemic. Victims are best placed to articulate what forms of reparation or acknowledgment, for example, will actually address the damage and harm from wrongdoing. Another reason for giving victims an important role in such decisions is connected to the importance of respect for agency itself.[86] Human rights abuses express a

---

[84] De Greiff, "Theorizing Transitional Justice," 38.
[85] Dixon provides some guidance on some models for coordination. See his "Reparations."
[86] On this point, see Radzik, *Making Amends*.

denial of the agency of victims, an agency in virtue of which they have dignity and that grounds human rights claims. By recognizing the agency of victims and giving them a space for exercising that agency in determining what happens to them, the decision-making processes related to transitional justice themselves are designed to counter the damage wrongdoing sought to inflict and grant the respect that wrongdoing denied.

Finally, responses to wrongdoing are pursued for the sake of fostering societal transformation, and this *jus ad bellum* analogue requirement will necessarily influence judgments of whether a given response was just. As I noted in the Introduction of this chapter, these processes must be holistic in a second sense: by fostering societal transformation as well as satisfying the victim and perpetrator specific demands. Holism in design and implementation of responses as well as holism in the pursuit of two distinct sets of requirements of transitional justice are complementary. There are both conceptual and empirical reasons for this complementarity. Empirical research supports the claim that combinations of processes of transitional justice are needed to actually contribute to the rule of law and other aspects of societal transformation.[87]

Conceptually, in making my argument for holism in the sense of coordinated combinations of responses, I showed that repairing damage from normalized collective and political wrongdoing and achieving recognition of victims as equal members of the political community entails dealing with structural inequality. Moreover, there is a further conceptual connection that Kutz himself recognizes. The forward-looking impact of accountability practices, he writes, can serve as "points of inflection in our relationships whereby new norms and expectations come to be warranted."[88] The circumstance of moderately severe existential uncertainty provides theoretical resources for explaining why this transformative potential is especially acute in circumstances of transition. With a fragile future, processes that in the circumstance of limited existential uncertainty may not have much impact on a community can come to play an important role in determining its future trajectory. How a society deals with past wrongs provides an indication of whether there is an acknowledgment of how the moral values of reciprocity and respect for agency were undermined in interaction in the past, and whether there will now be a serious commitment to build those values into interaction in the future. The legal responses adopted by the new government to deal with past abuses also have a bearing on any assessment of its authority to govern.

---

[87] Olsen et al., *Transitional Justice.*   [88] Kutz, *Complicity*, 47.

Taking seriously past abuses and responding legally to them provides, at least ideally, some initial evidence that those in power will utilize their power in a manner that comports with basic recognition of the rights, dignity and standing of all citizens. Thus far from balancing two separate moral imperatives, just practices of accountability for past collective and political harms are bound up with the very possibility of relational trans-formation, which is the overarching aim of transitional justice.[89]

[89] Here the political character of wrongdoing makes an important difference because by and large it is wrongs that were committed in the course of pursuing political objectives that are the subject of transitional justice responses rather than ordinary criminal wrongdoing pursued for the sake of individual and personal objectives.

Conclusion

Justly dealing with past wrongdoing stemming from an extended period of conflict and repression while attempting to transition is a fraught enterprise. In Chapters 1–4, I have developed theoretical resources for understanding and grappling with this issue. I first argued that transitional justice is not restorative justice. Forgiveness, often taken to be at the core of restorative justice, is neither necessary nor sufficient for transitional justice. Nor should the choices confronting transitional societies, I claimed, be framed as a principled compromise among familiar kinds of justice, such as restorative, retributive, or corrective justice. Previous attempts to articulate the principled compromise entailed by choices to deal with past wrongdoing in the midst of a transition abstracted concepts like retributive justice from their central moral principles. Such abstraction undercuts the basis for distinguishing among kinds of justice, such as retributive and distributive justice, and the reasons why we do not simply talk of "justice" but talk instead about "distributive justice" in the first place. Furthermore, the core moral question that theories of retributive, corrective and distributive justice address is not the central moral question confronting transitional societies.

Transitional justice, I argued, is a particular type of justice operative or salient in a specific set of circumstances of justice. These circumstances are pervasive structural inequality, where relationships among citizens and between citizens and officials are predicated on the unequal status of certain individuals or groups; normalized collective and political wrongdoing, where groups of individuals characteristically target groups of individuals for human rights abuses for the sake of achieving political objectives and such targeting becomes a basic fact of life around which individuals come to orient their conduct; serious existential uncertainty, in which the future political trajectory of a community is deeply unclear and the achievement of democracy is neither impossible nor foreordained; and fundamental uncertainty about authority, where the standing of the state to deal with past abuses is in doubt given its role in past wrongs and the incomplete establishment of democracy.

In the context of these circumstances, I claimed, the core moral question confronting societies and constituting the subject matter of transitional justice is the following: How to justly pursue societal transformation? Societal transformation is pursued in transitional justice via dealing with past wrongdoing. The circumstances of transitional justice help explain why societal transformation becomes bound up with the process of responding to wrongdoing in ways that do not occur in other contexts. Democracies characteristically treat the issue of reform of, for example, political or economic institutions as separate from the question of how to respond to perpetrators or victims of wrongdoing. By contrast, societal transformation becomes bound up with the process of responding to wrongdoing partly because of the circumstance of serious existential uncertainty. This is in part because pervasive structural inequality and normalized collective and political wrongdoing are tightly interconnected. As I argued in Chapter 4, dealing with the consequences of wrongdoing for victims often requires dealing with pervasive structural inequality. In addition, with the future of a community deeply ambiguous, the way that wrongs are dealt with can have broader implications for the future direction of a community.

The central question of transitional justice is how to justly pursue societal transformation. It should be seen as structurally analogous to another question that societies often face: How do we justly fight war? In the case of the latter question, just war theory articulates the *jus ad bellum* conditions that must be satisfied for a society to decide to initiate war justly. Here the cause being fought, the intention of political actors, and the likelihood of success, among other conditions, are taken to be relevant. The *jus in bello* criteria articulate conditions that must be satisfied for war to be justly conducted. Failure to satisfy either set of criteria undermines the justice of the war being pursued.

Analogously, societal transformation is the overarching *jus ad bellum* aim for the sake of which processes of transitional justice should be pursued. In the version of societal transformation I defended, the subject matter of transformation is the structure of political relationships among citizens and between citizens and officials. A central goal is to transform such relationships so that they are predicated on respect for agency and reciprocity. This exists when there is mutual respect for the rule of law, reasonable default political trust and trust responsiveness, and threshold levels of central relational capabilities. The pursuit of relationships of this kind must also respect the *jus ad bellum* analogue requirement that it be done in a manner that reciprocally respects agency.

Relational transformation is pursued in transitional justice by dealing with past wrongdoing. Specifically, transitional justice processes take up human rights violations that were committed for political reasons by groups of actors targeting groups in paradigm cases. To be fully just, processes of transitional justice must satisfy a set of *jus in bello* analogue requirements that fill out what constitutes an intrinsically fitting or appropriate response to victims and perpetrators of wrongdoing. Informing judgments of the fittingness or appropriateness of any response, I claimed, are four general factors: the specific nature of the wrong being addressed, the relationship between subject and respondent, the moral objectives of responding to victims or perpetrators, and the cultural context in which a response takes place. Achieving the moral objectives of responses to victims of normalized collective and political wrongdoing, such as acknowledgment that wrong was done, recognition of the victim's basic humanity and status as an equal member of a political community, reparation and nonrecurrence, I claimed, requires processes of transitional justice to be pursued holistically. That is, multiple responses to victims must occur. These multiple responses must be coordinated so that they can be mutually reinforcing and complementary, ensuring for example that the expressive functions of responses to wrongdoing are fulfilled and repair is apt.

Transitional justice responses can fail to be just in two senses: by failing to contribute to societal transformation or by failing to be appropriate and fitting responses to victims and/or perpetrators. There is reason to believe that processes can satisfy both sets of criteria if pursued with both sets in mind and if transitional justice processes are designed and implemented in a coordinated manner. Given that pervasive structural inequality compounds the consequences of wrongdoing for victims paradigmatically, adequately repairing the damage caused by such wrongdoing requires attending to such structural inequality. Insofar as normalized collective and political wrong-doing becomes more likely in the context of pervasive structural inequality, which provides a rationale for the targeting and mistreatment of members of certain groups, altering that context reduces the possibility for repetition of such wrongdoing. Thus, by pursuing societal transformation, societies are contributing to the aim of nonrepetition.

My account of transitional justice makes two distinctive kinds of contributions to the literature. The first is to articulate a basic structure for theorizing about transitional justice. This structure takes as its starting point the Humean insight that theorizing about justice is always context sensitive. It is against certain background conditions that certain questions or problems of justice arise, to which principles of justice provide solutions. Thus, in thinking through and about transitional justice, it is critical as a first step to know the circumstances and problem shaping this inquiry. In addition to framing transitional justice as responding to a particular problem or question that arises in a particular set of circumstances, I articulated the general form of this problem. Transitional justice is about transforming a community and dealing in an intrinsically fitting or appropriate manner with victims and perpetrators. Though both aspects of this challenge are highlighted throughout the literature on transitional justice, the relationship between these two concerns is very rarely made clear. Thinking of the relationship between the pursuit of transformation and the just treatment of perpetrators and victims using the analogy with just war theory makes the relationship less confusing and mysterious. Just war theory is a familiar structure for relating two distinct sets of concerns, and this structural analogy is useful in understanding the relationship between the two dimensions of transitional justice. Societal transformation is the *jus ad bellum* dimension of transitional justice, and the fitting treatment of victims and perpetrators the *jus in bello* dimension.

The second contribution of my account is substantive in nature. Beyond articulating a structure for conceptualizing transitional justice, I offered a particular substantive account of transitional justice. Specifically, I identified four particular circumstances of transitional justice, developed a conception of societal transformation, enumerated certain criteria that must be satisfied for societal transformation to be pursued justly, and argued that transitional justice will be achieved if responses to wrongdoing are designed, implemented and evaluated holistically. One may accept or reject parts or all this substantive analysis. What is key to recognize, however, is that accepting or rejecting the substantive account is distinct from accepting or rejecting the basic, more formal theoretical framework for theorizing about transitional justice. That is, one might accept the first contribution without accepting all or part of the second.

A significant benefit, in my view, of theorizing about transitional justice in terms of problems of justice and circumstances of justice is that it sheds light on the way(s) in which transitional societies, and the problems with which they deal, are similar to and different from other societies. My discussion in Chapter 2 concentrated on the differences between the problems of retributive, corrective, and distributive justice that theorists concentrating on stable democracies take up.

But of course actual societies will often exhibit combinations of the paradigm circumstances of transitional justice and of stable democracies. A society may have a legacy of normalized collective and political wrong-doing, but no serious existential uncertainty. The extent to which structural inequality remains may vary, present somewhere between a pervasive and limited extent. Debates in contemporary Spain surrounding how to deal with wrongdoing committed during Franco's reign illustrate this general category. In this set of circumstances, the problem of justice confronting such societies will be not exactly identical to the either the problems of retributive or transitional justice. Historical normalized collective and political wrongdoing may still need to be addressed, but it need not necessarily be addressed for the sake of achieving broader societal transformation. Such transformation may no longer be necessary if pervasive structural inequality has been reduced and there no longer exists a serious worry about the recurrence of normalized collective and political wrongdoing. Wrongdoing may remain important to address for the sake of satisfying the intrinsic moral claims of victims and on perpetrators discussed in Chapter 4. But because wrongdoing was normalized, collective and political, and was bound up with pervasive structural inequality, the standard for appropriateness will not be set by the retributivist or corrective justice standards. Such theories offer guidance for responding to deviant individual and personal wrongdoing, and have difficulty guiding responses to wrongs with a collective dimension. Thus, the insights from Chapter 4 concerning what is needed to achieve the intrinsic moral aims of responses to victims or perpetrators may be applicable to some extent to cases in which similar kinds of wrongdoing are being addressed in post-transitional contexts.

A different kind of hybrid case is a case in which individual and personal wrongdoing is committed against a background of pervasive structural inequality. Such cases can arise in the circumstances of serious existential uncertainty and fundamental uncertainty about authority. For example, the South African TRC explicitly required applicants for amnesty to demonstrate that their acts of wrongdoing had been done for the sake of furthering political objectives. Ordinary criminal acts of murder, abduction, and severe ill treatment were excluded. Left unaddressed by the TRC was how to deal with ordinary criminality committed by perpetrators acting individually and for personal reasons but acting against the background of structural inequality. Other societies may also face the question of how to respond to individual and personal wrongdoing committed against a background of structural inequality. Concern about the influence of background structural inequality, and in particular racial inequality, on criminal sentencing in the United States centers on the extent to which specific sentences or the sentencing guidelines enforced by the criminal justice system are in fact fitting and appropriate responses to deviant individual and personal wrongdoing. Differential sentences for white and black criminals guilty of the same crime suggest race, rather than the nature of the wrong done, determine the punitive response to a particular perpetrator by the state. Other discussions about this set of circumstances of justice focus on the ways in which poverty and disadvantage make lawful behavior much more difficult.[1] Scholars consider whether, and in what way, the fact that lawful behavior is more difficult should influence the amount of punishment we consider appropriate or fitting, as well as whether a punitive response to such perpetrators is indeed fair.[2]

One final version of the hybrid case worth mentioning is a response to normalized collective and political wrongdoing attempted in the context of pervasive structural inequality, but where there is no serious existential uncertainty. The absence of serious existential uncertainty in the cases I have in mind arises because there is little prospect of altering or over-hauling structural inequality. I argued in Chapter 4 that responding appropriately and fittingly to victims or perpetrators of such wrongdoing in a just manner requires taking into account the normalized and collective character of such wrongs, and the ways in which the consequences of being a victim are intertwined with and affected by pervasive structural inequality. Yet such a response would not have as its overarching objective necessarily societal transformation.

In the chapters leading up to this Conclusion I did not examine in detail any specific response to wrongdoing. That is, at no point did I articulate the general contribution of any specific kind of response to fostering societal transformation and to satisfying the moral claims associated with perpetrators and victims of wrongdoing. My silence with respect to a general analysis of particular types of responses to wrongdoing was delib-erate, and in the last part of this conclusion I want to explain the reasons behind this decision.

The first reason is that our understanding of the impact and expres-sive meaning of individual responses to wrongdoing, and combinations of responses, in the circumstances of transitional justice is still nascent. This is not surprising. Overhauling and transforming the terms struc-turing interaction among citizens and officials are by their nature

---

[1] See Wolff and de-Shalit, *Disadvantage*.   [2] On this debate, see Green, "Just Deserts."

complex undertakings. My aim in this book is to provide a theoretical framework for understanding (1) the components of transformation that are in need of cultivation, (2) the relationship among various components, (3) the circumstances in which that need arises, and (4) why such cultivation is an issue of justice. This understanding can inform the important empirical work being undertaken to explain what in fact happens in various contexts in terms of the promotion of the rule of law or trust when different process(es) individually or in combination are adopted.[3]

Our understanding of the role of particular responses to wrongdoing is limited not only because the promotion of societal transformation is complex. Many of the *jus in bello* analogue objectives of responses to wrongdoing, such as acknowledgment and recognition of the humanity and equal status of victims as citizens, are fundamentally expressive. Acknowledgment of wrongdoing occurs when condemnation of the permissibility of particular actions is communicated. Analyses of the expressive meaning of responses to wrongdoing in philosophy generally presume the circumstances of stable democracy. There are few inferences we can draw about the moral meaning and impact on the aims associated with responding to victims and to perpetrators of wrongdoing of particular responses in the circumstances of transitional justice. Margaret Urban Walker's important work on reparations provides a model for how research oriented around evaluating transitional justice responses like reparations should proceed.[4] But much further research into the expressive significance of responses to wrongdoing, individually or in combination, in the circumstances of transitional justice is needed before any general account of the moral functions of responses can be developed. Especially important in this context is filling out the impact of different kinds of respondents, such as domestic versus international actors, on the expressive function of responses to victims and perpetrators.[5]

---

[3] Examples of such studies include van der Merwe et al., *Assessing the Impact*; Olsen et al., *Transitional Justice*.

[4] Walker, "Restorative Justice"; Margaret Urban Walker, "Truth Telling as Reparations," *Metaphilosophy* 41, no. 4 (2010): 525–45; Walker, Margaret Urban, "The Expressive Burden of Reparations: Putting Meaning into Money, Words and Things," in *In the Wake of Conflict: Justice, Responsibility and Reconciliation*, ed. Alice MacLachlan and C. A. Speight, 205–25 (New York: Springer, 2013); Walker, Margaret Urban, "Moral Vulnerability and the Task of Reparations," in *Vulnerability: New Essays in Ethics and Feminist Philosophy*, ed. Catriona Mackenzie, Wendy Rogers, and Susan Dodds, 111–33 (New York: Oxford University Press, 2014).

[5] On this issue, see especially Teitel, Ruti, *Globalizing Transitional Justice: Contemporary Essays* (New York: Oxford University Press, 2014).

I did not discuss in detail particular responses to wrongdoing only because of existing epistemic limits. The second general reason I did not discuss particular forms of response is out of a desire to encourage expansion in the range of responses to wrongdoing considered when aiming to promote societal transformation in a just manner. The standard menu of such responses, as noted in the Introduction, includes one, all, or some combination of amnesty, criminal trials, truth commissions and reparations programs. Discussing in detail all or some of these responses reinforces these as constituting the complete range of options from which transitional societies should choose. However, as scholars and INGO organizations involved in transitional justice in specific settings recognize, the range of responses that might contribute to the just pursuit of societal transformation is potentially much broader. Acknowledgment of the wrongs victims suffered and recognition of the humanity of victims could take place in art, theater and television.[6] Debt forgiveness and land redistribution are additional areas where the reparative dimensions of economic wrongs may be pursued and where pervasive structural inequality may be mitigated.[7] Linking reparation programs with assistance programs is another alternative being advocated.[8] Education, and its contribution to our understanding of past wrongs and to the shaping of interaction among citizens, is increasingly emphasized.[9] By focusing on the overarching aims of transitional justice and the context in which these aims become salient, my hope is not to prejudge the question of what range of responses could plausibly be construed and defended as transitional justice responses.

The application of my substantive account to any particular transitional context will be complicated. Interpretation and detailed understanding of the particular society in question is needed to specify where exactly relationships need to be transformed and what form wrongdoing took. Another source of complication will be potential tensions that arise among the many demands that the pursuit of societal transformation and the

---

[6] On such cultural contributions, see Shandley, Robert, *Rubble Films: German Cinema in the Shadow of the Third Reich* (Philadelphia: Temple University Press, 2001).

[7] On these issues, see Sharp, Dustin N., "The Significance of Human Rights for the Debt of Countries in Transition," in *Making Sovereign Financing & Human Rights Work*, ed. Juan Pablo Bohoslavsky and Jernej Letnar Černič (London: Hart, 2013), 47–60; Gray, David, "Delivery, Complicity, and Greed: Transitional Justice and Odious Debt," *Law and Contemporary Problems* 70 (2007): 137–64; Moyo, "Mimicry."

[8] Dixon, "Reparations."

[9] Indeed, the ICTJ recently established an entire project dedicated to understanding the relationship between education and transitional justice. Information about that project is here: www.ictj.org/our-work/research/education-peacebuilding.

moral claims of victims and demands on perpetrators make. When dealing with land, for example, reparation for victims of unjust land appropriation and redistribution of land as part of a broader process of relational repair may point in different directions. A general theoretical conception of transitional justice of the kind developed in the previous chapters does not replace or displace the judgment necessary for determining what form transitional justice should take in any given society and how to resolve tensions that may arise in the pursuit of transitional justice. Rather, it is designed to guide policy makers and actors involved in transitional justice as they deal with particular contexts, by providing an articulation of what the standards for success in pursuing transitional justice should be, how they are interconnected, and why they are important to achieve.

Works Cited

Abizadeh, Arash. "Cooperation, Pervasive Impact, and Coercion: On the Scope (Not Site) of Distributive Justice." *Philosophy & Public Affairs* 35, no. 4 (2007): 318–58.

Alexander, Larry, and Michael Moore. "Deontological Ethics." In *Stanford Encyclopedia of Philosophy*, edited by Edward N. Zalta. 2015. http://plato.stanford.edu/archives/spr2015/entries/ethics-deontological/.

Alexander, Michelle. *The New Jim Crow: Mass Incarceration in the Age of Colorblindness*. New York: New Press, 2012.

Alkire, Sabine, and James Foster. "Counting and Multidimensional Poverty Measurement." *Journal of Public Economics* 95, no. 7 (2011): 476–87.

Allais, Lucy. "Restorative Justice, Retributive Justice, and the South African Truth and Reconciliation Commission." *Philosophy & Public Affairs* 39, no. 4 (2012): 331–63.

Allen, Jonathan. "Balancing Justice and Social Utility: Political Theory and the Idea of a Truth and Reconciliation Commission." *University of Toronto Law Journal* 49 (1999): 315–53.

Altman, Andrew. "Speech Codes and Expressive Harm." In *Ethics in Practice*, 4th ed., edited by Hugh LaFollette, 381–88. West Sussex: John Wiley and Sons, 2014.

Anderson, Elizabeth. "What Is the Point of Equality?" *Ethics* 109, no. 2 (1999): 287–337.

Arbour, Louise. "Economic and Social Justice for Societies in Transition." *International Law and Politics* 40, no. 1 (2007): 1–27.

Aristotle. *Nicomachean Ethics*. 2nd ed. Translated by Terence Irwin. Indianapolis: Hackett Publishing, 1999.

Arneson, Richard. "Liberalism, Distributive Subjectivism, and Equal Opportunity for Welfare." *Philosophy & Public Affairs* 19 (1990): 158–94.

Arthur, Paige. "How 'Transitions' Reshaped Human Rights: A Conceptual History of Transitional Justice." *Human Rights Quarterly* 31 (2009): 321–67.

Ashford, Elizabeth. "The Inadequacy of Our Traditional Conception of the Duties Imposed by Human Rights." *Canadian Journal of Law and Jurisprudence* 29, no. 2 (2006): 217–35.

Auf, Yussef. "The Egyptian Parliament: After a Lengthy Absence, an Uncertain Future." *Atlantic Council*, February 26, 2015. www.atlanticcouncil .org/blogs/egyptsource/the-egyptian-parliament-after-a-lengthy-absence-an-uncertain-future.

Baier, Annette. "Demoralization, Trust, and the Virtues." In *Setting the Moral Compass: Essays by Women Philosophers*, edited by Cheshire Calhoun, 176–90. New York: Oxford University Press, 2004.

Baker, John. "Trust and Rationality." *Pacific Philosophical Quarterly* 68 (1996): 1–13.

Barry, Brian. "Equal Opportunity and Moral Arbitrariness." In *Equal Opportunity*, edited by Norman E. Bowie, 23–44. Boulder, CO: Westview Press, 1988.

Barry, Brian. *Theories of Justice*. Hemel-Hempstead: Harvester-Wheatsheaf, 1989.

Becker, Lawrence C. "Trust as Noncognitive Security about Motives." *Ethics* 107, no. 1 (1996): 43–61.

Bedau, Hugo Adam, and Erin Kelly. "Punishment." In *Stanford Encyclopedia of Philosophy*, edited by Edward N. Zalta. 2010. http://plato.stanford.edu/ archives/spr2010/entries/punishment/.

Beitz, Charles. *Political Theory and International Relations*. Princeton, NJ: Princeton University Press, 1979.

Bell, Christine. "Transitional Justice, Interdisciplinarity and the State of the 'Field' or 'Non-Field.'" *International Journal of Transitional Justice* 3, no. 1 (2009): 5–27.

Bennett, Christopher. *The Apology Ritual: A Philosophical Theory of Punishment*. Cambridge: Cambridge University Press, 2008.

Benson, Paul. "Free Agency and Self-Worth." *Journal of Philosophy* 91, no. 12 (1994): 650–68.

Bergner, Daniel. *In the Land of Magic Soldiers: A Story of White and Black in West Africa*. New York: Picador, 2003.

Blake, Michael. "Distributive Justice, State Coercion, and Autonomy." *Philosophy & Public Affairs* 30 (2002): 257–96.

Blustein, Jeffrey. "Human Rights and the Internationalization of Memory." *Journal of Social Philosophy* 43, no. 1 (2012): 19–32.

Blustein, Jeffrey. *The Moral Demands of Memory*. New York: Cambridge University Press, 2008.

Borer, Tristan Anne. "A Taxonomy of Victims and Perpetrators: Human Rights and Reconciliation in South Africa." *Human Rights Quarterly* 25, no. 4 (2003): 1088–1116.

Braithwaite, John. *Restorative Justice and Responsive Regulation*. Oxford: Oxford University Press, 2002.

Brooks, Thom. "Getting Reparations Right – A Response to Posner and Vermeule." *Notre Dame Law Review* 80 (2004): 251–88.

Brownlee, Kimberley. "Civil Disobedience." In *Stanford Encyclopedia of Philosophy*, edited by Edward N. Zalta. 2013. http://plato.stanford.edu/ archives/win2013/entries/civil-disobedience/.

Buchanan, Allen. "Justice as Reciprocity versus Subject-Centered Justice." *Philosophy & Public Affairs* 19, no. 3 (1990): 227–52.

Carothers, Thomas. "The End of the Transition Paradigm." *Journal of Democracy* 13, no. 1 (2002): 5–21.

Carothers, Thomas, and Oren Samet-Marram. "The New Global Marketplace of Political Change." *Carnegie Endowment for International Peace*, April 20, 2015. http://carnegieendowment.org/2015/04/20/new-global-marketplace-of-political-change/i7fw?mkt_tok=3RkMMJWWfF9wsRoisq%2FBZKXonj HpfsX57OwrXKag38431UFwdcjKPmjr1YcGTsJoaPyQAgobGp5I5FEIQ7XY TLB2t60MWAemXSjrtqDIZoxAZZ13gZI3.

Carranza, Ruben. "Plunder and Pain: Should Transitional Justice Engage with Corruption and Economic Crimes?" *International Journal of Transitional Justice* 2 (2008): 310–30.

Christiano, Thomas. "The Authority of Democracy." *Journal of Political Philosophy* 12, no. 3 (2004): 266–90.

Christiano, Thomas. "Democracy." In *Stanford Encyclopedia of Philosophy*, edited by Edward N. Zalta. 2015. http://plato.stanford.edu/archives/spr2015/entries/democracy/.

Cohen, G. A. *Rescuing Justice and Equality.* Cambridge: Harvard University Press, 2008.

Cohen, Stanley. *States of Denial: Knowing about Atrocities and Suffering.* Cambridge: Polity Press, 2001.

Coleman, Jules. "Moral Theories of Torts: Their Scope and Limits: Part II." *Law and Philosophy* 2 (1983): 5–36.

Coleman, Jules, and Gabriel Mendlow. "Theories of Tort Law." In *Stanford Encyclopedia of Philosophy*, edited by Edward N. Zalta. 2010. http://plato.stanford.edu/archives/fall2010/entries/tort-theories/.

Collins, Cath. *Post-Transitional Justice: Human Rights Trials in Chile and El Salvador.* State College: Penn State University Press, 2011.

Coman, Julian. "Eighty Years On, Spain May at Last Be Able to Confront the Ghosts of Civil War." *Guardian*, May 29, 2016. www.theguardian.com/world/2016/may/29/national-museum-spanish-civil-war-barcelona?CMP=twt_gu.

Combs, Nancy. *Fact-Finding without Facts: The Uncertain Evidentiary Foundations of International Criminal Convictions.* New York: Cambridge University Press, 2010.

Combs, Nancy. *Guilty Pleas in International Criminal Law.* Stanford: Stanford University Press, 2007.

Cook, Karen S., Russell Hardin, and Margaret Levi. *Cooperation without Trust?* New York: Russell Sage Foundation Publications, 2007.

Crocker, David. *Ethics of Global Development: Agency, Capability, and Deliberative Democracy.* New York: Cambridge University Press, 2009.

Crocker, David. "Reckoning with Past Wrongs: A Normative Framework." *Ethics & International Affairs* 13, no. 1 (1999): 43–64.

Cudd, Ann E. *Analyzing Oppression.* New York: Oxford University Press, 2006.

Curry, Tommy J. "The Fortune of Wells: Ida B. Wells-Barnett's Use of T. Thomas Fortune Philosophy of Social Agitation as a Prolegomenon to Militant Civil Rights Activism." *Transactions of the Charles S. Pierce Society*. 48, no. 8 (2012): 456–82.

Curry, Tommy J. "Please Don't Make Me Touch 'Em: Toward a Critical Race Fanonianism as a Possible Justification for Violence against Whiteness." *Radical Philosophy Today* 5 (2007): 133–58.

Curry, Tommy J., and Max Kelleher. "Robert F. Williams and Militant Civil Rights: The Legacy and Philosophy of Preemptive Self-Defense." *Radical Philosophy Review* 18, no. 1 (2015): 45–68.

Daly, Erin. "Transformative Justice: Charting a Path to Reconciliation." *International Legal Perspectives* 12, no. 1–2 (2002): 74–183.

Daniels, Norman. "Equality of What: Welfare, Resources, or Capabilities?" *Philosophy and Phenomenological Research* 50 (1990): 273–96.

Danner, Allison Marston, and Jenny S. Martinez. "Guilty Associations: Joint Criminal Enterprise, Command Responsibility, and the Development of International Criminal Law." *California Law Review* 93, no. 1 (2005): 75–196.

Darwall, Stephen. "Justice and Retaliation." *Philosophical Papers* 39, no. 3 (2010): 315–41.

Darwall, Stephen. *The Second-Person Standpoint: Morality, Respect, and Accountability*. Cambridge, MA: Harvard University Press, 2009.

de Greiff, Pablo. "Justice and Reparations." In *The Handbook of Reparations*, edited by Pablo de Greiff, 451–77. New York: Oxford University Press, 2006.

de Greiff, Pablo. "Report of the Special Rapporteur on the Promotion of Truth, Justice, Reparation and Guarantees of Non-Recurrence." UN Doc. A/HRC/21/46. August 9, 2012.

de Greiff, Pablo. "Theorizing Transitional Justice." In *NOMOS LI: Transitional Justice*, edited by Melissa S. Williams, Rosemary Nagy, and Jon Elster, 31–77. New York: New York University Press, 2012.

Dixon, Peter. "Reparations, Assistance and the Experience of Justice: Lessons from Colombia and the Democratic Republic of the Congo." *International Journal of Transitional Justice* 10 (2016): 88–107.

Donadio, Colette. "Gender Based Violence: Justice and Reparation in Bosnia And Herzegovina." *Mediterranean Journal of Social Sciences* 5, no. 16 (July 2014): 692–702.

Drumbl, Mark. *Atrocity, Punishment, and International Law*. New York: Cambridge University Press, 2007.

Drumbl, Mark. "Collective Responsibility and Post-Conflict Justice." *Washington & Lee Public Legal Studies Research Paper Series*, Working Paper No. 2010. May 7, 2010. http://ssrn.com/abstract=1601506.

Drumbl, Mark. *Reimagining Child Soldiers in International Law and Policy*. New York: Oxford University Press, 2012.

Duff, Antony. *Answering for Crime: Responsibility and Liability in the Criminal Law*. Oxford: Hart Publishing, 2007.

Duff, Antony. "Legal Punishment." In *Stanford Encyclopedia of Philosophy*, edited by Edward N. Zalta. 2013. http://plato.stanford.edu/archives/sum2013/entries/legal-punishment/.

Duff, Antony. *Punishment, Communication and Community*. Oxford: Oxford University Press, 2001.

Duff, Antony. "Theories of Criminal Law." In *Stanford Encyclopedia of Philosophy*, edited by Edward N. Zalta. 2013. http://plato.stanford.edu/archives/sum2013/entries/criminal-law/.

Duthie, Roger. "Toward a Development-Sensitive Approach to Transitional Justice." *International Journal of Transitional Justice* 2, no. 3 (2008): 292–309.

Dworkin, Ronald. "What Is Equality? Part 1: Equality of Resources." *Philosophy & Public Affairs* 10 (1981): 185–246.

Dworkin, Ronald. "What Is Equality? Part 2: Equality of Welfare." *Philosophy & Public Affairs* 10 (1981): 283–345.

Dyzenhaus, David. "The Grudge Informer Case Revisited." *New York University Law Review* 83 (2008): 1000–34.

Dyzenhaus, David. "Judicial Independence, Transitional Justice, and the Rule of Law." *Otago Law Review* 10 (2003): 345–72.

Dyzenhaus, David. "*Leviathan* as a Theory of Transitional Justice." In *NOMOS LI: Transitional Justice*, edited by Melissa S. Williams, Rosemary Nagy, and Jon Elster, 180–217. New York: New York University Press, 2012.

Dyzenhaus, David. "Survey Article: The South African TRC." *Journal of Political Philosophy* 8, no. 4 (2000): 470–96.

Eisikovits, Nir. *A Theory of Truces*. New York: Palgrave Macmillan, 2015.

Eisikovits, Nir. "Truces: What They Mean, How They Work." *Theoria* 62, no. 145 (December 2015): 60–81.

Elster, Jon. "On Doing What One Can: An Argument against Restitution and Retribution as a Means of Overcoming the Communist Legacy." *East European Constitutional Review* 1, no. 2 (1992): 15–17.

Epstein, David L., Robert Bates, Jack Goldstone, Ida Kristensen, and Sharyn O'Halloran. "Democratic Transitions." *American Journal of Political Science* 50 (2006): 551–69.

Epstein, Richard. "A Theory of Strict Liability." *Journal of Legal Studies* 2 (1973): 151–204.

Feinberg, Joel. *Doing and Deserving*. Princeton, NJ: Princeton University Press, 1970.

Feitlowitz, Marguerite. *A Lexicon of Terror: Argentina and the Legacies of Torture*. Oxford: Oxford University Press, 1998.

Fletcher, George. "Fairness and Utility in Tort Theory." *Harvard Law Review* 85 (1972): 537–73.

Fletcher, Laurel. "From Indifference to Engagement: Bystanders and International Criminal Justice." *Michigan Journal of International Law* 26 (2004–2005): 1013–95.

Fletcher, Laurel E., and Harvey M. Weinstein. "Violence and Social Repair: Rethinking the Contribution of Justice to Reconciliation." *Human Rights Quarterly* 24 (2002): 573–639.

Fletcher, Laurel, Harvey Weinstein, and Jamie Rowen. "Context, Timing, and the Dynamics of Transitional Justice: A Historical Perspective." *Human Rights Quarterly* 31 (2009): 163–220.

Foster, James, Suman Seth, Michael Lokshin, and Zurab Sajaia. *A Unified Approach to Measuring Poverty and Inequality.* Washington, DC: World Bank, 2013.

Fuller, Lon. *Anatomy of the Law.* Westport, CT: Greenwood Press Publishers, 1968.

Fuller, Lon. *Morality of Law.* Rev. ed. New Haven, CT: Yale University Press, 1969.

Fuller, Lon. "Positivism and Fidelity to Law: A Reply to Professor Hart." *Harvard Law Review* 71 (1958): 630–72.

Gambetta, Diego, ed. *Trust: Making and Breaking Cooperative Relations.* Oxford: Basil Blackwell, 1988.

Gardner, John. "What Is Tort Law For? Part 1. The Place of Corrective Justice." *Law and Philosophy* 30, no. 1 (January 2011): 1–50.

Gerlach, Christian. *Extremely Violent Societies: Mass Violence in the Twentieth-Century World.* New York: Cambridge University Press, 2010.

Gert, Heather J., Linda Radzik, and Michael Hand. "Hampton on the Expressive Power of Punishment." *Journal of Social Philosophy* 35 no. 1 (2004): 79–90.

Gewirth, Alan. *Human Rights: Essays on Justification and Applications.* Chicago: University of Chicago Press, 1982.

Gibson, James. *Overcoming Apartheid: Can Truth Reconcile a Divided Nation?* New York: Russell Sage Foundation, 2004.

Gilabert, Pablo. "Comparative Assessments of Justice, Feasibility, and Ideal Theory." *Ethical Theory and Moral Practice* 15, no. 1 (2012): 39–56.

Goldhagen, Daniel Johah. *Hitler's Willing Executioners: Ordinary Germans and the Holocaust.* New York: Vintage Books, 1997.

Goldstone, Jack A., and Adriana Kocornik-Mina. "Democracy and Development: New Insights from Dynagraphs." George Mason University, Center for Global Policy, Working Paper #1, Fairfax, VA, 2005.

Gosepath, Stefan. "Equality." In *Stanford Encyclopedia of Philosophy*, edited by Edward N. Zalta. 2011. http://plato.stanford.edu/archives/spr2011/entries/equality/.

Gould, Carol. *Rethinking Democracy: Freedom and Social Cooperation in Politics, Economics and Society.* New York: Cambridge University Press, 1999.

Govier, Trudy. "Self-Trust, Autonomy, and Self-Esteem." *Hypatia* 8 (1993): 99–120.

Gray, David C. "Delivery, Complicity, and Greed: Transitional Justice and Odious Debt." *Law and Contemporary Problems* 70 (2007): 137–64.

Gray, David C. "An Excuse-Centered Approach to Transitional Justice." *Fordham Law Review* 74 (2005–2006): 2621–93.

Gray, David C. "Extraordinary Justice." *Alabama Law Review* 62 (2010): 55–109.

Gready, Paul, and Simon Robins. "From Transitional to Transformative Justice: A New Agenda for Practice." *International Journal of Transitional Justice* 8, no. 3 (2014): 339–61.

Green, Stuart P. "Just Deserts in Unjust Societies: A Case-Specific Approach." In *Philosophical Foundations of Criminal Law*, edited by R. A. Duff and Stuart P. Green, 352–76. Oxford: Oxford University Press, 2011.

Griffin, Christopher. "Democracy as a Non-Instrumentally Just Procedure." *Journal of Political Philosophy* 11, no 1 (2003): 111–21.

Griffin, James. *On Human Rights*. Oxford: Oxford University Press, 2008.

Haldemann, Frank. "Another Kind of Justice: Transitional Justice as Recognition." *Cornell Journal of International Law* 41 (2008): 675–737.

Hampton, Jean. "Correcting Harms versus Righting Wrongs: The Goal of Retribution." *UCLA Law Review* 39 (1992): 1659–1702.

Hansen, Thomas Obcl. "Transitional Justice: Toward a Differentiated Theory." *Oregon Review of International Law* 13, no. 1 (2011): 1–54.

Hardin, Russell. *Trust and Trustworthiness*. New York: Russell Sage Foundation, 2002.

Hardwig, John. "The Role of Trust in Knowledge." *Journal of Philosophy* 88 (12) (1991): 693–708.

Hart, H. L. A. "Positivism and the Separation of Law and Morals." *Harvard Law Review* 71 (1958): 593–629.

Hart, H. L. A. *Punishment and Responsibility*. Oxford: Oxford University Press, 1968.

Henham, Ralph. "Some Reflections on the Legitimacy of International Trial Justice." *International Journal of the Sociology of Law* 35 (2007): 75–95.

Herbst, J. "Political Liberalization in Africa after Ten Years." *Comparative Politics* 33, no. 3 (2001): 357–75.

Hieronymi, Pamela. "Articulating an Uncompromising Forgiveness." *Philosophy and Phenomenological Research* 62, no. 3 (2001): 529–55.

Hobbes, Thomas. *The Leviathan*. Introduction by C. B. MacPherson. New York: Penguin Classics, 1982.

Holder, Cindy. "Transition, Trust and Partial Legality: On Colleen Murphy's *A Moral Theory of Political Reconciliation*." *Criminal Law and Philosophy* 10 (2016): 153–64.

Hollander, Theo, and Bani Gill. "Every Day the War Continues in My Body: Examining the Marked Body in Postconflict Northern Uganda." *International Journal of Transitional Justice* 8 (2014): 217–234.

Hope, Simon. "The Circumstances of Justice." *Hume Studies* 36, no. 2 (2010): 125–48.

Hume, David. *An Enquiry Concerning the Principles of Morals*. Edited by Tom L. Beauchamp. Oxford: Oxford University Press, 1998.

Hume, David. *A Treatise of Human Nature*. 2nd ed. Edited by L. A. Selby-Bigge. Oxford: Oxford University Press, 1978.

Hurd, Heidi. "Correcting Injustice to Corrective Injustice." *Notre Dame Law Review* 67, no. 1 (1991): 51–96.

Hurd, Heidi. "Nonreciprocal Risk Imposition, Unjust Enrichment, and the Foundations of Tort Law: A Critical Celebration of George Fletcher's Theory of Tort Law." *Notre Dame Law Review* 78, no. 3 (2003): 711–30.

Hurka, Thomas. "Proportionality in the Morality of War." *Philosophy and Public Affairs* 33, no. 1 (2005): 34–66.

International Center for Transitional Justice. "From Rejection to Redress: Overcoming Legacies of Conflict-Related Sexual Violence in Northern Uganda." October 2015. www.ictj.org/publication/rejection-redress-overcoming-legacies-conflict-sexualviolence-northern-uganda.

Janoff-Bulman, R. *Shattered Assumptions: Towards a New Psychology of Trauma.* New York: Free Press, 1992.

Johnson, James T. *The Just War Tradition and the Restraint of War.* Princeton, NJ: Princeton University Press, 1981.

Johnstone, Gerry. *Restorative Justice: Ideas, Values, Debates.* Cullompton, UK: Willan Publishing, 2002.

Jones, Karen. "Trust as an Affective Attitude." *Ethics* 107 (1996): 4–25.

Jones, Karen. "Second-Hand Moral Knowledge." *Journal of Philosophy* 96, no. 2 (1999): 55–78.

Joseph, S., R. Williams, and W. Yule. *Understanding Post-Traumatic Stress: A Psychosocial Perspective on PTSD and Treatment.* Chichester, UK: John Wiley and Sons, 1997.

Julius, A. J. "Nagel's Atlas." *Philosophy & Public Affairs* 34, no. 2 (2006): 176–92.

Kaye, Mike. "The Role of Truth Commissions in the Search for Justice, Reconciliation, and Democratisation: The Salvadorean and Honduran Cases." *Journal of Latin American Studies* 29, no. 3 (1997): 693–716.

Khatchadourian, Haig. "Compensation and Reparation as Forms of Compensatory Justice." *Metaphilosophy* 37, no. 3–4 (2006): 429–48.

Kiss, Elizabeth. "Moral Ambition within and beyond Political Constraints: Reflections on Restorative Justice." In *Truth v. Justice: The Morality of Truth Commissions*, edited by Robert I. Rotberg and Dennis Thompson, 68–98. Princeton, NJ: Princeton University Press, 2000.

Krog, Antjie. *Country of My Skull: Guilt, Sorrow, and the Limits of Forgiveness in the New South Africa.* New York: Three Rivers Press, 1998.

Kutz, Christopher. *Complicity: Ethics and Law for a Collective Age.* New York: Cambridge University Press, 2007.

Hieronymi, Pamela. "Articulating an Uncompromising Forgiveness." *Philosophy and Phenomenological Research* 62, no. 3 (2001): 529–55.

Hughes, Paul M. "What Is Involved in Forgiving?" *Philosophia* 25 (1997): 33–49.

Kamm, F. M. "Failures of Just War Theory: Terror, Harm, and Justice." *Ethics* 114, no. 4 (2004): 650–92.

King, Charles. "Review Article: Post-Postcommunism: Transition, Comparison, and the End of 'Eastern Europe.'" *World Politics* 53, no. 1 (2000): 143–72.

Lagerspetz, Olli. *Trust: The Tacit Demand.* Dordrecht, the Netherlands: Kluwer Academic Publishers, 1998.

Lambourne, Wendy. "Transitional Justice and Peacebuilding after Mass Violence." *International Journal of Transitional Justice* 3, no. 1 (2009): 28–48.

Lamont, Julian. "Incentive Income, Deserved Income, and Economic Rents." *Journal of Political Philosophy* 5 (1997): 26–46.

Lamont, Julian, and Christi Favor. "Distributive Justice." In *Stanford Encyclopedia of Philosophy*, edited by Edward N. Zalta. 2014. http://plato.stanford.edu/archives/fall2014/entries/justice-distributive/.

Lang, Anthony F. "Crime and Punishment: Holding States Accountable." *Ethics and International Affairs* 21, no. 2 (2007): 239–57.

Laplante, Lisa. "Transitional Justice and Peace Building: Diagnosing and Addressing the Socioeconomic Roots of Violence through a Human Rights Framework." *International Journal of Transitional Justice* 2, no. 3 (2008): 331–55.

Lawson, Brian. "Individual Complicity in Collective Wrongdoing." *Ethical Theory and Moral Practice* 16 (2013): 227–243, 227.

Leebaw, Bronwyn Anne. "The Irreconcilable Goals of Transitional Justice." *Human Rights Quarterly* 30 (2008): 95–118.

Leebaw, Bronwyn Anne. *Judging State-Sponsored Violence, Imagining Political Change*. New York: Cambridge University Press, 2011.

Lenta, Patrick. "Transitional Justice and the Truth and Reconciliation Commission." *Theoria: Journal of Political and Social Theory* 96 (2000): 52–73.

Llewellyn, Jennifer, and Robert Howse. "Institutions for Restorative Justice: The South African Truth and Reconciliation Commission." *University of Toronto Law Journal* 49 (1999): 355–88.

Locke, John. *Second Treatise of Government*. Edited by C. B. MacPherson. Indianapolis: Hackett Publishing, 1980.

Luban, David. "A Theory of Crimes against Humanity." *Yale International Law Journal* 85 (2004): 85–167.

Luhmann, Nicklas. *Trust and Power*. Toronto: Wiley Press, 1979.

Mack, Andrew. "Global Political Violence: Explaining the Post–Cold War Decline." In *Strategies for Peace: Contributions of International Organizations, States and Non-State Actors*, edited by Volker Rittberger and Martina Fischer, 75–107. Opladen, Germany: Barbara Budrich Publishers, 2008.

Maibom, Heidi. "The Descent of Shame." *Philosophy and Phenomenological Research* 80, no. 3 (May 2010): 566–94.

Mani, Rama. *Beyond Retribution: Seeking Justice in the Shadows of War*. Cambridge: Polity Press, 2002.

May, Larry. *Crimes against Humanity: A Normative Account*. New York: Cambridge University Press, 2005.

May, Larry. "Complicity and the Rwandan Genocide." *Res Publica* 16 (2010): 135–52.

May, Larry. *Genocide: A Normative Account*. Cambridge: Cambridge University Press, 2010.

May, Simon Cabulea. "Moral Compromise, Civic Friendship, and Political Reconciliation." *Critical Review of International Social and Political Philosophy* 14, no. 5 (2011): 581–602.

McEvoy, Kieran. "Beyond Legalism: Towards a Thicker Understanding of Transitional Justice." *Journal of Law and Society* 24, no. 4 (2007): 411–40.

McEvoy, Kieran, and Lorna McGregor. "Transitional Justice from Below: An Agenda for Research, Policy and Praxis." In *Transitional Justice from Below: Grassroots Activism and the Struggle for Change*, edited by Kieran McEvoy and Lorna McGregor, 1–13. Portland OR: Hart Publishing, 2008.

McGeer, Victoria. "Trust, Hope, and Empowerment." *Australasian Journal of Philosophy* 86, no. 2 (2008): 237–54.

McMahan, Jeffrey. "The Ethics of Killing in War." *Ethics* 114 (2004): 693–733.

McMahan, Jeffrey. "Just Cause for War." *Ethics and International Affairs* 19, no. 3 (2005): 1–21.

McMahan, Jeffrey. "The Sources and Status of Just War Principles." *Journal of Military Ethics* 6, no. 2 (2007): 91–106.

Mendez, Juan E. "Accountability for Past Abuses," *Human Rights Quarterly* 19, no. 2 (1997): 255–82.

Mihai, Mihaela. *Negative Emotions and Transitional Justice*. New York: Columbia University Press, 2016.

Milanovic, Marko. "ICTY Convicts Radovan Karadzic." Blog of the European Journal of International Law. www.ejiltalk.org/icty-convicts-radovan-karadzic/.

Minow, Martha. *Between Vengeance and Forgiveness: Facing History after Genocide and Mass Violence*. Boston: Beacon Press, 1998.

Moellendorf, Darrel. "Amnesty, Truth, and Justice: AZAPO." *South African Journal on Human Rights* 13 (1997): 283–91.

Moffett, Luke. "Reparations for 'Guilty' Victims: Navigating Complex Identities of Victim-Perpetrators in Reparation Mechanisms." *International Journal of Transitional Justice* 10 (2016): 146–167.

Moore, Michael. "Justifying Retributivism." *Israel Law Review* 24 (1993): 15–49.

Morris, Herbert. "Guilt and Suffering." *Philosophy East and West* 21, no. 4 (1971): 419–34.

Morrow, Paul. "Mass Atrocity and Manipulation of Social Norms." *Social Theory and Practice* 40, no. 2 (2014): 255–80.

Morrow, Paul. "The Thesis of Norm Transformation in the Theory of Mass Atrocity." *Genocide Studies and Prevention: An International Journal* 9, no. 1 (2015): 66–82.

Moyo, Khanyisela. "Mimicry, Transitional Justice and the Land Question in Racially Divided Former Settler Colonies." *International Journal of Transitional Justice* (2014): 1–20.

Mulgan, Tim. *Ethics for a Broken World*. Acumen, 2011.

Murphy, Colleen. "Lon Fuller and the Moral Value of the Rule of Law." *Law and Philosophy* 24 (2005): 239–62.

Murphy, Colleen. *A Moral Theory of Political Reconciliation*. New York: Cambridge University Press, 2010.

Murphy, Colleen. "Political Reconciliation and International Criminal Trials." In *International Criminal Law and Philosophy*, edited by Larry May and Zach Hoskins, 224–44. Cambridge: Cambridge University Press, 2010.

Murphy, Colleen. "Political Reconciliation, *Jus Post Bellum* and Asymmetric Conflict." *Theoria* 62, no. 4 (2015): 43–59.

Murphy, Colleen. "Political Reconciliation, Punishment and Grudge Informers."
     In *In the Wake of Conflict: Justice, Responsibility and Reconciliation*, edited by
     Alice MacLachlan and C. A. Speight, 117–32. New York: Springer, 2013.
Murphy, Colleen. "Political Reconciliation, the Rule of Law, and Post-Traumatic
     Stress Disorder." In *Trauma, Truth, and Reconciliation: Healing Damaged
     Relationships*, edited by Nancy Nyquist Potter, 83–110. Oxford: Oxford
     University Press, 2006.
Murphy, Colleen. "A Reply to Critics." *Criminal Law and Philosophy* 10 (2016):
     165–77.
Murphy, Colleen. "Transitional Justice, Retributive Justice and Accountability for
     Wrongdoing." In *Theorizing Transitional Justice,* edited by Claudio
     Corradetti, Nir Eisikovits, and Jack Rotondi, 59–68. Burlington, VT:
     Ashgate Publishing, 2015.
Murphy, Colleen, and Linda Radzik. "*Jus Post Bellum* and Political Reconciliation."
     In *Jus Post Bellum and Transitional Justice*, edited by Elizabeth Edenberg and
     Larry May, 305–25. New York: Cambridge University Press, 2014.
Murphy, Liam. "Institutions and the Demands of Justice." *Philosophy & Public
     Affairs* 27, no. 4 (1998): 251–91.
Nagel, Thomas. "The Problem of Global Justice." *Philosophy & Public Affairs* 33
     (2005): 113–47.
Ní Aoláin, Fionnuala, and Colm Campbell. "The Paradox of Transition in
     Conflicted Democracies." *Human Rights Quarterly* 27 (2005): 172–213.
Ní Aoláin, Fionnuala, and Eilish Rooney. "Underenforcement and
     Intersectionality: Gendered Aspects of Transition for Women."
     International Journal of Transitional Justice 1, no. 3 (2007): 338–54.
Nino, Carlos Santiago. *Radical Evil on Trial*. New Haven, CT: Yale University
     Press, 1998.
Nozick, Robert. *Anarchy, State and Utopia*. New York: Basic Books, 1974.
Nussbaum, Martha. *Frontiers of Justice*. Cambridge, MA: Belknap Press, 2006.
Nussbaum, Martha. *Woman and Human Development: The Capabilities Approach*.
     Cambridge: Cambridge University Press, 2000.
Oberdiek, John. *Philosophical Foundations of the Law of Torts*. New York: Oxford
     University Press, 2014.
Ohlin, Jens David. "Three Conceptual Problems with the Doctrine of Joint
     Criminal Enterprise." *Journal of International Criminal Justice* 5 (2007):
     69–90.
O'Leary, Brendan, and John McGarry. *The Politics of Antagonism: Understanding
     Northern Ireland*. 2nd ed. London: Althone Press, 1996.
Olsen, Tricia D., Leigh A. Payne, and Andrew G. Reiter. *Transitional Justice in
     Balance: Comparing Processes, Weighing Efficacy*. Washington, DC: United
     States Institute of Peace, 2010.
Orend, Brian. "Justice after War." *Ethics and International Affairs* 16, no. 1 (2002):
     43–52.
Orend, Brian. "War." In *Stanford Encyclopedia of Philosophy*, edited by Edward
     N. Zalta. 2008. http://plato.stanford.edu/archives/fall2008/entries/war/.

Orentlicher, Diane F. "'Settling Accounts' Revisited: Reconciling Global Norms with Local Agency." *International Journal of Transitional Justice* 1, no. 1 (2007): 10–22.

Osiel, Mark. *Making Sense of Mass Atrocity.* New York: Cambridge University Press, 2009.

Periera, Anthony W. *Political (In)justice: Authoritarianism and the Rule of Law in Brazil, Chile and Argentina.* Pittsburgh: University of Pittsburgh Press, 2005.

Perry, Stephen. "The Moral Foundations of Tort Law." Faculty Scholarship 1153 (1992). http://scholarship.law.upenn.edu/faculty_scholarship/1153.

Pettit, Philip. "The Cunning of Trust." *Philosophy and Public Affairs* 24, no. 3 (1995): 202–25.

Pettit, Philip. "Legitimacy and Justice in Republican Perspective." *Current Legal Problems* 65 (2012): 59–82.

Philpott, Daniel. *Just and Unjust Peace: An Ethic of Political Reconciliation.* New York: Oxford University Press, 2012.

Pojman, L., and O. McLeod, eds. *What Do We Deserve?* New York: Oxford University Press, 1999.

Popovich, Neil A. F. "In Pursuit of Environmental Human Rights: Commentary on the Draft Declaration of Principles on Human Rights and the Environment." *Columbia Human Rights Law Review* 27 (1995–96): 487–603.

Posner, Eric, and Adrian Vermeule. "Transitional Justice as Ordinary Justice." *Harvard Law Review* 117 (2004): 761–825.

Postema, Gerald J. "Implicit Law." *Law and Philosophy* 13 (1994): 361–87.

Pouligny, Béatrice, Simon Chesterman, and Albrecht Schnabel. "Introduction: Picking up the Pieces," in *After Mass Crime: Rebuilding States and Communities*, edited by Béatrice Pouligny, Simon Chesterman, and Albrecht Schnabel, 1–16. Tokyo: United Nations University Press, 2008.

Prempeh, H. Kwasi. "*Marbury* in Africa: Judicial Review and the Challenge of Constitutionalism in Contemporary Africa." *Tulane Law Review* 80, no. 1 (2006): 1–84.

Radzik, Linda, and Colleen Murphy. "Reconciliation." In *Stanford Encyclopedia of Philosophy*, edited by Edward N. Zalta. 2015. http://plato.stanford.edu/archives/sum2015/entries/reconciliation/.

Radzik, Linda. *Making Amends: Atonement in Morality, Law and Politics.* Oxford: Oxford University Press, 2009.

Rawls, John. *Law of Peoples.* Cambridge, MA: Harvard University Press, 1999.

Rawls, John. *A Theory of Justice.* Cambridge, MA: Harvard University Press, 1971.

Raz, Joseph. *Authority of Law.* Oxford: Clarendon Press, 1979.

Reno, William, *Corruption and State Politics in Sierra Leone.* Cambridge: Cambridge University Press, 1995.

Richards, Norman. "Forgiveness." *Ethics* 99, no. 1 (1988): 77–97.

Ridge, Michael. "David Hume, Paternalist." *Hume Studies* 36, no. 2 (2010): 149–70.

Riley, Jonathan. "Justice under Capitalism." In *Markets and Justice*, edited by John W. Chapman, 122–62. New York: New York University Press, 1989.

Risse, Mathias. *Global Justice*. Princeton, NJ: Princeton University Press, 2012.

Rodin, David. "Terrorism without Intention." *Ethics* 114, no. 4 (2004): 752–71.

Roht-Arriaza, Naomi. "Reparations in the Aftermath of Repression and Mass Violence." In *My Neighbor, My Enemy: Justice and Community in the Aftermath of Mass Atrocity*, edited by Eric Stover and Harvey M. Weinstein, 121–23. Cambridge: Cambridge University Press, 2004.

Roht-Arriaza, Naomi. "State Responsibility to Investigate and Prosecute Grave Human Rights Violations in International Law." *California Law Review* 78 (1990): 449–51.

Roht-Arriaza, Naomi, and Javier Mariezcurrena, eds. *Transitional Justice in the Twenty-First Century: Beyond Truth versus Justice*. Cambridge: Cambridge University Press, 2006.

Roht-Arriaza, Naomi, and Katharine Orlovsky. "A Complementary Relationship: Reparations and Development," in *Transitional Justice and Development: Making Connections*, edited by Pablo de Greiff and Roger Duthie. New York: Social Science Research Council, 2009.

Rubio-Marin, Ruth, ed. *What Happened to the Women? Gender and Reparations for Human Rights Violations*. New York: Social Science Research Council, 2006.

Rundle, Kristen. *Forms Liberate: Reclaiming the Jurisprudence of Lon Fuller*. Oxford: Hart Publishing, 2012.

Rundle, Kristen. "The Impossibility of an Exterminatory Legality: Law and the Holocaust." *University of Toronto Law Journal* 59, no. 1 (2009): 65–125.

Rysiew, Patrick. "Epistemic Contextualism." In *Stanford Encyclopedia of Philosophy*, edited by Edward N. Zalta. 2011. http://plato.stanford.edu/archives/win2011/entries/contextualism-epistemology/.

Sangiovanni, Andrea. "Justice and the Priority of Politics to Morality." *Journal of Political Philosophy* 16, no. 2 (2008): 137–64.

Schmid, Evelyne, and Aoife Nolany. "'Do No Harm'? Exploring the Scope of Economic and Social Rights in Transitional Justice." *International Journal of Transitional Justice* 8 (2014): 362–82.

Sen, Amartya. *Development as Freedom*. New York: Anchor Books, 1999.

Sen, Amartya. "Elements of a Theory of Human Rights." Philosophy and Public Affairs 32, no. 4 (2004): 315–56.

Sen, Amartya. "Equality of What?" The Tanner Lectures on Human Values, Delivered at Stanford University, 1979. http://tannerlectures.utah.edu/_documents/a-to-z/s/sen80.pdf.

Sen, Amartya. *Inequality Reexamined*. Cambridge, MA: Harvard University Press, 1992.

Shafer-Landau, Russ. "The Failure of Retributivism." *Philosophical Studies* 82 (1996): 289–316.

Shafer-Landau, Russ. "Retributivism and Desert." *Pacific Philosophical Quarterly* 81 (2000): 189–214.

Shandley, Robert. *Rubble Films: German Cinema in the Shadow of the Third Reich*. Philadelphia: Temple University Press, 2001.

Sharp, Dustin N. "Emancipating Transitional Justice from the Bonds of the Paradigmatic Transition." *International Journal of Transitional Justice* 9 (2015): 150–169.

Sharp, Dustin N. "Interrogating the Peripheries: The Preoccupations of Fourth Generation Transitional Justice." *Harvard Human Rights Journal* 26 (2013): 149–78.

Sharp, Dustin N. "The Significance of Human Rights for the Debt of Countries in Transition." In *Making Sovereign Financing & Human Rights Work*, edited by Juan Pablo Bohoslavsky and Jernej Letnar Černič, 47–60. London: Hart, 2013.

Shaw, Rosalind, and Lars Waldorf. *Localizing Transitional Justice: Interventions and Priorities after Mass Violence*. Stanford: Stanford University Press, 2010.

Shoemaker, David. "Moral Address, Moral Responsibility, and the Boundaries of the Moral Community." *Ethics* 118 (2007): 70–108.

Sierra Leone Truth Commission. *Report of the Sierra Leone Truth & Reconciliation Commission*. vol. 2. Accra, Ghana: Graphic Packaging, 2004.

Smith, Nick. *I Was Wrong*. New York: Cambridge University Press, 2008.

Smith, Nick. *Justice through Apologies: Remorse, Reform, and Punishment*. Cambridge: Cambridge University Press, 2014.

Snyder, Jack, and Leslie Vinjamuri. "Trials and Errors: Principle and Pragmatism in Strategies of International Justice." *International Security* 28, no. 3 (2003–2004): 5–44.

Sriram, Chandra Lekha. "Justice as Peace? Liberal Peacebuilding and Strategies of Transitional Justice." *Global Society* 21, no. 4 (2007): 579–91.

Stewart, James. "Overdetermined Atrocities." *Journal of International Criminal Justice* 10 (2012): 1189–1218.

Stover, Eric. *The Witnesses: War Crimes and the Promise of Justice in The Hague*. Philadelphia: University of Pennsylvania Press, 2007.

Straus, Scott. "How Many Perpetrators Were There in the Rwandan Genocide? An Estimate." *Journal of Genocide Research* 6, no. 1 (2004): 85–98.

Strawson, P. F. *Freedom and Resentment and Other Essays*. New York: Routledge, 2008.

Subotic, Jelena. "Expanding the Scope of Post-Conflict Justice: Individual, State and Societal Responsibility for Mass Atrocity." *Journal of Peace Research* 48, no. 2 (2011): 157–69.

Subotic, Jelena. "Legitimacy, Scope and Conflicting Claims on the ICTY: In the Aftermath of *Gotovina, Haradinai and Perisic*." *Journal of Human Rights* 13 (2014): 170–85.

Swift, Adam. "The Value of Philosophy in Nonideal Circumstances." *Social Theory & Practice* 34, no. 3 (2008): 363–87.

Tanguay-Renaud, Francois, and James Stribopoulos, eds. *Rethinking Criminal Law Theory: New Canadian Perspectives in the Philosophy of Domestic, Transnational, and International Criminal Law*. Oxford: Hart Publishing, 2012.

Tasioulas, John. "Minimum Core Obligations: Human Rights in the Here and Now." World Bank.

Tasioulas, John. "On the Nature of Human Rights." In *The Philosophy of Human Rights: Contemporary Controversies*, edited by G. Ernst and J.C. Heilinger, 17–59. Berlin: Walter de Gruyter, 2012.

Taslioulas, John. "Punishment and Repentance." *Philosophy* 81 (2006): 279–322.

Teitel, Ruti. *Globalizing Transitional Justice: Contemporary Essays.* New York: Oxford University Press, 2014.

Teitel, Ruti. "Transitional Jurisprudence: The Role of Law in Political Transformation." *Yale Law Journal* 106 (1997): 2009–80.

Teitel, Ruti. *Transitional Justice.* New York: Oxford University Press, 2000.

Thompson, Leonard. *A History of South Africa.* New Haven, CT: Yale University Press, 2000.

Thoms, Oskar N. T., James Ron, and Roland Paris. "State-Level Effects of Transitional Justice: What Do We Know?" *International Journal of Transitional Justice* 4, no. 3 (2010): 329–354.

Truth and Reconciliation Commission of South Africa. *Truth and Reconciliation Commission of South Africa Report*, 5 vols. London: Macmillon Publishers, 1999.

UN Secretary General's Report. "The Rule of Law and Transitional Justice in Conflict and Post-Conflict Societies." 2004. www.ipu.org/splz-e/unga07/law.pdf.

Valentini, Laura. "Ideal vs. Non-ideal Theory: A Conceptual Map." *Philosophy Compass* 7, no. 9 (2012): 654–64.

Vallier, Kevin, and Fred D'Agostino. "Public Justification." In *Stanford Encyclopedia of Philosophy*, edited by Edward N. Zalta. 2014. http://plato.stanford.edu/archives/spr2014/entries/justification-public/.

van der Merwe, Hugo, Victoria Baxter, and Audrey Chapman. *Assessing the Impact of Transitional Justice: Challenges for Empirical Research.* Washington, DC: United States Institute of Peace Press, 2009.

Vanderschraaf, Peter. "The Circumstances of Justice." *Politics, Philosophy and Economics* 5, no. 3 (2006): 321–51.

van Ness, Daniel W., and Karen Heetderks Strong. *Restoring Justice.* 2nd ed. Cincinnati: Anderson Publishing, 2002.

van Zyl, Paul. "Justice without Punishment: Guaranteeing Human Rights in Transitional Societies." In *Looking Back, Reaching Forward: Reflections on the Truth and Reconciliation Commission of South Africa*, edited by Charles Villa-Vicencio and Wilhelm Verwoerd, 42–57. Cape Town: University of Cape Town Press, 2000.

Viaene, Lieselotte, and Eva Brems. "Transitional Justice and Cultural Contexts: Learning from the Universality Debate." *Netherlands Quarterly of Human Rights* 28, no. 2 (2010): 199–224.

Vincent v. Lake Erie Transportation 124 N.W. 221 (Minn. 1910).

Waldron, Jeremy. "Hart and the Principles of Legality." In *The Legacy of H. L. A. Hart*, edited by Matthew H. Cramer, Claire Grant, Ben Colburn, and Antony Hatzistavrou, 67–83. Oxford: Oxford University Press, 2008.

Waldron, Jeremy. "Why Law–Efficacy, Freedom or Fidelity?" *Law and Philosophy* 13 (1994): 259–84.